S A N D R A   K A Y

Diary

of a

Dogcatcher

These stories are a work of nonfiction and reflect my own memories and very personal recollections. I understand that there will be some who saw a different version, and that's the way life goes. Like the "telephone game," we all hear and see what comes to us and that, then becomes our own. Most of the names have been changed to protect individual privacy. It's my hope that every reader will recognize some of their own self in some of these stories, a shared experience, a shared adventure, a shared laugh or even a tear. We make our human condition more bearable by sharing.

Cover photo by Sandra Kay

Cover design and formatting by JD Smith

Published by Prairie Moon Press

All inquiries to SandraKayWrites1960@gmail.com

First published 2025

Scan QR for photos, sales, and book talk events. SandraKayWrites.com

Early Reviews

Diary of a Dogcatcher weaves the beautiful and sometimes brutal emotions and experiences of working in animal welfare with the tragedy and triumph of simply being human. Anyone who's worked in the animal world will recognize Peaches, Seymour, and Astro. This book makes us confront uncomfortable truths about animal welfare and memories of animals we think we failed, but also reminds us that we are not alone…and that our connection to other people, the animals we share the world with, and the world itself are what pulls us through the hard times.

Stacy Smith, Executive Director, Humane Tomorrow

"If you've ever been a horse-crazy child or shared your life with a beloved dog or cat, you'll see bits of yourself in Sandy's book. Her stories could be my stories, and reading her tales brings memories of long-lost and beloved pets back to life in my mind. If you've ever lived the life of someone working in animal welfare, you'll recognize the joys and sorrows in the pages of Sandy's book. And if you haven't lived this life but wonder about it, Sandy's depiction is perfect. There are struggles which she talks about, but there's also pride and a sense of satisfaction and that feeling of doing what you're meant to do."

Dr. Jennifer Williams, Executive Director, Bluebonnet Equine Humane Society

Dedication

For all the dogs who waited for me to come home, always forgiving me for smelling like someone else's dogs. And for Dave, who waited for me to come home one last time but was gone before I made it back. I will never stop seeing you everywhere I look.

And to all my animal family, past and present. Dogs, horses, cats, goats, sheep, chickens, parrots, and two fish. Each day of my life has been curated by you, all of you, and only you know how many stories are still left to tell. Some more than others, but you were all the love of my life. Giving you my whole heart will never be enough to repay what you've given me.

Table of Contents

PART ONE: WISCONSIN

"After nourishment, shelter and companionship, stories are the thing we need most in the world."
Phillip Pullman, English author

1. Patterns

I was about six when I brought home my first "lost" dog. I had seen it from the sidewalk and decided to set it free from the wet circle of dirt where it lived on a backyard chain. The dog was friendly, filthy, and smelled like dirty wet socks, but it was happy to follow me the several blocks home, where I proudly announced to Mom that it had followed me home. She noticed that I was holding a chain attached to its collar. In a few minutes, the owners came and reclaimed their stolen dog.

Everything in nature follows a set of patterns, from the cycle of the seasons to the paths animals follow through their environments. I would even bet that the push and pull of the tides is a metronome for aquatic life, providing a foundation for their patterns, too. As I looked back at the years of my younger self, it's true that I began to settle into my own patterns without even realizing. My earliest memories have stayed with me, a busy Wisconsin family full of brothers and laughter, tears and triumphs, with equal measures of discipline, sacrifice, generosity and love. The steadfast support and love from our parents played a huge role in our growth. As a result, I never focused on the moves our family made as Dad sought better-paying jobs in his new career of computer programming. Instead, I stayed busy exploring anything that caught my interest, always without worry of repercussions or harsh judgment. Even without a family pet in those first years, my need to connect with animals of any form was the foundation of my pattern. I was drawn to animals by a drive I couldn't identify and didn't understand.

A plastic rocking horse arrived one Christmas and instantly became real to me. How did Santa know I wanted a horse? I wondered. I didn't even send him a letter. It was like I had been born with that plastic horse, its stiff mane blowing in a pretend breeze, its legs folded in a permanent gallop as I rocked it down invisible roads for countless miles. The next Christmas a large stuffed sheepdog, as tall as I was, arrived and stayed with me a few years too many, a best friend for a kid in need of one. That same winter I clearly recall looking out the living room picture window to see Santa's sleigh being pulled by a set of big horses down the middle of the street one snowy afternoon. It was magical. Puffing out my cheeks, I blew a peephole in the frosty window just big enough to see the street. With my nose pressed to the window, I stared, mesmerized by the sight of the sleigh, the waving, red-suited Santa and the sweating, steaming horses. It was like being inside a snow globe. I was five years old, the first girl in the family, and hadn't yet learned to run like the wind from frilly dresses and everything pink.

Before long we moved to Neenah, just a few hours north. There I met a friend, a tiny, wily child whose parents I never saw. In my mind's eye, I still see her with me on the swing set, a slinky side-eye watching my every move. One afternoon during a little-girl argument, she bit a hole through the sleeve of my winter coat, drawing blood and leaving a scar. When I met my first feral kitten, many years later, I remembered her. It was also here that I had my first glimpse of the real Santa and his reindeer, flying through the stars one Christmas Eve. That night as I stood on my pillows to look out the winter window over the headboard of my bed, I was overwhelmed. I squinted my eyes, trying to make out the shapes in the sky. There they were, just as I had always known. Flying reindeer, fuzzy, furry creatures leading a blinking light through the dark skies. I had always known they were real.

The next family move brought us to Altoona, where a stray black and white cat stayed with us long enough to have a litter of kittens. Then one day she was gone, off to "live in the country" with her kittens, Mom explained. For some reason, those words left me uneasy, but I didn't know exactly why. Around 1967 or 1968, Mom and Dad built a home on Hillside Road, just a few miles from the Altoona duplex. The one-story ranch-style house had almost enough bedrooms for all of us. Brothers shared two bedrooms, and as the only girl, I had my own. We shared the neighborhood with other families and their similarly wild children, but still no permanent family pet joined us, other than a lonely basset hound for a short period of time. I rarely spent time with him. He just appeared one day and then one day he was gone. When I cried over his loss, Mom told me he went to a better home where he could get more attention. It was my first experience with deep and painful guilt. I deemed his sad life my fault.

But maybe I could have rabbits, and so I said my little girl prayers, made bargains I could never keep, and dreamed hopeful, bunny-filled dreams. Then one day, in the garage on Hillside Road, I watched Dad build a rabbit hutch in preparation for my first rabbit. I was ecstatic about bringing home a bunny, the begging and bargaining had worked, and all the usual promises had been made. Still stinging from the guilt of the basset hound, the promises were gospel to me. My bunnies provided the fix I needed for an animal in my life now that I was ready to care for one of my own. I learned quickly they were fragile creatures, providing plenty of drama and tragedy. Rabbits gave me insight into how babies are made, but the word "sex" was an awkward word that never seemed to fit comfortably in my head. Even so, the bunnies brought birth, then harsh lessons on keeping them safe and healthy, then more lessons on processing their inevitable deaths. Digging the tiny graves, I learned to handle a shovel before most girls my age could brush their own hair.

From the rabbits to the stuffed animals that filled my room, to the few animals that found our family as temporary pets in between moves, my days had a rhythm, a dependable heartbeat

I shared with them all. I absorbed and easily memorized every word of the animal stories on Walt Disney's Sunday night episodes and every detail on Mutual of Omaha's Wild Kingdom television show. All the animal books I read, every minute of every day, consumed me. Every detail about animals I read about, heard about, or learned in person was seared into my brain, wedged there and ready for instant recall whenever I needed. Learning things about animals was easy. I started and finished any book with animals as if the pages were on fire. *Ring of Bright Water, Weecha The Raccoon, Where the Red Fern Grows, Old Yeller,* virtually all of Walter Farley's *Black Stallion* series, Jack London's *White Fang*, John Steinbeck's *The Red Pony, National Velvet,* and *Black Beauty.* There were just so many books.

Great-Aunt Astrid Berthiaume gave me my first *Little Golden* bird book, and in those pages I read the first big word of my life, then with her help learned how to spell "Archeopteryx," the prehistoric bird. Going with Mom to the local library, I scoured its shelves for books with an animal as a main character. Whether in books or in real life, I sought the friendship of animals in every waking hour and even in my dreams. In their presence I was happy, content, settled, and focused. When I was with animals, either real or in a book, nothing else mattered. My own pattern was set. With animals, my heart fell in love, again and again. I never imagined that one day I would lose the strength, direction, and joy they gave me. One day it would all be gone, and I never saw it coming.

"Peace is the perspective found in patterns"
-Terry Tempest Williams

2. The Polar Coaster

I never forgot about the losses or disappearances of the few pets that came to our family early on. I can't imagine how challenging it must have been for our young parents as they made their way in the world back then. With a growing pack of children and another on the way, adding both the physical and emotional needs of a pet in a quickly growing family could not have been the best idea my parents had ever considered, but I suspect they both had a fondness for animals, too. They tried, but a pet was out of the question.

Dad had a childhood dog, Elmer, who he often mentioned over the years, and Mom was always enchanted with baby animals.

"Oh, if they would only stay this small!" she would exclaim, whenever holding a tiny kitten or puppy. She quietly dreamed of having her own horse again one day, but the times were different then. Raising a family was work, and my brothers and I would soon make five.

Maybe relieved to have left the demanding work of his parents' farm far behind, Dad discovered the opportunities within the fledgling computer industry. He was learning how to become a programmer, studying huge binders full of foreign computer languages. The computer jobs weren't plentiful, but they paid well, and we moved four times before I was ten.

Did Mom ever read those 1950s homemaker books with chapters of instructions on how to keep your husband happy and children quiet and clean? I'd like to think she never did, but she did become the nucleus of our family, the glue as we often said years later. Not because the pages of a book told her to, but because raising a family brought her joy. Her mornings were usually spent in pink fuzzy slippers and matching bathrobe, dancing circles and humming in a house filled with the noise that defines a growing family. She smiled, laughed, and hugged all of us often, especially when we weren't looking. Those were the hugs we needed the most, and she knew that piece of advice would not be found in the pages of the homemaker book. She was gentle, cheerful, and cleverly creative in how to keep us happy, entertained, fed, and clothed.

I'm sure there were days when both parents wished they had chosen a different path, as I think almost all parents must feel at some point. But for most of my childhood days and literally all my memories, I remember love, joy, discipline, and the strength and comfort of togetherness. Our parents held us safe and then, when the time came, sent us forward. Were they perfect? No. But they never failed to strive for perfection, all the while not falling into the trap of demanding perfection. Such instinctive wisdom made all the difference.

As Wisconsin kids, we loved snow days. No school and a playground of white stuff kept us outside from morning until dark, coming inside only to change soaked mittens or go potty. Northern moms never complained when school was closed on a snow day, her kids stayed busy outside, and our Mom was true to form. The year I turned eight, the home on Hillside Road in tiny Altoona, Wisconsin couldn't have been a better place to live. Neighbors with kids, school within a short walk through the woods, and the wooded hill, providing the best playground ever. And we would soon have a slide, one that none of us had ever seen, experienced, or could even imagine.

That first winter, Dad cleared a path on the hill for which the road had been named. On its slopes, he built a slide out of snow. The icy track, long and winding, was a work of art designed by Dad to be the perfect width for our round flying saucers. It started in the trees at the top of the hill behind the house, down past the kitchen sliding-glass doors and my rabbit hutches under the oak trees, made a steep bank around the corner and then ended in the neighbor's yard. As we flew up and around the steep banked curved, some centrifugal force gave us a stomach lurching drop and we would crash to a stop against the neighbor's basement foundation. Then up on our feet, fiberglass saucers in hand and we ran, laughing and gasping, to the top of the hill, to start all over again.

We learned to put our booted feet into the laps of the seated sibling in the saucer in front of us, making a linked train of kids on saucers flying down the hill, over and over again. Fall off the saucer and you'd be run over by the loaded saucers behind, sometimes five or six in a row. The more kids on saucers, the faster the train could go, making the banked corner and fast, final drop to the neighbor's basement wall that much more fun.

We knew Dad would spend hours at night with the hose, spraying down the saucer track so ice could form overnight, shoveling snow to repair and rebuild the banked corner, designing the edges and slope of the track to allow for maximum speed. We knew he, Mom and the neighbor parents would sometimes sit together inside the kitchen just behind the sliding glass door that looked out at the hill and our icy track. There, they sipped coffee, laughed at the kids, and enjoyed the company of good friends on those days when everyone had a little time to enjoy family and friends.

What we didn't know, not until a few years ago, was that Dad had dubbed this snowy hill the "Polar Coaster." It was nothing short of a miracle, our very own winter Olympic Luge run. As he worked outside in the dark winter evenings, shoveling snow and holding an ice-cold water hose while his hands and feet became numb, did he know what amazing memories he would create for all of us? I think he planned it just like that.

He's more than eighty years old these days, but still wrangles his snowblower, feeds his birds in winter, and stokes the fireplace on cold days so their indoor cat, Maxx, can enjoy the winter in comfortable cat style.

3. Real Horses

While I spent my summer days stalking chipmunks in the Hillside Road backyard, our parents searched for country property to move our family of seven. Four growing boys needed elbow room, and I kept bringing home every animal that "found me," even those that clearly belonged to someone else. Along with my love of dogs and fascination with the wildlife around our small-town home, I was also obsessed with horses.

On the dirt paths through the fields between home and school, my green Schwinn bike became a brown and white pony. My knees bent to absorb the concussions of bumps and holes, just like I'd seen the jockeys do on galloping racehorses. One day the chain slipped off the bike wheel and I had a real-life runaway down the hill in front of the high school. With no coaster brakes to stop or slow it, the bike went faster and faster, chain dragging on the tar, my canvas tennis shoes skidding along, no match for gravity. I don't remember being scared; after all, it was just a runaway horse, and of course I could stop it. I simply steered the bike into the gravel alongside the road and was promptly bucked off. With bleeding knees, I stood up, dusted off the gravel, replaced the slipped chain like I had seen my brothers do and climbed back on. Like every smart cowboy, I knew I had to show courage or forever lose the respect of my green metal horse. Putting mile after mile on the bike, there was no end to my horse-girl dreams. Then one day, like a miracle, Ginger came into my life, and the green bike was abandoned, relegated to duty rather than dreams.

Ginger was a medium-sized bay pony with a "side-eye" I could see from a hundred yards away. She had become a bit chubby in her early-retirement years, sharing the Leslie family's rolling 80-acre farm with their herd of Black Angus cattle and saddle horses. Their three kids were all within my age range. Kim, the oldest, had outgrown Ginger and graduated to a "real" horse. For a small fee, Mom had arranged to lease Ginger for me to ride and call my own, a deal that was a win for all involved except Ginger, who had perfected the art of retirement.

Ginger was thick and stout with a full black mane, long coarse tail and hard, dark hooves. She had no white markings at all to accent her color, but she did have a pretty Welsh-pony head with large, intelligent eyes and small, tight ears. She was slightly bow-legged in the front, even a bit over-at-the-knees and pigeon-toed, but that never slowed her down. All I needed to experience wind in my hair and the feel of a live horse under me was to catch this clever pony, climb on and stay on. Learning to catch her was my first lesson in horsemanship. On Saturday mornings, those 80 acres were an entire country, another world altogether for a nine-year-old girl. But somewhere out there was my pony.

On the drive to Leslie's farm, the butterflies in my stomach from the anticipation of riding a real horse would sometimes overwhelm. But the work and challenge of catching Ginger would quickly make them disappear. No matter how many hours it took, catching her became the lead story in my own adventures that made the Wild Kingdom adventures pale in comparison. She always treated capture as a life-and death event. I was bent on catching her, desperate to feel the horse under me, taking me places. I lost count of how many times I wished for Marlin Perkins's helicopter to zoom in over the pony and her herd as they disappeared 40 acres away.

Eventually, I learned to approach the herd with my head down, wrap the halter around my waist where it couldn't be seen by even the sharpest of pony side-eyes, and carry as much feed as the entire herd could enjoy. Once they were tricked into not running, they began lipping up the oats and corn from the grass. I would mingle with the herd, humming and acting innocent until I could inch myself close enough to Ginger. If the horses would let me, I could deploy my last weapon, flight. Tall for my age and thin, I'd slip behind one horse after another until I was close enough to almost touch her. Surely, the horses knew it. Then, with careful timing, I'd launch myself through the air at the pony and grab a handful of thick mane. It didn't always work, but when it did, her startled gallop would lift my feet off the ground. I held on for dear life as she ran, my free arm around her neck until she stopped. It sometimes worked. Riding my pony back to the house and barnyard for her weekend of labor, I just knew that even Mr. Perkins wished he was like me.

With me on Ginger, Steve on Tabby, his strawberry roan pony, and Kari on her fancy black Shetland pony, Midnight, we chased the cattle herd when no one was looking. We galloped as fast as we could down the cow paths in the woods, jumping fallen trees and ducking branches. Ginger was loyal, steady, and strong when we rode in the ditch of busy State Highway 12, where cars rarely slowed for children on ponies. She was smart to watch her feet as she obediently stepped across the creosote ties of the railroad bridge, the gully below it showing through the gaps between the wooden beams. I trusted her to be still when I stood on her back to pick apples from tree branches. She never complained about standing tied to the winter-pasture fence while we picked blackberries day after summer day. She was patient, kind and honest, and always worked her heart out for me, but I had to catch her first. That was her price. In this child's kingdom of tall grasses and even taller tales, we rode to our heart's content, imaginations soaring.

While I had spent the past couple of years riding Ginger to China, Australia, Siberia and on dozens of dusty cattle drives, all in the wild west of my imagination, a real horse had come into our lives. Sunny was born on the Leslie's farm in June 1971 to a family friend's palomino quarter horse mare, who had been mated with a chestnut Arabian stallion of local fame. I'm not sure what the arrangement was between Mom and the mare's owner, but Mom paid the thirty-five-dollar stud fee. On that warm summer morning, the herd didn't show for their usual trip to the water tank in the barnyard. Kari and I grabbed our ponies, obediently waiting in barn stalls, and galloped through the pastures, hoping we would see a new baby horse.

Then, there they were, the herd gathered around the mare, her colt still wet from birth but standing strong. I knew Mom had been excited to have her own horse, and here he was. Colored as bright red as the setting sun, he had the longest ears I had ever seen, three white socks and a wide white blaze from his forehead to the end of his nose. We sat there on our ponies, blending with the herd, sharing their curiosity. Our wonder at life's miracle was enough to take our breath. Mom had a horse.

From the very beginning, the colt was as spicy as his color implied. In his first week of life, he fought the halter so passionately he eventually threw himself on the ground in sweaty disgust. His mother looked bored with the theatrics. He fought the lead rope, disagreeing with any direction that wasn't of his choosing. Mom simply called him "Red" in those first weeks, and she loved him.

Around 1973, Mom and Dad found a quiet little farm for sale on County Line Road near the tiny town of Rock Falls. It would be our last move together as a family. From the very first time I saw the tidy white farmhouse, the hip-roofed barn standing empty and inviting, and the creeks that bordered both sides of the farm's 20 acres, it was more than I could have ever dreamed. It was pure magic. Living there would change my life.

4. Parents

I never knew much about the lives my parents lived as they were growing up, other than the memories of scattered conversations and a few brittle black and white pictures from those days. Larry grew up on the farm between Bayfield and Ashland, small northern Wisconsin towns near the tip of the Chequamegon Bay of Lake Superior. He was the only boy in a family of five girls, tending a rotating herd of cattle bought, sold and traded by his father, Hub.

His mother, Adele, worked always and rested little, skillfully managing the needs of six children, raising a summer garden for winter vegetables and tending chickens. She also worked as a nurse at the hospital in town. Somehow, she found time to cultivate flowers around the house on Cherryville Road. The color and cheer from the flower beds sent a message to all who visited that this house had love to share. It was where she could be found when she had time for herself.

Her husband was gone much of the time, hauling cattle or searching for the next deal, not much help when it came to the household or taking care of the farm. For those duties, I'm certain the only boy was pressed into regular service. Between barn and cattle chores, snow shoveling, lawn mowing, fence repairs and dozens of other tasks, there's a good chance that while his sisters were learning the work of future wives and mothers, young Larry carried much of the responsibility for the work outdoors. Despite the work, Larry loved cars, and his dreams were full of the new models being introduced. Like most young men his age, he saved his money and one day drove home a blue and white 1957 Chevrolet.

Mom and her older brother grew up in a tiny city house in Ashland, a town with a history of Great Lakes logging and iron-ore shipping. Her father, Melvin, worked a blue-collar job at the paper mill in town, where napkins and other paper products were made. On weekends he retreated to the lake for fishing or to the woods for hunting. Dorothy, her mother, always stayed fresh and pretty, keeping house for her husband and raising their two children in between secret card games with friends. Dorothy loved a good yard sale, loved a good game of cribbage, and loved to gamble.

Sometime during her high school years young Kay begged her parents for a horse, and one winter a horse arrived for her. Smoky looked stout and wild in the few pictures Mom had of him, but I never learned the whole story of the big black horse except she didn't have him long. Pictures in photo albums told the story of high school days that were not about horses and animals, but straight A's on report cards and parades and football games as a drum majorette. Tall, vibrant and always pretty, she loved to dress the part and throughout her life, always turned heads.

Dad fell in love and soon proposed, but Kay wasn't a country girl and didn't attend regular church, to the dismay of Larry's parents. When they married, it was without their blessing. Despite that, their marriage lasted 32 years, happy and full until Mom's death from cancer in 1990.

5. The Greatness of Grandparents

All my life there have been waves, sometimes wind-whipped and white-capped, sometimes serene. I've learned that they can be wild or gentle, and I'll never have control over which. Waves hid the lives beneath them, a protective wall, dark and frothy or smooth and round but impenetrable except by children's imagination and the knowledge of those who take the time to study them. For children and scholars of the lake, the mysteries revealed brought riches. My grandfather Melvin was a Lake Superior fisherman and knew this about waves.

Every summer, my brothers and I would beg to take a trip to Ashland, hoping to spend time with grandparents. One summer we boarded a Greyhound bus, four elementary-aged kids without an adult guardian for the trip north from our central Wisconsin home. It was a different time then, and we survived without drama, but it was more than a bus ride on our own that made that summer memorable. That was the summer I learned to fish.

To us, Dorothy and Melvin were always "Grandma and Grandpa in town." Their tiny house was just a few city blocks from Ashland's iron ore docks on Lake Superior's Chequamegon Bay. It was a time when giant ore carrying ships, like the ill-fated Edmund Fitzgerald, would still come to be loaded with ore mined from the region. Dad's parents, "Grandma and Grandpa on the farm," lived a few miles outside of town, their small dairy farm sat precariously on a handful of wetland acres, a battle with water and nature they fought every day and in every season. Whittlesey Creek was the heart and soul of the property, its never-ending current dividing the tall, hip-roofed dairy barn from the white farmhouse. A wooden bridge spanned the creek just outside the squeaking screen door of the back porch. It provided access to the barn, the trout ponds, the creek banks, Grandma's spectacular summer garden and all the acres of the farm. We took turns visiting each of their homes, a few days here, a few days there. Tractor rides with Grandma on the farm through the low brush of chokecherry trees brought us to the beach, where we lost our breath in the icy summer water of the lake. There, we hunted agates and driftwood treasures for hours, listening to Grandma tell stories about where the waves had come from and what might be hidden under them.

On the days we spent in town, we'd hide for hours in Grandpa's wooden garage with its musty smell of fish, stale cigarettes, dried grass, and lawnmowers. I still smell those layers of life and can still close my eyes and see the scarred wooden walls of the garage. During summer there was always a pail along the wall of the garage filled with minnows, tiny silver fish held captive, flashing with panic when I looked under the clipped-on lid. I was drawn to their misery like a magnet. I would study them for hours, their unblinking eyes rotating upward occasionally. Watching them dart back and forth in the little bucket, I wondered what fish think.

The minnows helped him catch fish but needed oxygen to live in the bucket, Grandpa said. This first lesson in life, how air comes to be in water was a simple fact for him, but to me the words were golden gospel. He said oxygen in the water that the fish used to breathe is made by the sun, the plants underwater, and the animal life there. In a bucket, there is only enough oxygen for a day. I simply could not imagine how fish breathed air underwater. But I fizzed the water with the garden hose as he had shown me, and the minnows stayed strong for days. I imagined that the little fish swallowed the small bubbles of air. While I tried hard to tame the minnows to be pets, I wondered how Grandpa caught the big lake fish he brought home. He must have heard my unspoken question.

One morning he lifted me into the passenger seat of his butterscotch-colored Chevy truck. His aluminum boat, its sturdy hull and Johnson outboard motor built to manage the demanding waves of Superior, was hooked to the bumper. Years would go by before I learned that Grandpa Johnson was not the inventor of the boat motor. But on that day, I was headed to the ocean, going to sea with the tallest man I had ever met, to learn how to catch fish. I thought I might explode.

On cloudy days, the lake was dark. Its chilly mood was usually accompanied by a north wind rushing sharp weather and foamy waves to shore, their journey powered by foreign, damp winds. On this shiny blue day, the hesitant northern sun pierced the crystal water, illuminating its floor at 50 and then even 100 feet and more out from the boat docks. Leaning over the gunwale I watched the bottom slip under our boat, an undulating gossamer window framing my child's imagination where silver-green mermaids beckoned, ancient whales sang, and long-dead iron ore sailors looked back at me. On this day, on this lake with this man I loved and adored, I knew my heart was home. It was the only place I wanted to be.

We rode the waves together, he in the rear guiding with a push or pull of the motor handle, me in the bow in my orange canvas life-vest, white-blond hair flying in tangles behind me. I relished the smell of the lake on the wind and the sound of the water slapping and sliding under the boat's thin metal floor. Who knew what Grandpa thought as he navigated those waves with his tiny granddaughter riding forward, blue eyes wide, pink cheeks flushed with cold. I would like to think that he was filled with love for the small life before him that he was just getting to know, just as he was filled with a love for the life all around him, the life of the lake that he knew so well.

We fished together more than once, and on days when the lake was too wild for our boat, he drove to the small bridge over the Kakogan Slough, a quiet backwater of the Chequamegon Bay, which is now a protected wildlife refuge. On the bridge, I caught my very first fish, a young, muscular northern pike. Grandpa made me hold it in my tiny hands as he removed the hook. In my craziest dreams, I could never have imagined so many teeth on a fish. As he worked with his tools to get the hook out, he explained that young fish, returned without harm to the water, would live, maybe one day finding another hook but only after making many more families of fish. As the fish slipped from my hands back into the slough, I turned just in time to see a pair of ivory-white Trumpeter Swans as they flew just a few feet over our heads. We could hear and feel the whistling air from each stroke of their wings. As they passed over us, I ducked my head. I had never seen birds so big. He laughed, holding my hand as we watched them fly away, low over the slough, gliding, then disappearing into the cattails.

As I sit here today, I watch a snowy egret climb through the morning haze over our small Texas stock pond. The egret is a rare visitor for us, and my dreamer's imagination makes it a message from Grandpa, from that day so many years ago as we stood holding hands on the bridge, marveling at the swans. With my own age creeping in and tomorrow's world a bit unsteady, I miss the days we spent together and miss even more the days we never had. But my memory of his love, for the lake and for me, has become enough.

When I'm lucky enough to visit the lake on a trip north, I see him there, always. "Happy birthday, Cotton Top," he said in his sharp northern accent. "I love you." The lake holds our love in place, the waves a reminder of where it began.

6. Whittlesey Creek

Staying on the farm while visiting grandparents meant early to bed, early to rise, homemade donuts and eggs from the hen house for breakfast. We pulled vegetables from the smooth red clay of Grandma's gigantic garden and drank fresh milk brought in from the milk cans standing patiently in the water-filled cement cooler in the barn. The glass bottles of milk gathered layers of thick cream at the top, skimmed off for the adult's coffee, home-churned butter, and Grandma's home cooking.

Days were spent trampling paths on the banks alongside Whittlesey Creek, the "crick" that carried Lake Superior water through the acres of the farm. The distinction between the vowels, creek or crick, was the way my northern clan of German and Scandinavian heritage talked. Most vowels were pronounced hard and long; boat was always bote, Minnesota was always Minneesoda. My ears were deaf to our accent, and I always wondered why the rest of the world, all, that is except Walter Cronkite, had a different one. But the crick's voice was always the same, welcoming us, offering adventure, and inviting us in. The water was never too deep and always too cold, but we couldn't resist.

The banks sloped steeply to the water just ten steps off the back porch, where Grandma preserved meat, fish, and garden vegetables for winter meals. I can still hear the thousand slams of the wooden screen door as we ran in and out like untrained puppies masquerading as children, filled with excitement at the sight and sound of the creek. On every visit to the farm, we ran to the creek first, not stopping for greetings, looking under the wooden walk bridge where the turn in the creek had carved out a hole. Aunt Ruth's trout was almost always there, staring back, daring us to step in. She tried but never caught it, the magic of the current made it a giant of a fish, smarter than all who had come before it, destined to live forever. Every year I imagined it was the same fish, and maybe it was.

But as much as the farm held adventures, our childish preferences clamored for the buzz of life in town with late-night television, secret bowls of ice cream and neighborhood games with friends long after dark. We begged for more time with grandparents who kept few rules and enforced even fewer. But then over the years it happened that the childish need for the sugar high of freedom was replaced by memories of days at the farm. The simple beauty there and its own special freedom was as invisible to me then as a grain of sand on a beach. I heard but didn't understand the whispered stories told by the steady flow of Whittlesey Creek. I saw but didn't look deep enough into the dark secrets of the trout pond in the cattle pasture. I chased but never caught even one frog from the hordes of leopard frogs near the pond. The sun, dappled in the long grass, took the frogs further than my hands could reach and deeper behind the verdant door of their secret lives.

I didn't notice the small seed planted in my heart on the day I accidentally hooked a German brown trout from the pond, my excited shouts bringing Grandma on the run. Together, we marveled at the stunning treasure of the fish, its ruby red and golden spots glimmering in the sun like polished jewelry, its mouth opening then closing, desperate for life. Her hands removed the hook, then held mine as together we slid the fish back into the water. It lingered there a moment, stunned. Then, with a jolt it disappeared, leaving expanding ripples on the surface of the pond and a story for us to share. The seed began to grow.

My love for the farm is permanent, and the memories of its riches return when I close my eyes. In that private darkness, I remember the tender taste of sweet baby carrots stolen from Grandma's garden. In one exhale I am back there again, a kid in striped coveralls, skinny arms swinging a matching engineer's cap. But maybe it was all the things, the million tiny things that keep our memories alive no matter how old we get. Today, the moments of our time while staying in town during visits up north set a distinct parallel to the peace and wholeness of the farm, the garden, the pond, the creek, the never-ending squeak of the screen door on the porch. With the scent of ripening bananas, yeast rising and percolating coffee embedded forever in my sensory memory, I have never stopped yearning to live more like my country grandparents. Without Grandma's voice to answer my adult questions, I've surfed the internet for organic gardening tips, how to store and preserve produce, and how to make the homemade noodles she added to her chicken soup.

The white farmhouse with the magical porch is now almost completely reclaimed by vegetation, weather, and time. It's nothing more than a crumbling relic now. The welcoming voices behind the screen door are just whispering ghosts. There is no sweet smell of Grandma's kitchen filling the porch and welcoming us home. The vaulted attic space is now collapsed onto the living room floor where Grandpa would hide behind tall newspapers in his big chair, smoke hand-rolled cigarettes and growl sideways at grandchildren.

In that sacred attic, we would lay doubled together under mountains of Grandma's quilts, surrounded by the sounds of the bats in the walls coming awake, flying out to greet the stars in the cool summer dark. It was where in winter we'd wait for morning's light and then watch our breath curl up from the warm quilts, then we'd squeal and fling them back, braving the winter-cold air, using only our toes to navigate the narrow, curved wooden stairway, down to where Grandma's donuts and family voices warmed us again.

The property was purchased years ago, establishing Whittlesey Creek National Wildlife Refuge. There is even a multi-story visitor center now with an observation deck where the choke-cherry sloughs and distant beaches can be seen, and maybe even a trumpeter swan family for the very lucky few. The fields and ponds of the old dairy farm are gently but purposefully being reclaimed by nature, returning it to the lake-level wetland area it should have always been. Smelt, the tiny fish first found in northern lakes back in the early 1900s, can once again spawn, schooling upstream in waves a thousand deep, their Whittlesey Creek path now safe from the nets of pink-cheeked grandchildren. The early spring migration always brought us to the banks of the creek, excitedly waiting for the first rolling silver wave of Smelt to come around the bend in the chilled hours of gray spring mornings.

Grandma and the adults sat in the kitchen tucked alongside the big porch, playing cards, gossiping, and catching up on family news while drinking coffee from a pot that never grew cold. As we netted the first fish and poured them into buckets, she would meet us at the big wooden table on the porch to begin prepping them for the fryer, the freezer, or for canning and pickling.

Grandma's skills are now uncommon. In her day, she was formidable, her family's food mostly homegrown, her hands strong, calloused, and gentle, years before disfiguring arthritis would steal their strength. Her smile for us always came from the heart. It was easy to feel and made her more beautiful than words could say. I wish I could have told her that.

On a recent visit I searched the lake shoreline for agates under the surface, my shoes abandoned in the sand and bare feet turning blue as the waves curled against my legs. Each rock I picked up was illuminated, the wet layers and colors revealed, telling stories of where it had come from, how it was made, and what it might one day become with the help of the waves. Who hasn't picked up a rock on the beach and then dipped its dry smoothness into the water to see its colors and layers?

I am a rock, a layered agate polished by the lake, my purpose not yet defined, the past becoming clearer as the years go by, each layer telling a story of the elements that made me. I am a rock, the lake's work in progress. I am drawn back every year to the waves, washed and polished a little more, then sent home with another layer revealed, another part of me complete.

Why didn't I pay more attention? I finally understand the truth of the farm and the lake. It's become the place all of us, brothers and cousins, retreat to in our memories and return to in person year after year, some of us with adult children in tow. Like a gift made by hand, our grandparents gave each of us a lifetime love for the lake and its simple but glorious treasures. I am a rock, an agate in progress.

7. Our Own Farm

I was about to turn 13 when we moved to the farm in Rock Falls. It had once been a hard-working family dairy farm but its acres, covering a good portion of the 16-square-mile county section, had been divided and sold off over the years. Even though the move from Hillside Road to this farm had ended my weekend adventures with Ginger, I loved everything about this farm immediately.

There were woods bordering all four sides of the 20 acres, deep, mature and filled with wildlife. There was a small, spring-fed creek running through the backyard and away to the woods on the other side of the quiet road. Better yet, there was a much larger creek to the south of the property boundaries, once a part of this farm but now fenced off and belonging to an absentee landowner. It was perfect. The creeks were my refuge and my classrooms, providing countless hours of joy and adventure.

While roaming the banks of the big creek, I often heard partridge, or "ruffed grouse," drumming their wings deep in the woods to gain the favors of a mate. It's the first place I saw a covey of woodcock rise from the brush, strong, tiny little birds with the most amazing camouflage color patterns. It's where I learned about beaver families and saw first-hand and up close the astonishing architecture and engineering genius of the beaver. It's where I first heard the slap of their startled tails on the surface of the pond behind the dam they built, warning their own families of the danger in the stranger sharing space on the banks of their pond.

It's where I heard the sap exploding inside maple trees, as loud as gunfire, those few winters when the temperatures fell into the double-digits below zero, freezing the air to stillness, making the blue morning snow hard as diamonds under my boots. I learned to separate the different calls of owls in our northern woods. Gray, Great, Screech, Barn, and Snowy, all made their homes in or near our little farm. I tracked raccoons in the woods to their secret nests in the trees and discovered one warm afternoon if I sat quietly amongst the leaves, the woods would soon burst with activity, revealing the lives of the animals there. There could have been no greater gift from my parents than the wonders of this farm.

I avoided the loud competition with brothers, choosing instead to spend time with my dog or on the horse, following the trails through the solitude of the woods and along the creek banks. I never felt alone.

8. Sunny

I was painfully shy, awkward, and struggling as the only girl. My voice was often drowned out by four noisy brothers. School was no help, nor was it an escape from my introverted self. I found peace and joy in the woods, near the wild animal families I observed there routinely, and in the companionship of the farm animals.

Mom's horse was also growing up, and by now she had named him Sunny. He continued to be a headstrong young horse with his own ideas and opinions, none of which had anything to do with becoming a compliant riding horse. His explosive energy scared me, so I avoided him completely. Instead, I rode the new pony, Star, logging a million pony miles around the quiet back roads and animal trails through the surrounding woods. One summer afternoon, Star and I came upon a skunk caught in a steel-jaw leghold trap. I tied her to a tree, stripped off her saddle and used the saddle blanket to throw over the suffering skunk. With a stick, I sprung the jaws of the trap, and the skunk ran off on three legs. I had never learned how to unlock those cruel traps before that moment, and while I worked to figure out how, the skunk didn't spray me. I never wondered why.

I learned to leverage the weight of summer hay bales, even though they often weighed as much as I did. Working as a team with brothers, I learned by watching, throwing them off the field wagon and onto the motorized and chain-driven hay elevator which carried the bales up into the huge attic, or "hay mow" over the stalls and stanchions of the barn. In no time at all, I had another menagerie of rabbits. Then a rotating series of barn cats, all destined to receive short but sweet names that would fit on tiny grave markers. Their time with us as outdoor cats was a near-guarantee to short lives with tragic endings.

King, the Labrador dog, filled the footsteps of our family's first Labrador, Barney, who disappeared one night into the woods and never returned. King was soon joined by Trooper, an awkward German Shepherd puppy who arrived one Easter weekend. Both lived long lives with our family. In that first year, Dad helped us buy a bred Hereford heifer from the neighbor, and one year we had a hundred yellow chicks in the old brooder house, our parent's adventure into self-sufficient farming.

And I rode. I rode Star even further than I had ever ridden Ginger. Star was easy to catch and didn't mind spending hours as my personal chauffeur down the roads and across the creeks and fields of the new farm. But she was small, and I was tall. It wasn't a match made in heaven. Coming inside one late afternoon after hours on Star, Mom exclaimed, "You've ridden everyone else's horses, but you won't even look at the one we have in our own barn!" She was right, of course. Even the cows avoided me, learning quickly if I poured a pile of feed on the ground next to the fence, enticing them to come closer to where I stood waiting, I would ride them too. But Mom had a point. I thought Sunny was crazy.

I was convinced that the wild red horse would run me down or drag me through the pasture at the end of his lead rope or buck me off at every opportunity. Terrified, I stayed as far from him as I could get. Best just to pretend he didn't exist. But one night I dreamed I rode Sunny in the 4-H fair horse show. In my dream, he was the horse I had always wished I had. We won ribbons, we received applause, we were glorious together. After that, I looked at him differently. Could I ride him?

Certainly, I had ridden wilder horses without a second thought. Goldy, the mare that had run away with the Kim and bucked her off, breaking her collarbone. I rode Goldy without thinking twice. Whiskey, the huge bay gelding who belonged to family friends. He was used for barrel racing, and he was so big, so strong and so powerful only the family's oldest girls rode him. But I begged, and Whiskey was a thrill. There weren't any horses I wouldn't try to ride. But Sunny was the monster under my bed.

Mom tried to train Sunny on her own, succeeding in teaching him a slew of horrible manners. When she tried to set the saddle on his back, he simply stepped away or into her space, achieving either a dropped saddle or a squashed toe. If she managed to get the saddle on and safely cinched up, there remained the bridle and bit. His response to that was to clench his teeth completely and raise his nose so high in the air that Mom needed a bucket to stand on to reach the top of his head. If she managed to get the bit to his lips, he perfected the art of rearing high and twisting sideways to prevent having to accept the bit and thus, the indignity of both bridle and saddle. On the few occasions when Mom won both these battles and managed to mount up, it was predictable that he would either buck, flip his head so adamantly as to make the ride miserable, spook violently at imaginary plastic bags or dandelion fluff, or all the above simultaneously. It was during these early rides that she learned, in no uncertain terms, that he would never tolerate a spur or a whip. Ever.

Eventually, we tried a different approach. She would lead and I would ride, and with two against one she hoped we could gain some ground. For a short time, we did. It wasn't long until I was riding Sunny somewhat on my own, around the barnyard and occasionally even across the little creek and down the mini-bike trails. But Sunny still called the shots.

Prodded by Mom's hope, Dad began construction of a riding arena using rough-cut oak planks and cedar posts. He measured and then laid out an oval arena that encompassed the entire large garden space and most of the yard around it. The brothers were delighted with no more garden to tend. We all helped dig holes, learning from Dad how to use post-hole diggers and how to tamp the dirt firmly around the post's base for a solid, level post. I still bury fence posts the same way, preferring to patiently tamp the dirt firmly and still taking pride in the sturdiness of my fence posts.

I was riding Sunny in the new arena long before all the rails were attached, which, as it turned out, would be the turning point. Even though Mom and I had gotten past the bridle and saddle issues with help from a cowboy friend, Sunny hadn't given up his preference for criminal behavior. As we would learn over the years, if we didn't give him something challenging to think about and learn, he'd dream up something on his own. He had learned every quick way to get out of being compliant, but Mom had a plan. As horse people do, word-of-mouth references had recommended local horse trainers, Amy and Alma, a mother-daughter duo.

On the day they came to meet Sunny and watch me ride, he put on a show as only Sunny could do. As I rode him around the arena, he spooked at every blade of grass, ran sideways back toward the barn more than once, and then spun a few circles before stopping dead in his tracks in front of one of the cedar fence posts. I tried, but no amount of urging could get him to move on. With his long ears laid back and his nose flipping the bit up and down, he brought the demonstration to a close in style. Deliberately, he reared straight up in the air, hovering over the top of a cedar post for what felt like the longest minutes of my life. As I had done before, I instinctively threw myself on his neck, reins dangling, and hung on until he came back down to earth, after which I meekly asked him to move on. Clearly, the handsome three-year-old gelding had my number. Amy and her mother looked at each other, horrified.

It's a safe bet what would have happened had Mom not found Amy and Alma. It was the early 1970s and there was a local mink ranch that routinely advertised a free pick-up service and base payment-per-pound for unwanted horses, ponies and "downers," the industry term for livestock animals no longer able to walk on their own. I had seen their big green trucks rumbling around the area, sometimes empty, sometimes with startled equine eyes peering out between the slatted sides of the trucks. Those trucks stole many brave red colts and countless others, all destined to be made into meat for the sharp teeth of tiny carnivores, housed by the hundreds in mink farm cages awaiting their own tragic fate.

After watching his display of bad manners, Amy agreed to take him on, laying out a plan which included 60 days of training for the horse at their farm, during which we would not be able to ride or take lessons on him. This time would be dedicated to teaching the horse what he needed to know, and what he needed to forget. Once Sunny demonstrated a level of competence and compliance, I could begin to take lessons on him, with the goal of continuing his training and eventually even competing in the show ring. In the meantime, I was welcome to observe any of Amy's riding lessons in the area, and we were also welcome to watch Sunny's sessions with Amy. I learned that a few girls from my school were taking regular lessons from Amy, and so I made plans to watch them on the days when I was able.

I was 13 years old, soon to be 14, and had not yet reached the peak of my adolescent awkwardness, but I knew that I was different. I was much less outgoing, I struggled more with direction and instruction, and it always seemed to me that I had to work a bit harder to understand concepts. But learning from Amy was effortless. Her style of teaching and quiet, strong guidance during the inevitable challenging moments with a young, talented, and headstrong horse was perfect for my style of learning.

Sunny found a fit with her, and he blossomed with her training. She expected nothing less than the best try from her students, both human and horse. She didn't hold impossible standards over our heads. Quietly, she shared her belief in her students, encouraging us when we had frustrated tears, keeping reality close at hand when we became over-confident, and always showing us a path forward to success, one step at a time. Sunny didn't know it yet, but I had found a fit, too.

In group lessons with girls my age riding their horses, Amy took time to observe the latest practice demonstration from all of us, then gave us exercises tailored to address the issues she observed. When we practiced the exercises, she always included the reason why these exercises were important. Why keeping our heels down would help with strengthening our seat, why keeping our chin up would help with the steadiness of our hands and the effectiveness of our weight in the saddle. Amy's explanation of "why" always made sense. She never shouted, belittled, or threatened, instead choosing to observe, listen, and understand the hurdles standing in the way of success in every exercise. Her lessons were much more than riding lessons for me. I learned to work harder to understand what Sunny was thinking, how he was feeling, and how to work with a smart, ambitious horse and stay ahead of his game.

I was becoming a rider, not just a passenger. Gone were the days of a scared kid hanging on for dear life. In its place now there was a studious teenager, my dreams grown larger than life itself, riding a talented and beautiful bright red horse. With Amy's help and mentorship, a lifelong friendship had begun with the horse and with the teacher. My life would forever be brighter.

As the months tracked by, Sunny and I began to bond. Not every day was easy, but every time we worked together, we learned more about each other. Within a year I was riding Sunny bareback and bridle-less, loping big figure-eight circles in the pasture where he would do anything I asked of him, not only because he wanted to, but because he understood what I was asking. We had found each other as friends, his sense of humor and strong personality a fine and perfect contrast to my inward-seeking, shy temperament. Our adventures had begun.

Together we followed the deer we'd see on our rides around

the Rock Falls countryside. When we saw roaming dogs, his step quickened, waiting for my cue so he could pin his ears and thunder after them. He never liked dogs of any size, but he always had a soft spot for cats. The barn cats knew this, and they stayed close to Sunny in the winter, getting through the frigid nights and snowy days perched in the middle of his broad back. Lying comfortably with paws folded in, the cats would ride Sunny for hours on end. It was a common sight, the fuzzy red horse standing quietly in the winter sun, chewing hay while one cat or another was asleep on his back. I never thought twice about it.

Then, just like I had dreamed, we attended the county 4-H Horse Show the summer I was 14. Sunny and I won enough first-place ribbons to qualify for the state championship show to be held at the Wisconsin Dairy Expo Center three hours from home.

It was Mom's first long trip pulling a trailer. I remember her excitement and nervousness, especially as we drove across the interstate bridge spanning the Wisconsin River, high winds making the trailer sway behind the brown Chevy blazer. It was decades before GPS and Siri, and Mom had mapped out her route before we left home. As we approached Madison, the state capital, it was my job to read the directions to her, street by street and turn by turn, in order. It goes without saying that she missed a turn or two, but we survived and eventually arrived in one piece at the largest 4-H Horse Show in the state. I don't remember bringing home any ribbons or awards from that show, but I do remember the fun, adventure, laughter and tears as Mom and I shared the biggest moment of our time together with Sunny, up to that point. Our shared dream had come true.

9. Once a Thief

Between horse shows, Sunny had become my best friend and the teacher I instantly understood. I held a retirement party for my dependable friend Star, and Sunny and I began our travels across the universe. We ran through hundred-acre cornfields, the huge ears of corn slapping my boots, the tassels on the stalks spraying my face with dust and pollen. Stopping in the middle was brave. There were no landmarks but our tracks in the dirt. With my head barely above the stalks, I couldn't see where our exit from the field would leave us.

Other days, we followed paths outlined with beaver-chewed stumps of oak, mulberry, willow and maple saplings to the banks of the beaver pond, occasionally catching a glimpse of a beaver as it went about its work. We ran like the wind through the trees when the biting flies were on the hunt, clouds of insects like flying vampires, with a bite that would draw blood and leave a scar. On the run like this, I would look behind us over Sunny's galloping haunches to see the angry, hungry flies trying to catch us. Occasionally we'd see a deer, a brief flash of summer sorrel among the foliage my first hint, and then the flag of its tail through the trees as it leapt away. If I let his reins go slack, it became a wild ride. Sunny kept his ears trained on the deer as we crashed through the woods after it, stopping only for the fence lines the deer had cleared with ease.

High school had started, and ninth grade brought a new friend. Janet was also awkward and a bit of a loner. On a midsummer day during summer break, Janet and I saddled our horses.

She and her parents had worked out a temporary arrangement with my parents to keep her new horse at our farm for a few weeks until a closer location could be found. For our adventure that day, we had secretly planned to steal a feast. Nothing good comes to thieves, but we didn't know that then, and anyway, our plan was solid. There was a rumor about a hidden watermelon field, the biggest field of watermelons you could ever imagine, owned by a local corporate produce farm. The farm was home to the country's most popular horseradish, but every year the owner offered melons and strawberries and cantaloupe for sale. Some local boys had discovered the secret melon field, and word spread quickly. The boys said the field was guarded by the farm's employees, men in trucks carrying shotguns loaded with rock salt. It wouldn't kill anybody, but it will sure as heck leave a mark, the boys said knowingly. Janet and I didn't worry. We were sure we would be faster on our horses.

The day of the heist was a hot day by Wisconsin standards. After an hour or two of riding, we found a path towards the field, winding through a stand of young lodgepole pine trees. We turned our sweating horses up the path. The trees made a 12-foot-tall forest, just high enough to hide us and the horses as we worked our way toward the watermelons. "Someone needs to trim these tree branches!" I said to Janet.

She said, "Well, if a truck comes after us, it won't be able to fit between them!" and we laughed together, sure in our plan. What could go wrong?

Whiskey and Sunny were ready for a break when we saw the edge of the field through the branches ahead of us. There were acres and acres of watermelons, huge, dark green and just waiting to be stolen. Who would miss a few watermelons? Working quickly, we removed the bridles from the horses, hung them on the horns of the saddles and put their halters on. We tied them each to a tree so each horse could enjoy his own watermelon while we ate ours. We had brought two jackets each to use to carry our watermelons, and we had also packed a pocketknife, forks, and napkins. We thought of everything.

"Don't forget to loosen your girth," Janet reminded me. The horses were quietly standing tied to their trees, grateful for the break. Janet and I were getting ready to go choose our melons from the field.

"Right!" I said.

"That way the horses can cool off a little while they eat," she added. With the horses settled and the girths loosened, we made our way to the edge of the trees, scanning the watermelon field for trucks or men with shotguns. The coast was clear.

"Ready?" she asked. I nodded.

Here we go. Do thieves remember the first time they broke the law? Do they remember the thrill of getting away with the crime or the sweaty fear of getting caught? What mysterious force causes children to celebrate becoming tiny, joyful criminals?

We stepped out from behind the trees and quickly ran towards the biggest melons to steal. "They're GIANT!" I shouted.

"Just grab some and let's go!" she hollered back. She was already on her way back to the horses with two fat watermelons wrapped in her jackets. Janet was short and she struggled to keep the weight of the melons off the ground. I'd chosen two huge watermelons and was losing time, trying to get them zipped into my jackets. Just as I hoisted my two, I heard Janet yell "TRUCK!"

I didn't even turn to look. Dropping the watermelons like two burning logs, I ran as fast as I'd ever run in my life. How much does rock salt hurt? I wondered as I bolted for Sunny.

By now the horses knew something was happening. They were yanking their ropes, nervously swinging around, heads high, on full alert. Janet was ahead of me and reached Whiskey first, grabbing his lead rope and swinging up into the saddle in one smooth motion. They tore off down the path at a dead run. I was struggling with Sunny's rope as he spun and turned in circles. His horse friend was gone, and something large rumbled toward us from somewhere out there. As the lead rope finally came free in my hand, Sunny took off after Whiskey with me running next to the saddle, grabbing for the saddle and moving as fast as I could to keep up. My steps next to Sunny were getting longer with every stride. I took two giant steps and pulled on the saddle horn to swing up, like I had done so many times before. I was up and we were on the run.

Once in the saddle, I looked through Sunny's ears and saw Whiskey's black coat and appaloosa spots ahead of us on the path. Then they veered right at a dead run, following the path to head for home. At the same time, Sunny turned right too, except we were not on the path. He had turned directly into the thick trees, with no regard for the branches. At the very same moment the saddle slipped sideways, the loose girth finally yielding to the force of a running horse and his quick exit stage right. What a picture I must have made, a skinny girl hanging on sideways, her dear life flashing before her. Before I could blink, pine tree branches were slapping my face and arms with enough force to break the skin. If we didn't stop soon, I was going to be killed by Christmas trees.

Janet and Whiskey were gone, and I feared I would have to face the wrath of the truck guys by myself. It was either that or bleed to death right here in the pine trees. Finding a clear thought, I managed to put enough pressure on the lead rope to convince Sunny to slow down, then stop. I slipped from the saddle just as it turned completely upside down under him. I didn't hear any truck; all I could hear were the sounds of Sunny's heavy breath and my own gasping. Where were the men and their shotguns? Why weren't they charging after us? I touched my hand to my face. Yep, that's going to hurt, I thought, wondering how I was going to explain this to my parents. But the men and their truck never followed. Maybe the trees prevented the truck from racing after us, or maybe the men were laughing so hard they couldn't see to drive. I righted the saddle, tightened the girth and put the bridle back on Sunny. We set out for home. As we stepped out of the pine trees, Janet was waiting. Making our way home, we didn't speak. Even the horses were quiet.

Finally, Janet broke the silence. "Looks like we should have brought band-aids, too."

I have never cut into the first watermelon of the summer without the best bits of that day returning to make me smile. The companionship of a best friend, the sharp smell of sweating horses, the taste of blood in my mouth as Sunny, Whiskey, Janet and I, a ragged band of fresh new criminals, ran through the pines towards freedom.

I can't call Janet and laugh with her over our adventures as kids. She lost her battle with breast cancer before she turned 35. But maybe somewhere in Wisconsin under a pine tree or two there's a couple of rusted old forks and a random watermelon plant that still grows.

The year I turned 37, I buried Sunny. He was 27 then. I had brought him to Arkansas to live out his life with me. The time he had spent as a riding horse for the children of friends was over. He was with me for the first and last ten years of his life. His life-long habit of cleverly opening gates and doors with his horse-nose, so he could steal with practiced perfection from feed bins, barrels, and bags, had taken a toll on his hooves. As a result, he had been foundered for some time, but it had worsened in his old age. While good hoof care had mitigated much of the pain and discomfort associated with this condition, there came a time when nothing helped anymore. He spent days lying down, and on the occasions when he had to stand, the pain he experienced was visible.

On the day I had chosen to put him down, I bought a six-pack of Pepsi in cans, one of his favorite treats, and in the hour before the vet was due to arrive, we stood near the hole where he would soon rest and I held the cans, one at a time, in the air for him to swallow, the way we had done for years when we traveled to horse shows. He drank all six. Then, like he had done since he was a young colt, he stuck his tongue out and closed his eyes, his cheeks pulled in hard, savoring the flavor lingering in his mouth.

After the vet left and my friend's still body lay at the bottom of the hole, I wished him a speedy journey and then I cried. I cried for our life together, the adventures we had shared, his friendship and familiarity, and the sweet horse smell that was all his own. Would I remember everything about him now that he was gone? Grief can be irrational like that. I cried for my mom, my carefree child's life, now so far behind me. And I cried for the memory of that June day in 1971 when he was a wet, hours-old colt and I was a gawky ten-year-old girl on a tired pony. He was gone from me but would join Mom wherever it was that good horses and the people we love find each other again. Maybe this time they would have the friendship she had always yearned for, at long last with a horse of her own. It was fitting that I give Sunny back to her, the horse she had always wanted for her own and the horse she had unselfishly given to her equally horse-crazy only daughter. I hoped that when they did meet again, she'd forgive me for my time with him. Maybe she'd meet him with a summer-warm watermelon, cut just right so his white nose could again turn pink as he ate from the top down, like any good thief would do.

The memories we hold can carry us forward if that's where we keep our focus, and that's probably the best lesson I learned from Sunny, Mom, and Amy. Every time he and I struggled with a challenge, it was because I failed to keep moving forward. As I learned about dressage from Amy, and other instructors through the years, I often heard the word "forward" combined with instruction and wisdom as it related to success while working with a good horse. All my life, that word has haunted me nearly as much as it has helped me.

As I go forward with these last chapters of my life, I'll remember the lessons learned about "forward" taught by Sunny in those days of my younger self. I see now that the forward steps I took back then have changed. Years of living have brought a slower roll to my days now and a recognition that all good things have an ending. But the "why," the reason that made all the difference when learning, hasn't changed. The why remains the same, and with luck will again guide me in the moment I need it most.

10. Pheasants Come to the Farm

High school terrorized the most introverted side of me, the side I hid behind while being awkwardly immature with the few friends I did make. My odd clothing choices and secret, solo lunch hours taken in library closets helped preserve a bit of confidence, but I hid through most of the noise and lights of high school. I was at my best when it was just me with a peanut butter and jelly sandwich and a good book. Classmates excelled in debate class, on basketball teams, designing yearbook pages, learning theories of global economics, dissecting frogs, and reading Shakespeare. Friday pep rallies were particularly painful. The girls screaming and fawning over the sports team stars made no sense to me.

High school was supposed to launch us into pre-adulthood with an introduction to career choices, college options, communities of like-minded friends, against-the-rules alcohol drinking and learning about the opposite sex as an interest rather than an anomaly. With my horses and dogs waiting, I wanted to be rid of high school and graduate. My own life was waiting. But there was one saving grace for me. Agriculture 101 and FFA with Mr. Donald.

Ag class was held at the end of a long hallway leading to the back parking lot. It was well known that this was where the "stoners" hung out. The closer to the Ag room door, the stronger the smell of fresh cigarette smoke, old nicotine and marijuana. These were the kids I never made eye contact with. They swaggered, they swore, they drove their own beater cars, or trucks with full gun racks in the rear window. Shop class and Ag classes were the two rooms at the end of this hallway, so naturally the kids who took these classes would not be the same kids in debate class or chess club. I had no interest in chess and barely passed ninth grade debate. I didn't want to rebuild a tractor like all the boys were fighting to do, but I did want to learn about animals. When I got my class curriculum for 10th grade at the start of that school year, I was ecstatic. Agriculture 101 was one of my electives.

In Ag class we learned how to test fresh dairy milk for its butterfat content, how to determine feed-to-meat conversion ratios for beef cattle and feeder pigs, and how to judge dairy cattle and recognize many of the different breeds of cattle. We raised money for class projects by selling candy bars and popcorn, but also by meeting in local farm fields on late-fall weekends to pick corn. The fields had already been picked by the corn-picking machines, but hundreds of pounds of broken corn cobs were left behind in the stubble. We collected truck-loads of corn, taking it all to local feed mills for cash. Hard work, but the money went to pay for the projects Mr. Donald knew wouldn't get funded by the school board. One of those projects was raising wild pheasants.

Wisconsin has a state Department of Natural Resources, or DNR, that did a fair job of protecting natural resources like the bald eagle, wild rivers, and the state's white-tailed deer herds. The DNR also offered a Ringneck Pheasant re-population program for regions around the state where the species needed a population boost. One year Mr. Donald arranged for his classes to take part in the program as volunteer pheasant raisers. Student volunteers had to agree to raise the birds to a certain age and then release them into wild areas where they could thrive and repopulate. I begged my parents. The Rock Falls farm had an old chicken brooder house where the pheasants could live and grow until time for release, and I made, of course, all the usual promises. My parents relented, and immediately I signed up to receive 50 baby pheasants. All that corn picking had paid for the delivery of hundreds of baby pheasants, and one Saturday in early March we drove into town to collect mine.

They were tiny. The tiniest little birds I had ever seen. They looked like bumblebees. Round and fluffy with tan stripes on black bodies, their impossibly miniature legs carried them all over the slippery cardboard box at 100 miles per bird hour. I was warned by the DNR representative to keep the lid on the box until I got them safely home, but I had to peek. Could they hear my heart pounding?

Dad had set up the brooder house with a heat lamp designed especially for poultry, tiny feeders and waterers and a corner with a pile of loose hay for hiding. As Dad helped me release them into the brooder pen, I watched them in awe. So tiny. So fast. So many of them. I had no point of reference as I watched the baby birds figure out their new surroundings.

A week or two went by without event, the little pheasants acclimated to my coming and going, cleaning their enclosure, refilling their food and water dispensers, adjusting the heat lamp. Even though they were still tiny, they were growing. Then one night there was trouble.

It was late March, when Wisconsin weather can be wet, frozen, windy and cruel. Without a mom pheasant to keep them warm, the chicks depended on a heat lamp. When they arrived, Dad had strung an extension cord to the house to provide the electricity for their lamp. Wedging it between the doors, he plugged it into the nearest interior outlet.

For the first two weeks, the heat lamp had done its job, and the pheasants were comfortable and healthy. We had all gotten used to stepping over the cord on our daily trips in and out of the house. All was well until the night a brother came home in the wee frozen hours after a night out with friends.

Trooper, the German Shepherd, always made it a habit to sleep in front of the door like any good dog, doing his job to keep potential intruders out. Brother Dave, sneaking home after

2 a.m., managed to roll into the driveway without alerting our sleeping parents. Cutting the engine on his 1970 Monte Carlo, he successfully glided into the drive on silent wheels. Even Trooper didn't hear him. But getting into the house would be another thing altogether. As he eased open the door and stepped inside, his foot fell on Trooper's tail, who howled in surprise and leaped up, barking. Dave tripped over the swirling dog, lights came on, and loud words were exchanged. Dad, dog, and brother finally settled after the usual parent discussion, and finally the lights were turned off again. No one noticed the unplugged extension cord on the dining room floor.

A few hours later, I rose and dressed for school. I had chores to do before the bus came, so I went out into the wet cold, heading to the barn first to drop hay for the horses and cows, then to the brooder house to check on my pheasants. When I opened the door to the brooder house, the heat lamp was dark. All my pheasants were dead. I stopped breathing.

All 50 were on their tiny backs, spindly legs pointed to the ceiling, motionless. Kneeling and sobbing, I gathered them up, hot tears rolling down my cold cheeks. One by one, I dropped them into my coat pockets. Then I saw a leg move. Looking closely, I could see some of the fluff moving, just the smallest of breaths. They were alive! I stuffed the rest of the baby birds into my pockets and ran to the house.

"Mom!" I yelled. "MOM!"

She came running, her pink bathrobe wrapped tightly around her waist. "What in the world?" she asked.

Between loud, choking sobs, I told her the light was out, the birds looked dead, but one was still moving and could she save them? The words came out in one long, wet sentence.

"Blow your nose," she told me.

Then she went to the kitchen, turned on the stove and grabbed her favorite cookie sheet. It had baked thousands of cookies for us, Christmas cookies, birthday cookies, chocolate chip, oatmeal. It bore the scars of a lifetime of spatulas and spoons and baked-in stains of cookie ingredients. The cookie sheet was love.

"Start handing me chicks," Mom said.

One at a time, I handed her the pheasant babies, and she placed them on the cookie sheet in rows. Not bumblebees anymore, now they looked like tiny blobs of cookie dough. When my pockets were empty, Mom slid the cookie sheet into the warming oven. Then we waited, shoulder to shoulder, on kitchen chairs there in front of the oven door.

What does a mother feel when she needs to summon a miracle for her children? I'll never know, but I think for mom, her worry and love provided an extra boost of creativity that brought forth miracles she may never have imagined otherwise. When I was a spindly seven-year-old, I spent the better part of one day crying over my upcoming role as a princess in our ballet-school recital. I needed a fairy-princess wand. Like most future fairy princesses, especially those without magic wands, I was prone to drama. I went to bed the night before the recital completely devastated that I had no wand. The next morning, there on my bed lay the most perfect fairy princess wand my seven-year-old eyes had ever seen. A wooden dowel and a cardboard star wrapped in aluminum foil. It was my very first mom-miracle. Then came the pheasants.

"Look!" she exclaimed.

About ten minutes into the cookie sheet experiment, Mom and I saw the first pheasant baby pop up and stand on the cookie sheet inside the warming oven. I couldn't believe it. Soon after, another chick righted itself and stood, then another, then another. Together we started collecting the peeping, re-warmed chicks. All 50 babies had survived. While Mom and I sat by the stove, Dad had gotten a large cardboard box ready and had already rigged the heat lamp to the edge, hoping for the best. Into the box went the chicks, and as they began to peep and eat and drink, my tears were replaced with grins. Down to the basement went the box with the heat lamp firmly secured. The chicks would be warm and safe for the day.

After the heat lamp disaster, the pheasant babies grew, molting from tiny chicks to pre-adult birds, becoming wilder each day. I learned how high these birds can jump from the ground, and I learned how quickly they could take cover and blend in with the leaves and dirt of their surroundings. The mortality rate for them was high, but by the time late summer promised a new school year, 25 grown birds were set free in the woods surrounding our Rock Falls farm.

11. Wisconsin Winter Mornings

I heard an owl this morning in the dark. Muffled by some distance, it sounded like it was on the pipeline clearing, just a few hundred yards to our east here in Texas. Just like that, I was a teenager again, stepping out into the silent night that is deep-winter morning in Wisconsin. With bed hair and big boots, mittens and two layers of coats, I fed the cows and horses waiting in the barn, then hurried back in to clean up for school. Somehow, without much bloodshed, we navigated the rotation of five kids in one bathroom, then a breakfast of Cheerios and the school bus by 6 a.m. The hectic, loud mornings always began with that first quiet step outside. The cold, sometimes more than 20 degrees below zero, was always a reason to hurry. We were rarely late to start, and even more rarely late to finish.

Texas makes me miss the sharp northern cold, when my fingers grew numb in the three-layered chopper mitts and toes stiffened in boots, despite thick felt liners. There was always something real about the kind of cold that can kill a person. Snow crystals creaked and squeaked with each step as I walked to the barn, head bent and breath curling in frozen fog. I played a game as I walked in the cold, huffing frosty breath out from under my scarf and closing my eyes. The frost made my eyelashes fuse together with frost, and I'd walk blind for a few steps, eyes frozen shut until finding forgotten muscles in my eyelids to pull them open again. Then I'd do it again.

Sometimes on these mornings, colder than anything I'd ever felt, I'd hear the maple trees along the creek, their sap freezing hard until the tree heart exploded. The noise split the hardwood silence and carried for probably miles, frozen in the air forever. Other times, if I was lucky, I'd hear a Great Gray owl, its voice so large and full it could have been on my shoulder, yet I knew that was a trick of winter's cold. It would be half a mile or more away, probably on the giant dead oak tree along the creek. Once when I walked there, I found a tragic story on bloodied snow. Broken bones and tufts of fur, the last life of an unlucky rabbit. I didn't hear it often, but the owl's baritone song found a way into me, leaving traces of wonder that have lasted the years without tarnish.

Inside the barn, the warmth from the animals greeted me in a rush as I hurried to close the door against the cold. The moisture from their overnight manure filled the air with richness and thickened their whiskers with frost. The low barn beams over their heads had sheltered generations of farm animals from the stark and unforgiving cold of Wisconsin's country winters. I opened grain bins, poured scoops of feed for the horses and then more for the cows.

While they ate, I climbed up the ladder to the attic of the barn to drop a few bales of hay down. Standing there, I looked around at the hundreds of bales stacked in rows, all the way to the barn's roof beams. We had to use the hay on top first. "Breathe," I told myself. And in that breath, I found calm coming through me. Just breathe.

I worked my way up in the darkness, feeling my steps one bale at a time and, as I went higher, finally guided by the thin light of a single, flickering bulb at the peak of the hay loft roof. The air here smelled of summer dust and secrets, allergies and arguments. Occasionally the bales hid an unfortunate creature dried stiff between alfalfa leaves and clover blossoms. Mice, snakes, one time a whole skunk.

A first exploratory kiss from a boy was stolen here once, in this dark cave. An awkward moment hidden behind the tall wooden walls and then packed tightly between layers of hay bales. A shy girl's secret carefully kept, never shared.

Clumsy boots don't slip, I thought to myself as I climbed down the ladder. It could be a hard fall. I spread the hay out on the snow, in equal piles under the now-melting stars. As I opened doors and gates, the farm animals walked out into the cold, heads dropped low. In between my foggy breaths, I could hear the school bus shift down and turn off Highway 37, at least five stops yet to go before arriving at ours. Between the now-gray light of winter morning and the sounds from the bus, I didn't need a clock to know it was time to hurry, or I'd miss my ride to school.

12. On My Own

With high school graduation fast approaching, I was like most teenagers, ready to run free and hard at work testing the limits of my parents' patience. By the time I turned 17, I was sure I knew all I would ever need to know, and so, on the first day after graduation, I packed my things into a few boxes and moved out. I had a part-time job at a burger joint in town, a bicycle and my dog. I don't think Mom and Dad expected me to succeed, but I thrived on my own even if I wasn't completely successful right off the bat.

The relationship with Amy had evolved from student and teacher to friends. When she heard of my plans to move, she let me sublet a small room in the house she shared with several other college students. I had no real bills to pay except monthly rent, a portion of the utilities, and my own needs. Sunny stayed on the farm with my parents. For the first time in my life, I was on my own. I loved making my own decisions, good or bad. If my work shift ended late at night, I called my roommates to let them know I'd be late coming home. One night, Amy answered.

"You don't need to call us and check in," she said.

It was one of those moments where you said Oh! I really was on my own, as much as I could be. The freedom to choose my own day, my own groceries, when to wash my own clothes, what time to be back home at night was so new to me I didn't even recognize it. But the feeling was a comfortable fit, and I never looked back.

13. The Shawtown Bridge

It was early spring in Wisconsin, 1979, the first winter after high school graduation. I accepted Amy's offer to partner with her on a horse training barn and in no time, 30 stalls were filled with paying customers and a few good school horses for the lesson program. Neither of us had ever worked so hard, but we were paying our bills.

On a gray, damp day, I was driving to town after cleaning horse stalls to run a few errands on my to-do list. Taking a favorite shortcut, I turned the car towards the Shawtown bridge, an aging iron bridge over the Chippewa River. It was the time of year when the river was deep and unpredictable, its black current in sharp contrast to white stretches of ice sheets lining the banks. No matter how cold our winters were, the middle of the river always flowed with deceptive speed, darkly menacing any time of day. Every year the river swallowed someone. A child, a college student, a sleeping driver, someone died every year, and we all knew it.

As I drove across the bridge, the pale late-afternoon sunlight made me glance at the dark beauty of the water, as I usually did. I loved this river, and I loved its moods even more. Then I saw it. There, in the rolling current of the river's deepest middle, was a black dog, spinning and struggling to keep its head above water. I braked hard, threw the car into park and jumped out onto the bridge roadway.

Watching the desperate dog caught in the current, I leaned over the railing and threw a loud whistle down to the dog. It was all I had to give, and it wouldn't be enough. Hearing the whistle, the dog struggled harder, raising its body out of the water with effort and answering with a weak bark. I whistled again, my brain whirling, trying to think of how to save this dog. It spun around one more time, looking in my direction, legs flailing against the surface of the river, and then it went under. I watched until I was chilled, waiting for the river to blink and give the dog back, but it was gone.

There was nothing I could do. As I stood there, I was completely submerged by the hopeless feeling of seeing an animal suffering and having no way to help it. I was not prepared for the profound sadness that swept over me when I finally accepted the dog was gone. It wasn't even my dog, but without the ability to help it, it may as well have been, so deep was my heartbreak. Standing there on that windy bridge watching someone else's dog drown, I didn't know that instant would become one of those memories where the picture never fades and the feeling never ends. Do any of us ever recognize life-changing moments like that at the precise minute we experience them? I had no idea that in the years to come, my memory of this day on the bridge would come back to remind me why I did what I did as an animal control professional. The black dog's tragedy would give me a reason to keep trying, despite the challenges I would face as an animal control officer. Never again would there be nothing I could do.

14. New Jersey

Still holding onto my inner-child's dream of someday riding in the Olympics, in the summer of 1981 I accepted a position as a working student for a former Olympic equestrian coach, taking my first airplane flight to New Jersey and the farm he shared with his wife. Both still competed, and they had dozens of horses needing daily care. Too many horses for only two people. Nervous and excited, I thought I was more than ready.

But even at 20, I was still too emotionally unsure of myself to settle into the routine. Hours of horse care, stall cleaning, daily lessons from the coach, and other routine assignments would have made this job one in a million for any other talented horse girl. But day after long day I watched the planes fly overhead, my homesickness taking hold until it was overwhelming. I called Mom and begged to come home. She tried to soothe my homesickness with care packages and phone calls, prompting me to tell her stories of the horses I was riding and the lessons I was learning. Eventually, she relented.

By then, Amy had closed the training barn, married a veterinarian, and moved on with her life. I came home to Wisconsin with reality right in front of me. What did I want to do with my life? I had no idea. Needing a job, I learned to drive a school bus.

By then, my parents had sold the Rock Falls farm. Soon after the sale was completed and in a stroke of circumstance, I met the new family and arranged to move into the basement bedroom. They offered free room and board in exchange for training their horses, a schedule that fit perfectly between bus driving routes. It was an odd arrangement, but in some way matched the moment, segueing between the child I had been and the adult I was struggling to find. I still didn't see much in my future, but for a girl who lived in the moment, staying on my beloved farm, riding someone else's horses, and driving a school bus was enough for a while. Growing up could wait.

Ticking off the months like this, I began to take stock. I had no career. My work was just a job. I loved the horse work, but where was the future in that? I sensed a need for more stability, something with an income I could depend on and work that had meaning. Maybe college would be the answer, a way to build equity in a life of work while shaping a career. I applied for grants, took out a loan, and enrolled.

15. Coming Out

While attending college in Eau Claire, a door opened from a closet I didn't even know I was in. As a twenty-something school bus driver, I often put my name on extra driving assignments, especially a coveted spot for a summer youth sports camp. It was an easy gig. Over the weeks the program lasted, I became friends with the two "counselors" assigned to ride my bus. I admired these girls with their easy confidence and good looks, both of whom were clearly at the top of their athletic community's food chain. Watching Lexi and Kate interact with the other counselors, it was obvious I wasn't the only one who admired them. Their outgoing, easy manner and slight swagger made it clear that both women were comfortable in their roles of leading and inspiring others.

I wanted to be more like them, but I had never been particularly clever at sports, and I certainly wasn't used to being a leader. I spent too many hours alone in my woods, riding Sunny solo down the quiet roads around the farm and reading books in my room. I couldn't throw a softball with any kind of accuracy, discovered during snowball fights with neighbor friends and brothers. While my snowball intentions were accurate, even the barn door knew it was safe from my throws. I had always been tall for my age and usually ran rather than walked, but I was still an awkward girl with big teeth, knobby knees and pigeon toes. These sleek and confident athletes played softball, volleyball and basketball and were the college team's scoring stars. They wore their hair in stylish cuts that dared anyone to disagree with them. I was a dusty horse-girl, driving a school bus in worn-out barn boots to pay the rent and buy a few beers along the way. Despite those differences, I made them laugh, and we became easy friends.

Each morning I drove the bus on a set route, stopping to pick up groups of children waiting in their camp t-shirts and colored shorts, ready for a day of games and camaraderie. Lexi and Kate, my first passengers of the day, greeted the campers when they boarded and made sure each found a safe seat. With the route complete, I drove to the sports fields on our college campus to drop my passengers. In the afternoon, I returned to pick them up for the ride home. The counselors managed the kids and cleaned up any trash left on the bus at the end of the route. All I had to do was drive the route and be on time.

It was a Friday, the last day of the summer camp. The kids had been good, tired from the last-day festivities. With the bus empty, I looked up in the mirror just before arriving back at the bus barn. Lexi and Kate met my gaze, leaning forward in their seats.

"Hey," Kate said, her chin lifting with the word. Her elbows rested on her legs, spread comfortably in the small bus seat. Her hands were folded together.

Meeting her eyes, I said, "Hey."

"We're having a party tonight at our house, why don't you stop in?" she said.

I glanced at them both. Did I see sly smiles? I slowed down for the last red light, pushed in the clutch, slipping the stick shift into neutral. With the bus stopped, I took a moment. Parties really weren't my thing. And even though I had just parted ways with my boyfriend, I wasn't ready to put myself in a room with college boys just yet, if ever.

My boyfriend of several months was a hardworking guy, with a quick smile and friends who adored him. He was a sweetly attentive and gentle man with a sense of adventure and a need for companionship. But no matter how many hours we spent together, our relationship just didn't feel like a fit. I was struggling with what my "thing" was, whatever that meant. I had no clear picture of what a relationship could be for me. Leaving him was hard. Through his tears he asked, but I had no reason to give him, and the phrase "It's not you, it's me," was a sorry cliché that did nothing to ease his hurt.

After our breakup, I basked in being on my own again. Go to a party? I wasn't eager to meet any new boys just yet, and my experiences with group parties, although admittedly limited, usually led to expectations of some sort of relationship thing. I looked up in the mirror again. Kate sensed my hesitation and doubled down.

"It's just a bunch of us counselors and a few other people, you don't have to bring anything or anybody else, just show up."

I saw her exchange a glance with Lexi. Had they discussed this invitation? It seemed that way but maybe I was just being skittish. I breathed, then put the bus back into gear, let the clutch out and headed for the last turn into the bus lot. I knew I'd miss my daily camaraderie with these two. What did I have to lose?

"Sure," I said. "Where?"

Lexi gave me a slip of paper with the address and said, "Great! See you tonight!"

I parked the bus, followed them into the break room and then they were gone. I'd see them soon, but in an entirely different light. It was July 23rd, 1983. I had no idea my entire world was about to spin on its axis.

16. The Sty

Music has a way of defining bits of our lives, staying in our heads, shaping experience through sound, giving voice to emotions not yet known. Music can be a vehicle for change, especially, as I soon discovered, at the parties of the women athletes. That summer, everyone was listening to Michael Jackson's new album, Thriller. The Police had a number one hit song "Every Breath You Take," which was destined to become an anthem for the women I would soon meet. With music leading the way, I sang along and lifted new wings.

That evening, I pulled up to the address Kate had given me. After finding a parking spot, I made my way to the house. Standing in front of it, I took a deep breath and swallowed hard, stepping up onto the wooden porch. Through the open door I saw a darkened room. Maybe a living room, I wondered. As my eyes adjusted, I saw it was filled with couples dancing to a slow song. My heart sank.

"Just great," I thought. "Men are here."

As I stood there looking in, I had no idea of the threshold I was about to cross. Behind me was my childhood with all its innocence, imagination, and solitude. In front of me was music, laughter, and a mystery that beckoned so deeply it felt as if I was being pulled forward by magnets. I felt like a late summer weed, rooted forever there on the porch. Before I was ready, I was met by a dark-haired woman in a loose-fitting white shirt with sleeves rolled up to mid-forearm.

"Welcome to The Sty," she said with a twinkle. With a big smile, she added, "Come in!"

I gulped and followed her into the house. Who names houses, I wondered. She led me through the dancing couples towards the kitchen, shouting over the music about daiquiris, bananas, and blenders, then pointing to a beer keg, wedged in ice in a plastic barrel.

"Help yourself!" she shouted and then disappeared.

I grabbed a red Solo cup from the table and poured a beer from the keg. Then I looked around. All I saw were women. I don't remember ever hearing the term "lesbian" as a kid. Not in our Catholic grade school nor in any of the public-school systems we attended with each of our family moves. Sure, occasionally a kid would get in a disagreement with another kid, and slurs would fly, especially if no adult was within earshot. We practiced cuss words in those spaces, we practiced with anger and even hate, although the latter was always a temporary thing. We practiced forgiveness, and we practiced joy. We practiced becoming adults. Two of the terms we saved to sling at each other, which held a lot of weight and left some of the deepest bruises, were the terms "lesbo" and "homo." Just like the term "rape," which I heard on the Walter Cronkite news all the time, I wasn't sure exactly what the words meant. But I didn't miss the fact that they were evil words used to hurt others.

I marveled as I stood there, beer in hand and slow dance music fading. Women dancing with women! Lesbians! Gone was my dread at being at a party as a single woman. There wasn't a man in sight. It was the first time I used that awkward word. The term had never been part of my regular vocabulary, nor did it exist in any other aspect of my environment. Up until that moment, I had never knowingly met any gay people. I had no gay friends that I knew of and understood absolutely zero about what being gay meant. Neither did anyone I knew. The depth of my naivety had not even registered yet, that would take some time.

I wandered back through the living room where the music was playing again, this time David Bowie's "Let's Dance" had couples twirling and swinging together. Stepping around the dancers, I went back out to the porch, and found a folding chair. The night air was a familiar friend. Surrounded by music and a house full of women I had never met, I felt like I was back in my woods, leaning against the trunk of a warm oak tree in the morning sun, with sounds of birds replaced by the sounds of women laughing together. I had never felt so completely at home.

Arguments are made among academics and psychologists, those who strive to understand the habits of people or at least explain away our varied humanity regarding the origins that comprise and define our species. What I have learned through the years is that this homosexual "lifestyle" is not a choice. If homosexuality could be a choice rather than a genetic blueprint, there might not be many gay people at all. I haven't met any gay person who would purposefully choose to live this harder, often hated and almost always misunderstood life. The terms depicting gay people, and there are many, should never be paired with "choice." Choice has as little to do with being gay as it does to being straight or even being another ethnicity.

There was a joke shared back in those days: "What's the difference between being Black and being gay? If you're Black, you don't have to tell your mother." We laughed to hide our pain. For many, these parties represented their only family.

I believe that, just like puppies, we are born to be the way we are. Yes, there are environmental factors to be considered as a person develops from infant to adult. Yes, there are influences that undoubtedly shape our lives and behaviors in ways we couldn't possibly predict but must learn to live with, like a timid puppy exposed to frightening factors at an early age, who then learns to bite and snap in fear to protect itself. Or the same timid pup exposed to the same frights but provided a supportive, learning environment where the pup can develop coping skills to manage their instinctive fear, discovering ways to deal with the challenges of real life in positive ways.

People too are either left to fend for themselves in a scary world, or provided support to help them build positive inner resources to manage what life throws at them. There are puppies and children born to be extroverts or introverts, bullies or care-takers, leaders or followers. The point is, nothing but genetics dictates who a baby is born to be. The factors that influence that baby from the day of birth onward are what make all the difference. I was raised in a home with everything I would need to find success. My parents protected me, pushed me, cheered me on, shared their values, showed me right from wrong, set examples for decency, compassion, and consideration, and nurtured my love for adventure, other people and for life itself. Together, they set expectations, gave me responsibilities and levied consequences that enabled learning and growth. Even with all this, I was born to prefer women as companions, con-temporaries, peers and partners. But I didn't know it until that night at The Sty.

As the months went by, I would learn that it wasn't an easy assignment, this gay thing. While I never wished to erase the part of me that was most comfortable and happy in the presence of women, I did wish many times that I could do what straight people took for granted. I wished I could walk down the street holding hands with the person I loved. I wished I could assume that a lifetime together would result in the legal sharing of our hard-earned savings and properties. I wished that employers and government entities would consider a same-sex partner as a legitimate family member in terms of insurance coverage, medical decision-making, and other inclusions. I wished the church I'd grown up in didn't interpret the love I felt as wrong and immoral. It felt right to me. My love was honest. I prayed every night to God, never asking for anything, but always thanking Him for what I had. God made me and my friends in His own image, the same as He made my family. For that, I gave thanks with every prayer.

Dad had worked hard to provide each of us with a foundation

in the religion and spirituality that meant so much to him as a kid and which provided him, all his life, with his strongest support and moral compass. Like I had learned from Dad, I offered a thank you to God for each day I had been given. But still, I wished I didn't have to hide my love and my joy from my family, my church, and the communities I lived in.

As gay women, we mattered in more ways than that simple word implies. We mattered as part of an ever-growing community of increasingly visible gay people with skills, dreams, and talent. What is that worth to a community? How is that value measured? What was true then is that the contributions of gay people were rarely recognized without the specter of ridicule, the threat of hate, or at the very least, misunderstanding and disdain.

With all this, I felt complete. I knew I had found what was missing. That the discovery came with so much challenging and painful baggage was just part of the deal. It would have been so much easier to "just be straight." But it wasn't me.

17. Relationships

With each tentative step in this new world, I searched for something lasting, a relationship worthy of building bigger, worthy of the hard work I knew it would need. My joke to friends was that I was looking for someone to soak my dentures with. I was searching for someone to fill the hole I felt when I was dating the two serious boyfriends I had. Relationships for me never felt frivolous or temporary. I went into them with eyes wide open and my heart right behind. With my dogs, cats and horses, I had become used to the hard work and eventual pain of commitment. I buried more than a few favorite pets, but people aren't pets. Sure, there were fun, extemporaneous moments between friends, the kind of play that provides more questions than answers and leads to lessons learned, but a real relationship, one that could be built and would build in return, was still waiting for me, somewhere.

My first kiss with a woman was that night at The Sty, a midnight moment that took me by surprise and left me with the seed of confidence I would need in the years to come. There on the porch, with slow dance music gently trickling out the screen door, it was the dark-haired woman who greeted me at the threshold who gently took my face in her hands. Her eyes told me to just be still and, for God's sake, to shut up. I did. Then she leaned forward, her lips touched mine, and she gently kissed, then teased for a tiny second, then leaned back, a slow smile growing as she saw my expression.

"There," she said.

I met my first girlfriend at a party just a few months after that night at The Sty. Joan and I soon found a house to rent together, blended our random collections of mis-matched furniture and housewares and promptly adopted a cat. Russell Sprout would go on to live a long and glorious life with Joan, but in those first years he helped us both learn about the value of relationships. The next months were a blur of friends, parties, final exams, money woes, broken-down cars, blizzards, and lessons in life. Not any different than any other college kid. After less than two years, Joan and I split up, for the most part amicably, and as the years went by, we hung onto our friendship. We are still close friends today. The foundation of our short time together stuck with us and provided building blocks for the trials and successes we found as life took each of us on our travels.

Over the next few years, my confidence grew. Not overnight, but bit by bit. I learned to express consideration and kindness to others, while laughter, adventure, and exploration provided the spark of the real me. I loved the newness of this life. Each day was like pointing your car in a direction not yet traveled, heading for destinations which promised to leave you wanting more. I met so many amazing women, most of them college athletes in sports ranging from softball to basketball, volleyball and soccer, rugby and lacrosse to swimming and even bowling. There weren't any horse girls; in that fact, I remained an anomaly.

"Perhaps one did not want to be loved so much as to be understood." -George Orwell

18. Linda

Not many of the girls I met were as naïve as I was. They were comfortable with who they were, and not all of them were gay. With very few exceptions, the straight girls were accepting of the gay girls, their friendships and camaraderie as strong as any friendships could be. One of those straight girls was Linda, who became my best friend in 1979, that awkward year I spent living as a guest on the Rock Falls farm. She is still my best friend today, a treasure and a comfort that defies definition.

Linda was 18, and I was 19 years old when we first met. She was engaged to be married to the younger brother of the man who bought our farm for his family. Linda was the athlete I wished I was, and the best listener I've ever met. Together we went to too many dive bars, drank too much Jim Beam and chased it with never enough beer. We threw darts and played pool with foolish boys who underestimated our skills in the game. And we talked. We drove through the night on back roads, crossing county lines and crossing them back again, laughing, crying, sobering up. With the windows rolled down to welcome the fresh breeze into the car, the fumes of whiskey, beer and cigarette smoke would leave, replaced by the scent of wet farm fields and earthworms. Who knew that we each needed someone to listen to our hopes and fears? To listen as we reached back in our pasts and dreamed about our futures, looking for ways to reconcile things that seemed irreconcilable. From the first day we met, we knew each other. We were solid.

On one of our last nights out together, just days before she was to be married, I looked at her as she sat across from me, laughing at something silly we had just shared. It was like a movie when the scene suddenly changed; the light dimmed, and her face wasn't 20 years old anymore. It was wrinkled and worn with years not yet lived, her gaze smart and thoughtful with lessons not yet learned, her smile a grandmother's smile, her eyes filled with patience and weariness, joy and laughter, the look that only comes from experience, and I knew.

"You'll be a grandmother one day," I told her.

"I hope so!" she said, and we laughed at the idea of growing old and wrinkled. As the moment passed, her face was smooth and young again, her eyes bright with hope.

Today, she is the best grandmother her grandchildren will ever know, full of adventures and always cheering for them, whether wiping tears or celebrating smiles. She caught a few curveballs but eventually married again to the love of her life. She worked with her whole heart and changed lives in her career of speech therapy. She finds time every spring to bring new life to their little farm by planting the huge garden she always dreamed of when we were young and wild. We still laugh about getting old and wrinkled, but our laughter rings true now, just like our love for each other always has.

19. Coming Home

Shortly after college let out that spring, I found a job with friends in Colorado. Looking forward to adventure, I loaded my 1974 Ford pickup truck with a few boxes of belongings. The next morning, I left Wisconsin for Colorado. The only directions I had were "Go south to Iowa, then go west." Driving to Colorado with no real destination in mind was the road trip experience of my life up until then. I didn't need to be convinced to leave college behind, exchanging it for three jobs in the mountains to keep my bills paid and have enough money to spend time with friends. I met more women than I can remember.

There was the women's amateur hockey team in Aspen, known fondly as The Aspen Mother Puckers. They formed the nucleus of much of the lesbian social life there in the Roaring Fork Valley between Glenwood Springs, where I worked, and Aspen.

Before fall set in, it was clear that I had worn out my welcome with friends. I'd rented a small room from them in the loft of their tiny A-frame cabin, and the floor plan was only big enough for two. With the offer of another job back in Wisconsin, I again packed up my blue truck and headed back east and north. I had one tank of gas and $64 in cash. I would turn 26 years old in a month, and that small wad of cash was all I had to show for my time on this planet. Maybe it was time to grow up.

I hadn't told anybody, not my friends, not my family, that I was coming back. The day I arrived, I drove straight to Mom and Dad's to surprise them and say hello. I hadn't been there for more than 20 minutes when the phone rang.

Mom answered, "Hello?" then she paused, her eyebrows knitting. "Just a moment. It's for you," she said.

"Who even knows I'm here?" I asked. She shrugged and held out the phone. "Hello?" I said.

"HEY! It's Chris!"

The excited voice on the other end of the line was my college friend Chris, one of the girls I knew from college parties with the other women athletes. Chris and her partner had also just arrived in town, driving from their home in Arkansas to visit Chris's grandmother. Chris had graduated from college the previous year and went on to graduate school in Arkansas. We made plans to meet for a few beers the next night. Any friend of Chris was a friend of mine, and when we met, her partner and I hit it off immediately.

But soon enough the two returned to Arkansas. I returned to my jobs driving school bus during the school year, delivering packages for a delivery company during the holiday season and tending bar at night at the new "gay" establishment in town. By the end of that long winter, I was ready for a change of scenery. Most of my friends had graduated and work was beginning to seem like a dead end. When I had an opportunity to split the cost of gas in a friend's car for an impromptu spring break trip to Arkansas, I was all in. I called Chris, and the dates were set.

It was March 1987. On a frosty early morning, my friend Kevin and I left Wisconsin in his tiny beat-up car with a Canadian blizzard chasing us south. We took turns driving through the night, navigating the dark through an ice storm in Iowa but pressing on, knowing the weather would only get better if we could stay ahead of it. Exhausted, we arrived in Arkansas to green grass, dandelions, the songs of birds and the hum of lawnmowers. I couldn't wait to get a sunburn.

In less than a week, I was in love with the climate and community of Arkansas. Impulsively, I made plans to leave my Wisconsin friends and jobs. I didn't know it, but Chris and her partner were struggling to maintain their relationship. Within a month after my arrival in Arkansas, the rift between them became a chasm, and their young relationship fell to the earth burning. I didn't know how to take responsibility for someone else's relationship woes, but I clearly played a part in the ending of their time together. It was a confusing and exciting time in my life, so many new things, so many challenges, so many adventures to be lived. I grieved the loss of a friend just as I celebrated the beginning of a new relationship.

Immediately I thought I had found the long-term relationship I yearned for. With any kind of luck, I could also find a job to grow into. I was off and running, discovering, exploring, learning, loving, living. All I needed was a job. Finding work in a state filled with blue-collar culture was not as easy as I had assumed. With some college, I found myself over-qualified for the factory jobs that paid well and offered benefits. Without a southern family tree or an accent that boasted southern pride, I was vastly under-qualified as well. Running out of money and without any job prospects, I called the local animal shelter on a whim. What would it be like to volunteer at a dog pound? There was only one way to find out.

PART TWO: ARKANSAS

*There is no communication in this world
except between equals."* Ken Burns

20. The Volunteer

After I found the number for the shelter in the yellow pages, I took a deep breath and made the call. I had never been inside an animal shelter and knew nothing about what a "dogcatcher" did, if that was what they were really called. I had never volunteered anywhere, ever. But I'd spent too many restless nights wondering what the world held in store for me. I needed to quit sitting around wringing my hands, waiting for life to happen to me.

The woman who answered the shelter phone may have gone into shock when she heard me inquire about volunteering there. In that short quiet pause on the phone, I imagined seeing her eyebrows raise.

Then she said, "Come in any day," with a smile in her voice. "We're open from 10 a.m. to 5 p.m., but you'll have to meet our director first."

I told her I would see her the next day. My excitement began to build. I've always loved something new — a new adventure, a new season, a new friend, a new puppy. This felt like all those things and more. Shortly after ten the next morning, I pulled into the shelter parking lot, angled my truck into a visitor slot, and walked into the first animal shelter of my life.

The smell of bleach made my eyes burn, and under the bleach smell was wet dog fur, fresh dog waste, tomcat urine, cigarette smoke, and spray-can air freshener. I was glad for the bleach smell as I stood there, surrounded by the blue haze, but I was thoroughly comfortable. Like that first night at the threshold of

The Sty, standing on the outside looking in, I knew with every part of my soul that this was where I belonged.

21. Meeting Lib

There was no pamphlet or brochure to explain the career benefits or pitfalls of animal shelter work. There were no college professors to teach me about parvovirus, possums, how to get a raccoon out of a chimney or how to guess the sex on a fuzzy, fluffy kitten. There was no one I knew who had the experience and patience to explain it all so I could make an informed decision. No. On that day all I had to go on was a gut feeling that here, in this smelly, tiny cement-block building surrounded by lost and unwanted animals was something I could fix. Never in a million years could I have guessed it.

My self-esteem had recently taken a beating at several chicken-factory interviews. At the last one, I lost a decent-paying egg-candling job to a badly dressed young girl wearing a grimy, once-pink baseball hat stuffed down over her large ears. On the front of the hat a slogan proclaimed "49% Sweetheart, 51% Bitch." Walking out to my car that day with just a few dollars left to my name, I sagged, wondering what the hell I was going to do. But as I stood there that first day at the shelter, I looked around and recognized a world that made complete sense to me. It was as natural as breathing.

The cramped front office had an old, cracked linoleum floor. On the right, as you entered through a screen door, stood a tall receiving counter. Behind the counter sat Theresa in her tie-dyed dress and Birkenstock sandals. You could almost see the small cloud of patchouli. She was on the phone, and as she flipped her long dark hair back, she made eye contact and offered a smile.

As I smiled back, she pointed wordlessly to the door opening behind me. Clearly, I was the hopeful volunteer who had called the day before. I wasn't even holding a sign.

I turned to see the shelter director, lit cigarette poking out from the side of her mouth as she clenched it tight, surveying the tall blond girl in her shelter.

"Can I help you?" she asked.

All I could smell was the blue haze, but I kept my focus on the tiny woman in front of me.

"Hi," I said. "I called yesterday about volunteering."

I had to look down at the top of her cigarette as I asked the question, but she didn't flinch. She may have squeezed the damp cigarette a little more as she squinted up at me, this fresh-faced girl with a northern accent who was asking about volunteering.

"Sure," she said. "Nice to meet you. I'm Lib Horn." Looking up at me, she reached a hand forward, and we shook hands. "What do you know how to do?"

Lib was a tiny woman, dressed in tan pants with side pockets, a short-sleeved button-down plaid shirt and well-worn canvas tennis shoes that had never seen a tennis court. The wrinkles on her clothes and on her inquiring face were well acquainted. She had dark salt-and-pepper hair, cut straight and short, her face framed by the practical style. Her bright eyes were quick and thorough, not piercing, but they didn't need to be. One look and it was easy to understand that she needed only about seven seconds to toss you back into the river you came from if you deserved it. When we first met and for years after, Lib was rarely without a long, skinny cigarette between her teeth, always clenched on the side. Sometimes it would even be lit. That she could walk around and have entire conversations while holding a cigarette in place was crazy enough, but most of the time she managed to balance a long ash on the end, ash that never seemed to fall off on its own, no matter how long it grew. It seemed permanent.

When we met, Lib had been on the job for about a year. Hired for a job very few wanted, she had inherited an agency that city leaders had all but abandoned. The 1940s-era kennel had been built on low-lying and low-value property on the south side of the growing Ozark Mountain town. It was a sad piece of land where the rainwater runoff took its final plunge into antique city drains that had long been over-tasked. Her job was to bring the city shelter into some sort of humane compliance under the watchful eyes of a small but vocal group of local animal lovers. Her previous jobs as a schoolteacher, government employee, and part-time rat-lab inspector for a university research department had not prepared her for the reality of this aging shelter and the harsh, brutal moments that had defined it for years. Into that reality I stepped, a naïve girl from the land of cows, cheese, and beer. Lib was the bridge between the ghosts that haunted the history of this shelter and its future. She was five feet one inch tall and weighed maybe 115 pounds. I loved her immediately.

Our friendship, even with a few ups and downs, would last years until her death in November 2015. Her question that first day, "What do you know how to do?" prompted a surge of confidence I didn't know I had. I stood taller, straightening my t-shirt.

"Well," I started, "I love animals." She stood there, unblinking. "And I've trained and shown horses," I blurted.

She waited. I noticed the long ash on her cigarette, slightly drooping now. Would it fall? Confidence disappearing, I began to panic. What else did I know how to do? Mom had always told me I had to learn how to toot my own horn, and now I really had to if I wanted to work here as a volunteer. I took a deep breath and continued.

"I've had dogs and cats and raised rabbits for 4-H when I was a kid," I said hopefully. "My parents bought a farm when I was 13, and I loved it there. The woods, the horses, the beavers." I hesitated. The beavers? Why did I mention beavers? They weren't pets. My imaginary hand slapped my forehead. But then I saw her eyes sharpen.

"Tell me about the beavers," she said.

And I spilled my heart out. I told her about the two creeks on our farm, about the paths through the woods where I rode my horse and where I walked with my dog behind me and the barn cat riding on my shoulder. I told her about the beaver lodge, the trees chewed next to the banks of the pond they built and about the time I tried to walk across their dam. I also told her that I once got in trouble with the law for stealing the neighbor boy's traps one winter, all two dozen of them.

"Did he get his traps back?" she asked.

"Yes," I replied sheepishly. "And I had to apologize to him. But he was killing the beaver family," I added with emphasis. She looked at me again, measuring my words.

"Can you come in tomorrow?" she asked. I said yes.

Did I shout my answer? I wondered. You know those times when you're so excited inside that your ears become deaf to the sound of your voice? This was one of those times. Standing there with Lib Horn that first day, talking about horses and dogs and beavers, I felt a change coming over me. I didn't stutter in the telling of my story. I didn't look down at the floor when answering her questions; instead I met her gaze with strong and steady assuredness. I knew what I was talking about. The awkward high school girl I had always been, the same one who struggled to fit in among the confident and handsome women I had met, began to fade. I knew this place, and I knew the work like I had lived it all my life and I was a hundred years old already. Did she see me stand a little taller? Did she watch the tentative college girl metamorphose into a woman filled with purpose and mission? Maybe so.

For the years we knew each other, I wouldn't be the first nor would I be the last person she took a chance on. Lib cared about people, and I quickly learned that was the core of her own heart. It was the same instinct that she could tap, calming almost any conflict, quieting the most opinionated moment. Such a skill was as hard to find then as it is today, especially in the world of animal sheltering and animal advocacy. Lib Horn was the first person I met who cared as much or more for people as she did for the animals in her care. She taught me to embrace this basic founding principle; doing so would hold me steady for the course of my career, failing me only at the very end. By then, many friends and colleagues had already fallen victim to the realities of shelter animal euthanasia, the heartbreak of relentless death. The overpopulation problem that we all battled was no one's fault and everyone's fault.

But on that fresh new day, I knew none of this. All I knew was that this was another life-changing moment before me, and I needed to grab it. She said I would start by learning how to clean kennels and maybe if it worked out and I liked the work, someday there might be a job available. I drove back to my shared duplex rental, head swirling in a blue haze of my own making. What I didn't know then was that the days and hours to come over the next year and a half would become the first miles of the greatest adventure of my work life. The learning curve would be a straight-up climb, the steepest I'd ever experienced, but it would bring me the most rewarding work I'd ever known.

22. An Animal Shelter Meets My Heart

In addition to Theresa, the receptionist, there were two animal control officers, both large, gruff men who had seen better days, and three animal caretakers. Richard, who told me his title was "kennel master," was easily my favorite. He was a tall, thin young man with a shock of dark hair that rarely lay smooth. Richard rode a little battered moped to work every day, rain or shine, knees folded up under his chin, elbows tucked in, no helmet. He was a colorful figure in a town not short on color. On my first day, Lib told me to follow Richard everywhere. Over the next few weeks, I learned how to clean a kennel, calm a frightened cat, taste-test dog food, and eventually, how to help euthanize the animals who hadn't found a home or who were sick or injured. He was kind, gentle, and soft-spoken; he and the animals he cared for could have been their own fairy tale. He loved them all.

The shelter was a long, narrow building with 20 indoor-outdoor kennels in the first half, and 20 identical kennels in the rear half of the building. The two banks of cat cages were in between, hoses and supplies tucked into the few spaces in and around the cages. Like most animal shelter kennels of the day, the building was cement block and chain link, each kennel with a sliding metal guillotine door on the exterior wall so that dogs could have access to individual outside kennels and some fresh air. It was an awkward and inefficient system, especially for cats and very old or injured animals, but it was all we had. With hoses and buckets of soapy water, we cleaned cages first thing every morning and then worked hard to keep them decently clean throughout the day. For the most part, we succeeded.

The building was severely outdated, and too many years of poor cleaning practices and shoddy maintenance created more problems than solutions. This wasn't lost on Lib; she recognized the challenges ahead and had been actively working to resolve each problem as it landed on her desk. Solutions of that scale required money, the kind that doesn't fall from the sky, especially in a city where money to help stray animals had never been a priority. As I got to know her better, I saw that Lib had been working as hard as a television evangelist to recruit people to her cause. By the time we met, her efforts were gaining momentum. In the meantime, there wasn't much to prevent us from doing our best with what we had, except for the day we were faced with an epic Ozark Mountain rainstorm.

The city was built in the heart of the Ozarks, one of the oldest mountain ranges in the United States. The town and surrounding landscape were breathtaking, but with its aging water infrastructure, any rainstorm of more than a few inches usually caused backed up-sewer drains. With the shelter located at the end of a main drainage system, we faced this every time the system failed. We were used to the office being flooded, sometimes more than a couple inches of standing water would need to be squeegeed out so we could clean and dry the floor in time to open to the public. The kennels, however, were always spared. The sheer size of the floor drain in the middle of the kennel building was enough to prevent the kennels from being flooded like the office.

The big drain did require some attention from time to time to keep it functioning. Once, when our morning cleaning routine stopped due to the drain being plugged, Lib offered to be lowered into the problem drain to fish around for the problem. Usually, it would be wads of animal hair wrapped around a nylon leash or two, but there was no telling what would end up in the drain. I learned quickly to pick up those things as I cleaned each cage. That morning, Lib donned some over-sized yellow rain pants and matching Playtex Living gloves, the kind Madge wore for those Palmolive TV-commercial manicures. We laughed. She made quite a vision. Suited up, she eased herself down into the muck. After some time poking around with her yellow gloves, she was lifted back out, sweaty and covered in sewer water. The drain was still plugged. She hosed herself off as best she could and called the city public works department.

The man who responded, a grizzled gentleman named Harold, removed the clog and got the drain working. Over the years Lib worked for the city, she and Harold remained close friends, sharing sewage stories and city political news, often confusing the two and laughing at their own cleverness. But one night there was a storm, bringing consequences that were more than we could have imagined.

23. The Storm

The rain had been coming down off and on for days, saturating the ground. Drain systems throughout the city were at full capacity, and the nearby Arkansas River was at flood level. But the system that brought the rain wasn't done. In a surge one night, the storm dumped six to eight inches of water on the city, pushing city services, including the shelter, to crisis mode. As we arrived at the shelter, we expected a mess and hard, dirty work ahead, but we didn't expect what we found.

Desperate barking greeted us, the tone different from the excited barking we were used to hearing at the beginning of the day. Hurrying through the flooded front office, we were stunned to see the kennels. There was over a foot of dirty black water covering the entire kennel floor. Human excrement floated with dog excrement and even a few feminine hygiene products. The aisle and every cage were flooded. As we hurried to set up temporary cages outside so we could move the frantic dogs, I saw our kennel master stop.

The kennel he was standing in front of held a family of small dogs; the mom and dad and their four half-grown puppies. We put them together in a large kennel run, hoping they would acclimate easier and thus, be easier to adopt. They were all dead. The water had been too deep. He was motionless, his face impossible to read, then I saw his shoulders shudder as he sobbed. There was nothing to be done but get to work.

24. The Tan Tomcat

I hadn't been a volunteer for very long before Lib offered me a job as an animal caretaker. Within a few weeks I was getting paid minimum wage, working for animals who appreciated every little thing. When I left each day, I knew I had done my best to provide something of value to each animal in our care. A blanket, a bowl of wet food, a kind word or a soft scratch behind the ears; for the ones who feared strange people, a blanket hung on the doors of their cages to offer some privacy and a sense of safety, and maybe help them cope with the environment they were now in. Maybe those little comfort things could help them get adopted into a loving family home, leaving the shelter and its noise and smell far behind to begin new lives. Good care could make the difference between life and death, I was sure of it.

I was in my element. I proudly told my parents that I had found a job I truly loved. More than a job, I had discovered a career, a future, and a purpose. After five years in college, I had never felt so motivated each day as when I rolled out of bed to get ready for work. It was truly difficult to go home every evening. With this job, I could help the lost, terrified, injured, and sick animals, even if I couldn't save all their lives. My care could make their lives better, even if just a little bit. But not every animal who came to our shelter for a new chance at a better life would find it. It was 1987, and animal sheltering was in the earliest stages of being re-branded from "dog pound" to "shelter." Even so, no matter how hard we worked, many of the animals we took in and cared for ended up being euthanized. It was one of the most important parts of our job, said Lib. She reminded us every day that it was our job to care for them the very best we could, and when it came to their last day, as was inevitable for so many, Lib was there to help us understand that we were the last person those animals saw, and we needed to give them our best. It was one of the toughest assignments we faced every day.

After she was hired, one of the first changes Lib made in the euthanasia procedures at the shelter was to require an injection of sedative prior to actual euthanasia-by-injection. While this procedure has since become outdated as better drugs, more efficient procedures and employee education efforts have changed the field, at the time it helped provide a kinder, more humane euthanasia. To sedate means to induce "sleep," and with sleep came unconsciousness and, most importantly, no pain. It was a huge step in the shelter's prior policies and one that made Lib a hero in my eyes instantly.

On the schedule to be euthanized just a few weeks after I had been hired was a tan-colored feral tomcat. His wide, blocky head was covered in scars and wounds, his ears were tattered from battle, and he even had a few broken teeth. His unblinking eyes dared a human hand to cross the threshold of the cage door. Today I think back to this tough old tom and still marvel at the skill he must have had to survive in a world bent on his destruction. I have since been humbled by hundreds more just like him, all of them earning my respect and admiration for their fierce spirit.

To safely and quickly sedate animals like this feral tom we had a homemade syringe pole, nothing more than a wooden dowel rigged to hold a simple syringe and needle. With a small injection of a drug sedative "cocktail," we could safely sedate animals like the tomcat without fear of losing a hand in the process. One of the tasks for the kennel master was to double-check paperwork and then inject all the animals scheduled for euthanasia that day. His quiet approach combined with his gentle voice and comforting touch would settle the most fearful dog, most of the time. In a few moments, the animals were all lying in their kennels or cages. Some had vomited, a common response to the drug mixture, and were lying in their own vomit. It was my job to reposition them, so they weren't in their own mess while the correct dose of euthanasia solution was pulled up for each animal on the schedule. The tan tom was on the schedule that day.

The dogs on our list all died quietly, and we worked our way down the row of kennel cages. Sitting or kneeling on the floor with them, I would hold the dogs next to me or in my lap, one front leg in my hand, my thumb providing pressure on the cephalic vein so my partner could find it with the needle easily. After all animals had been injected and were lying prone in their kennels or cages, he would again go to each cage or kennel and verify death with a stethoscope. I would follow behind and bag up each animal for the freezer. Shortly after she was hired, Lib had put a stop to immediate incineration of euthanized animals. I never asked her why, but in just a few months I would understand, finding a deeper appreciation for the wisdom of this woman and the depth of her compassion.

As we got to the cats, sedated and prone in their stainless-steel cages, we went to the tan tom first. My partner laid him flat out on the small table in the cat room and prepared to inject him with a "heart shot" of euthanasia solution, at the time an acceptable method with the use of a pain-blocking sedative, which we had already administered. But at the millisecond the needle pierced the skin of the cat's rib cage, he jumped into the air and flew off the table, landing crookedly on the cement floor, his claws scrambling for traction. In a flash he was out the door, into the parking lot and running drunkenly in great bounds through the grass lot where the police department trained their K9 dogs. We followed at a run, not sure what to do if we caught him but amazed that he had fought off the effects of the drug.

The cat didn't see the chain-link fence between him and freedom, and he crashed hard into it, head on and going full speed. I don't know what the measurement of a chain link diamond is, all those shapes that make up the integrity of the fence itself, but I know for sure that it's much smaller than a large tomcat's head. Somehow, in the speed of his freedom flight or maybe the effects of the sedative, the cat's head went clean through the fence and there he stuck.

We looked at the stuck cat, then at each other. Our eyes met, and we both knew that this cat deserved to live. With a borrowed pair of bolt cutters from one of the animal control trucks, we worked to cut the chain link from around the cat's neck, and then he was free. We watched him run into the woods across the road. We never knew if he lived or died during the days that followed his great escape, but there was no way either of us could have euthanized him after that. We never told a soul, and for months I would see that cat-sized hole in the chain link and smile.

25. The Hardest Lesson

I had been an animal caretaker for just a few months when one of the animal control officers suddenly quit. Lib encouraged me to apply for the job. The interview process was fast, and within a week I was being fitted for a brand-new uniform. At last, I was going to learn how to catch dogs. Finding my way around town behind the wheel of the animal control truck, I memorized the streets and alleys, highways and hollers of the college town.

As I drove, I saw owned dogs and clever strays roaming, many of them routinely out on the streets, and found pockets of feral cat colonies, some with dedicated caretakers and some fighting for every bite of food available. Through it all, I was amazed by the hidden numbers of unwanted companion animals, especially in a town that prided itself on image. I was also amazed at the survival skills these animals had. Many of them were living decent lives with no help from people except some free food from time to time. My admiration for them grew, and it wasn't long before I began to rebel against the daily euthanasia list. Without a backward glance, I fell victim to wide-eyed idealism for the first time in my life. Why bring animals into the shelter at all if they were just going to be sentenced to death in less than a week?

I had learned to gain the trust of wary stray dogs using a quiet voice, slow movements, treats and sometimes even toys. I was good at it. But most of the dogs I worked so hard to catch never left the shelter alive. It was a different time then. While the early 1980s ushered in many new concepts in the world of animal welfare, the public had yet to be convinced. For many, the pound was just an agency that provided rabies control by getting rid of stray and unwanted animals. Who would want to adopt one of those mean dogs? Despite the public perception, animal shelters began to promote adoptions of unclaimed animals. Our shelter, like many others across the country, began community education and outreach programs. The concepts of humane sheltering and compassionate care began to be accepted. The image of the dogcatcher from the cartoon *Lady and the Tramp* was fading.

Even with these changes, our euthanasia rate was depressing. In those early days, I was sure that being out on the streets was a far better option for stray animals. As my new uniform began to lose its shine, I let more than a few stray dogs run through the alleys, across the roads to another backyard, down through the drain tunnels and into the woods, following them only with my eyes. I sent them on their way with the hope that they would be safe, that someone would put out a bowl of water, a bit of food, or even open a door. For those animals who had a home but couldn't resist the call of the wild, I often let them find their own way back home, learning that less than 10% of our stray animals would ever be reclaimed by worried owners. I especially believed that the feral cat colonies were far better off on their own than in our tiny, smelly shelter.

For months this outlook sustained me as I learned about our "regulars," the dogs who knew where the hole in their fence was, or who were let out the front door by owners without a worry. It would be many more months before I understood that these unwanted animals and the ones whose owners failed to keep at home were the main source of the many hundreds we euthanized each month. That's a hard truth to accept when the ones I left to roam always looked so carefree. It would be years before community-wide spay/neuter or trap-neuter-return programs, designed to help curb the explosive growth in the pet population, became commonplace for shelter animals. In the meantime, I didn't see the connection.

26. The Sins of Our Pets

Euthanasia is a term that literally means "kind death." To some people, there is nothing kind about death, not theirs, not their loved ones, and certainly not for an animal in a shelter. Death brings out the passion in animal people. Most of us deny it will ever find us, then weep for years afterward when we lose a beloved person or pet to the finality of death. Death is almost always personal, and that makes it worse.

I've wondered if these were the people whose parents gave them abstract reasons for loss like "Grandma is gone now" or their dog or cat was "living on a farm in the country with lots of room to run." But I grew up that way, too. Then why? Why can't parents offer softness, sympathy, and support to a child when a profound loss threatens the stability of their emotion? Why do we hide from death?

When it comes to death, truth is elusive, especially when it concerns a young heart being guarded by a parent, and that is our foundation as a culture.

My parents meant no harm, it's how they were taught as children, too. As I started this new job, with my excitement at a zenith I had never experienced, euthanasia of the animals I had promised to help was at the core. I needed to understand why it was ok. I needed to find a way to reconcile my feelings towards ending an animal's life with the reality of an overflowing shelter, or sick and injured animals on the streets with nowhere to go, no comfort, no second chance. I needed to know how to do my best for them, even as I learned that far too often, my best was to give them a kind death. How could I accept their death, especially when I was the one who ended their lives?

I wondered back then, in my new uniform and shiny badge. Was there a heaven or hell for an innocent creature like a pet? What about the unwanted dog who landed in our shelter because of a dog bite, or pooping on the carpet, or chewing a shoe for the last time, or digging in the flower beds, or chasing the chickens? What about the cats who came to us because the children developed an allergy? Are the sins of the pet deserving of a death sentence? Are our pets even capable of committing a sin?

What about all the different religious and spiritual beliefs of so many different people, many of whom are pet owners? Then, there are those who ask why death must be bundled emotionally with spirituality or the rules of a specific religious denomination at all. And the biggest question that plagued my young dogcatcher mind; was euthanasia just for the sinners? Or was it a reward for the ones who suffered?

It was just all so complicated.

My work always had to be better for the animal in need, and better didn't always mean more weeks or months in a cage, waiting for a family. Sometimes better was a kind death, a release from loneliness, an exit from fear, an alleviation of chronic pain. The animals themselves asked for nothing less, and they asked for nothing more. In this way, I knew I was still helping the animals who needed me. It never occurred to me that some would think it was wrong, but I wouldn't meet those people until years later, when I was beginning to accept that my own time in the world of animal sheltering needed to come to an end.

To some animal advocates, any life was life enough, and the No Kill community, initially begun in 1944 began to gain ground in the mid-90s. Soon after, influential voices helped it explode in the early 2000s, bringing shelter animal euthanasia, and all the baggage that accompanied it, to the forefront. By 2004, No

Kill and animal euthanasia had become household words. In the mud that flew between advocates on both sides, unleashed passions clouded any solution or agreement between opposing principles. From the noise of this division within the animal welfare community, I learned that not everyone agrees that the term "suffering" can and does encompass emotional and mental anguish, such as that of a caged or kenneled companion animal, removed from basic physical comforts like routine quiet, regular touch, and human companionship. Unlike visible suffering, when an animal spends its life waiting in a cage, no blood is shed, no scars are ever seen. But not everyone saw it that way.

It's a human condition to disagree, especially when our hearts are involved in the conversation. But the basic tenet I still believe in today remains the same. From the very first day as a volunteer in 1985, I gave every animal my best effort and an honest chance at a better life. I didn't save every life, like the slogan for one national animal no-kill declares we must. Instead, I worked hard to make every animal's life better, even if I only had a short time to do so and even if that "better" didn't meet the expectations of an idealistic public. I had more than just the animals in my kennels to care about, there were animals on the streets who needed a chance, too.

I was just beginning to understand that I could no longer do the work I had loved so much. I could no longer walk through the aisles of my shelter kennels, or the rooms with rows of cats hiding in plastic boxes and sequestered behind stainless steel cage doors or plexiglass windows. When I did, the stress of each animal found me in waves, their loneliness, exhaustion, fear and worry drowning their hope right before my eyes. Sometimes I just had to go sit somewhere, like a bout of heat exhaustion, waiting for the strength to return to my knees. But the strength that was missing was from my heart, something I never expected to lose. I had seen it happen to other people, friends who left because they couldn't do the work anymore. But I never thought I would be them. I was stronger. I wondered if I was going crazy.

27. Astro and Seymour

Being an ACO was not a job for the weak of heart or slight of spirit. What I knew for certain was that I enjoyed being with animals all day, every day. Working with them, helping them, keeping them comfortable, learning how to solve the problems they found themselves in, and forging relationships with the people who either caused the problems or offered a solution. When the shelter was full and every kennel or cage occupied, I struggled with the reality, knowing that bringing in one more stray would mean another animal would have to die.

But I also learned that leaving them on the streets wasn't the answer. They all needed another chance. Lost animals needed a way to get back home, giving their owners another chance to be better caretakers. Unwanted animals needed a safe place to sleep with food and water, and another chance to meet a new family that would love them. My own truth was that my new boss, Lib, was the champion of second chances. I followed her lead.

So, I began to make notes, mental and real, about the dogs and cats I saw in neighborhoods. With these mental notes and some creative problem solving, I discovered there were a lot of animals that could be helped without having to come into the shelter at all. It would just take a little extra effort and, always, a little extra time. I was getting paid by the hour anyway.

There was the black lab who belonged to a local attorney, a "repeat offender" we called her, many times she would get a free trip home rather than a ride to the shelter to wait safely for her furious owner to reclaim. Even with free passes, the owner of this beautiful and funny Labrador wrote multiple checks to the city to reclaim her pet, giving Lib hours of entertainment and conversation about the future as plans for a new and bright facility began to take shape.

Then there was the large, bright Pyrenees dog, Astro. About once a week, Astro could be found galloping joyfully among the kids on the school playground near his home. School administrators were tired of hosting the big dog, and the owners didn't seem to care that Astro wasn't welcome. After a few free returns, we were instructed to take him to the shelter so his owner would have to come in and reclaim him with fees, hoping that the increased fines would inspire the owner to be more responsible. We learned quickly that Astro, while cheerfully willing to be caught and always a good boy around the kids, turned into Cujo the split second he was behind a cage door. It was like a switch went off in his head. Instantly unrecognizable with his charging, aggressive snarling and challenges to the human on the other side of the cage, the behavior would prove to be Astro's undoing. After multiple trips into the shelter to reclaim his dog, his owner surrendered him to the shelter. It was years before shelters had behavioral experts on staff, but even without an expert evaluation, we all knew there was no safe home for Astro and his unpredictable aggression. I always wondered why his owner just didn't fix his fence.

One afternoon, I was on duty alone when a call came about a dangerous cat in a garage. The older couple who lived there barricaded themselves in their home while the strange-acting cat turned in circles in the garage, yowling loudly, occasionally growling and spitting at nothing. This was the scene when I pulled up at the address and walked toward the garage. As I watched the cat, the hair stood up on the back of my neck. What was wrong with it? I spoke to the homeowners through the door. No, they had never seen this cat. No, they didn't know any neighbors who owned cats, and they had lived here for years and knew most of their neighbors. They had made a few phone calls before calling the pound, they said, but none of their neighbors knew anyone with a cat, either. I looked back at the cat, still circling, still growling and yowling, its own hair on end and its tail puffed up like a raccoon's.

I went to my truck and fetched a net, a transport crate and a pair of gloves, thinking maybe this cat had rabies, but there was only one way to find out. As I approached the cat, I carefully aimed the net and captured him in one swoop. The result was instant and dramatic. The cat leaped into the air, straight up into the body of the big net, and screamed as if it had just been lit on fire. With the cat twisting, screaming, fighting, I managed to get it contained in the net long enough to dump it into the plastic carrying crate and slam the door shut. Sweating, I carried the cat and my equipment to the truck to head to the shelter. Once there, the decision was made to euthanize the cat and send its head to the lab for rabies testing, the only way to accurately diagnose the fatal disease. The results would be back the next day. That night I was the ACO on call.

I've spent many days and nights thinking how things could have been different, how we could have arrived at a different conclusion and how the ultimate tragedy that occurred that day could have been prevented. Around 11 p.m. that night, my pager went off, and I called into police dispatch. The dispatcher told me she had a distraught caller on the phone who wouldn't take no for an answer, so she had agreed to call the animal control officer on duty to ask if we had picked up any stray cats that day.

I asked for the address and a description, and when I heard the dispatcher, my heart fell off a cliff. The address was two doors down from the couple's garage. I called the number, introduced myself, and listened to the perfect description of the cat I had picked up. As I listened, I knew I would have to tell them the horrible news, that their beloved cat was dead, and that we had made that decision in error. I knew my reasoning for why we had euthanized their cat wouldn't matter to them. I knew they would be devastated, grief-stricken, angry, heartbroken. The man told me their lost cat was older and had been blind all his life. He had never been out of the house except that day when a visiting relative left the door open. A terrified, lost cat, completely out of his element and in fear for his very life with every strange smell, sound, and feel. A cat without a lifeline. A cat that needed a second chance.

It was years before microchips for shelter animals were common, a little thing that would have made all the difference that day. It was a time before mandatory hold periods for injured or ill animals were standard policy, those decisions left to shelter and municipal administrators, as this decision had been.

His name was Seymour.

28. Peaches

It was summer, and I was still wide-eyed and learning fast about all the skills I would need to be a decent animal control officer. On patrol with the senior officer one afternoon, we were casually driving the streets keeping an eye out for stray or loose dogs, making our presence known in the neighborhoods. When the truck was more visible, less animals found their way into the streets. A call came over the two-way radio. The dispatcher gave us the address for a citizen who needed help with her own cat. We weren't sure of the details, but she told us the elderly lady was in tears on the phone, and a cat had cornered her in her bedroom.

When we arrived and knocked on the door, a woman's voice inside the house told us to let ourselves in. When we entered the home, we saw packing boxes everywhere, all in various stages of being filled. There was no sign of a cat or the owner, but we could hear the caller crying behind a door in the hallway off the dining room.

"Don't hurt her!" the lady cried. "Her name is Peaches. My daughter wants me to move, so I've been packing for a week, and today Peaches just went crazy and attacked me. I ran to my room and closed the door, but she wouldn't let me come out! I didn't know what to do, so I called you."

The senior animal officer I was training with took charge of the moment. "Do you know where she is now?" he asked.

"No," came the tearful reply.

He told me to go back to the truck and bring in the net, an

animal crate and handling gloves. While I was outside gathering the equipment, he learned that the owner would be moving into a nursing home and wouldn't be able to bring her cat. She planned on taking her to the shelter the day before she left her home for good. She told him that Peaches had been her only companion since the death of her husband, and she had never been aggressive in any way.

"She must be upset about all the boxes," she said as I returned with the tools.

He told her to stay in her room, and we went to work looking for Peaches. Her owner described her as a red tabby with long hair and a few white markings. It wasn't long before I found her tucked under the couch in the living room. My training partner came over with the net, and after a few minutes of fishing around under the couch, pulled her out. He had been able to get the aluminum rim of the net over the cat, leaving her plenty of space to run into the length of the net itself as he pulled her forward. A quick and expert twist and flip, and Peaches was secure in the net. I opened the wire door to the crate, and he inverted the netted cat over the door, giving it another twist except this time in the opposite direction, and into the crate plopped the overweight, and by now extremely frightened, Peaches. With the crate's door secured, he told the owner it was safe to come out of her room.

She emerged in tears. It was obvious that this was as traumatic an experience for her as it had been for the cat. The two old friends, now separated by the wire door of the crate, looked at each other. In that moment it was clear to me that no church existed, no preacher alive would ever have the words of comfort, and no senior-center activity counselor would ever be able to measure the loss that was happening as we stood there in the living room, surrounded by cardboard boxes holding the remnants of the old woman's life. Her children, her husband, and now her cat, all gone.

Her goodbye to the cat was seared into me. The training

officer picked up the crate and turned to leave. As I was gathering the remaining equipment, she came to me and handed me a crumpled $20 bill.

"Promise me she'll be safe!" the woman begged. "She won't be hurt, will she?"

From my few days of city personnel training classes, I knew we were forbidden to accept tips or money of any sort while on the job, instead we were told to encourage the potential donor to designate the money to the shelter or the humane society group so the money could be accounted for and properly documented. She continued to insist, and my explanation about city policy couldn't change her mind. I sensed that maybe the money was a contract, a promise of sorts, a way to seal the deal and give her an assurance that no matter what happened, I would respect the offering and see my promises through to the end, no matter what the end may be.

I guessed she was in her late 70s, from a generation of folks to whom the definition of animal control evoked cruel and unbearable images of the ending of animals' lives. It was this perception that I had vowed to fight against. Today, I knew I could assure this lady that Peaches would be fine. I couldn't promise her that the cat would get a home, but I could promise that she wouldn't be hurt. She had my word. As for the crumpled money, I would turn that over to Lib or Theresa when we arrived back at the shelter. I turned to make my way to the waiting truck.

When we arrived back at the shelter, Lib looked at the terrified cat and made the decision. It would be far kinder to euthanize Peaches. Our shelter was no place for an old, frightened cat who would likely never get accustomed to the noise and smells. The trainer instructed me to bring the cat into the euthanasia room. There, he met me with a syringe of euthanasia solution and a tool he called "the cat grabber." Designed with a long handle and padded, crescent-shaped dual jaws, with a squeeze of the hand the jaws could close. It was built to fit around a cat's throat.

Using the tool, he pulled the terrified cat from the crate and swung her up onto the stainless table. I cringed as he pinned her to the table with the tool, all the while giving me instructions.

Without the courage to tell him no or to insist he follow Lib's protocol of pre-euthanasia sedation, I followed his instructions and held her still. She must have been in a state of shock from the day's events, not moving once while he quickly slid the needle between her ribs and with a quick rush, injected the solution. Peaches went limp under my hands. "Put her in the freezer," he barked, and so I did, placing the limp, chubby red cat into the frosty interior of the chest freezer. I laid her on top of a black plastic bag, the frozen animal inside likely euthanized the day before.

He had already left the room, so I cleaned the small stainless-steel table, put away the equipment, and turned in the $20 bill to Theresa. I found my own lunch and went back to the euthanasia room where I sat on the same table, eating my sandwich and chips. I thought about what had just happened, clear in my own mind that there had to be a better, gentler way to handle frightened cats. And how could I explain the mistake the training officer had made by not administering the sedation drugs? Even with that, I took some comfort knowing I had done the best I could to keep my promise to the old lady and to Peaches.

The next day, the trainer and I were assigned to shelter duty, cleaning kennels throughout the day and euthanizing any animal that came in injured or ill. A dog was on our list to be euthanized. It had been hit by a car and was in critical condition. Without any form of identification, the kindest thing to do, and our policy at the time with the participation of a veterinarian, was to euthanize it.

With the veterinarian consulted and Lib's initials on the intake form, the trainer and I carried the injured dog to the euthanasia table and without incident, the suffering dog died quickly. Once again, I cleaned up the room, bagging the dog's body so I could put it in the chest freezer, adding to the number waiting in frozen solidarity to be placed in the incinerator. I went to the freezer first to open the lid, knowing I wouldn't have enough hands when I was carrying the bagged and lifeless body of the dog. When the lid opened, my heart stopped, and suddenly I couldn't breathe. There was Peaches, just like I had left her, but now her entire body was shivering, vibrating in a subconscious response to stay warm. Her red tabby fur was covered in a fine frost. She was not conscious, but she wasn't dead, either.

I don't know the science behind why the drug we administered didn't work for Peaches. I learned years later that the pink pentobarbital solution, commonly used then in shelters and by vets for animal euthanasia, could sometimes yield unpredictable results. It would be several more years until a new and improved pentobarbital-based animal euthanasia drug came on the market. But there I stood in front of the freezer, devastated. I grabbed the shivering cat, wrapped her in a towel and ran to get Lib. Through our tears, we completed what should have been done the day before. Peaches was finally at rest.

From Lib, I learned that Peaches wasn't the only animal whose body had fought off the effects of the euthanasia drug we used. It was the same one used by virtually all shelters and veterinarians. That day, Lib was as horrified as I was, and within a week she had written new procedures for the euthanasia of all our shelter animals.

Working with a veterinarian, we received training to look for three sure signs of death. First, after the drug is administered, we learned to check the palpebral, or eye, reflex. Tap a corner of the eye, and if the brain is dead, the eye will not subconsciously react with a blink to protect itself. With brain death comes a complete lack of consciousness, most importantly there is no perception of pain. Secondly, the heartbeat must be stopped, and the only true way to determine this is to insert a needle directly into the heart muscle after the animal is unconscious and the brain cannot perceive pain. The needle will move with each beat of the heart. When the needle stops moving, the animal is dead. We learned that even the most sophisticated stethoscope lacks the sensitivity to detect the very last heart-beat. The final and most undeniable form of death verification is rigor mortis, the muscle stiffness that sets in due to lack of circulation and brain death, combined. Verification of death using these proven techniques was not yet standard practice in many animal shelters, but it wasn't long before it would become an industry-wide focus.

I didn't know any of these things then, having been on the job less than a month. What I did know was that I had broken my promise to the woman. Had I caused the suffering of her beloved friend Peaches? Did the cat suffer? I was inconsolable.

I doubt the training officer knew how much his actions influenced me, and there's no way he would ever know how many times over the years I mentally referred to a moment with him and told myself *never again*. In my mind, he became an electric fence.

Goats can be clever, and I had one that liked to jump and go exploring, so I added a strand of electric wire to the fence of their yard, securing it at goat-nose-height. When I was done stringing the wire around the perimeter, I plugged in the charger that would deliver alternating electric current to the wire. Ah, electricity! When my darling goat touched her nose to the wire, it would pack a punch. I knew she would never forget the experience, and she would be unharmed and safe behind her fence. All that remained was a test to see if it was carrying a current. I was a girl farmer, and my man-farmer toolbox didn't have an electric fence tester, the kind with a tiny light that blinks as the current shoots through the tool harmlessly. So, I touched the wire with the pointed tip of my pliers.

It turned out to be a close call. The shock of electric current caused my plier-hand to jerk straight back towards my head where the pliers, perfectly glued by electric current to the grip of my hand, whizzed by my forehead so close and so fast I didn't even have time to blink. I can tell you one thing about this experience. I still have two eyes. But perhaps the most important thing I learned is to never again touch an electric wire with a metal tool in your hand.

That's how I learned from the man who was my first introduction to some of the most critically important tasks for an animal control officer to perform perfectly. Every time he showed me the way he did things, the shock would hold me captive, and my brain couldn't let go. Because of him, I learned quickly what *not* to do and how *not* to do it. Most importantly, I learned to trust my own instincts about right and wrong, no matter the circumstance. If it had to do with the care and comfort of an animal, it had to be right. If it wasn't right, it may as well have been an electric shock.

I can't imagine what it would have been like to lose an eye that day, but it would have left a scar for the world to see. Emotional scars are invisible. I return to that living room in my mind, remembering an old woman and her cat, friends for years but separated by circumstance, as they said their final goodbyes.

29. A Wagging Tail Is Not Always a Happy Tail

Eventually, I was liberated from the oversight of training and began to handle public calls on my own. I cleaned and organized the animal control truck I'd been assigned, a hefty white Ford 3/4 ton with a big fiberglass "dog box" mounted on the chassis. Being in the field on my own had a certain romance for me, but it could also be life-threatening. Not all dogs wanted to meet me.

One of the first calls I took without backup was a benign-sounding dog-at-large call in a quiet neighborhood. The other ACO on duty besides me had gone to lunch, so I was on my own. As I drove down the street, I saw the dog a few hundred yards ahead, a medium-size, tan pit bull type dog, nose down in a yard, tail up and wagging. As I approached, I rolled the window down and gave the dog a whistle.

"Hey sweetie! Where do you live?"

One look at the truck and the dog panicked. It's true that dogs get to know the dogcatcher truck, especially those whose owners are often less than diligent about being responsible or respectful, letting their dogs run loose throughout neighborhoods. This dog was a regular and knew the truck, but as the new girl, I didn't know her. What's more, it was clear that she either had a current litter or had just weaned a litter of puppies based on the size of her teats. She ran in front of my truck, tail tucked, ears flat, looking back over her shoulder as I slowly followed her down the street. She turned into a driveway at full speed and then disappeared behind the house. Casually, I parked my truck, put on the yellow warning flashers and climbed out, glad she was home. I wouldn't have to bring this dog into the shelter. I'd just close whatever gate she had run through, then leave the owners a note.

By now it should be obvious. I was making not one, not two, but a giant pants-full of mistakes, one of which I was very soon to warmly experience. Mistake number one: The dog was obviously not in her own territory when I first saw her in the neighboring yard. The evidence would have been her demeanor the moment she saw the truck and knew she was in trouble. She tucked her tail, lowered her head, and ran for familiar ground, which I correctly guessed was her own yard, several driveways ahead. Mistake number two: When she did get home and disappeared around the back side of the home, my failure to appreciate the fact that she might have puppies there, thereby increasing the potential of a protective attack, and failing to fully understand her comfort level in her own territory, increased exponentially the chances of my being seen as an intruder or a threat. Mistake number three: leaving the security of my truck without telling the office where I was, requesting back-up assistance, or bringing with me any type of tool so I could either capture the dog safely or at the very least defend myself if necessary.

I needed a sign that said, "Bite Me, I'm a Rookie."

But I wasn't done making mistakes yet. Next, I stepped out of the truck without so much as a leash, put my hands in my pockets, and strolled out across the street to close the gate, which had to be just around the corner of the house, I thought. I'd close the gate, leave my note and be on my way. I was going to be a hero, such a nice animal control girl, bringing the dog home safely and just leaving a little note to please make sure the gate stays closed and get a rabies shot for your dog as soon as you can, thank you.

I looked up from my idealistic joy to see the dog coming at me down the middle of the street, silently but at full speed, which looked to me like a hundred miles an hour. Her head was up, ears in full bloom, tail straight up in the air and wagging as fast as a pit bull tail can wag. The dog had home-field advantage. I could see her eyes drilling right into my own from 50 yards out, then 30 yards, then 10, and I had nothing.

I'm-going-to-die-I'm-going-to die-I'm-going-to-die. I thought. Right here, right now. It was true, then, what I had heard about wagging tails. Leave it to me to make that lesson as hard as I could. And for those who think, "Aww! It's only a dog! You weren't going to die!" I would suggest stepping into a yard, or in this case, personal territory, that belongs to any dog. Any decent mail delivery person will agree with me. It's dangerous.

At about five feet out, I could see her eyes. She was not blinking as she hurtled towards me, staring right into my own eyes. Then she launched into the air and straight at my face. I remember lifting my hands out of my pockets and raising them next to my face. I also remember yelling something loud and pointless as I side-stepped the airborne dog. I turned in time to see her drop to the ground behind me. We faced off again, and again she launched into the air at my face, still soundless. Again, I yelled and side-stepped. By now I realized, on top of everything else, that my dark brown uniform pants were a shade darker. And damp. The dog landed behind me, and I turned to face her again, hands still next to my face as if the dog was pointing a gun at me. I was face to face with an aggressive momma pit bull in what was clearly her territory.

I was too far from the truck to make a run for it, and too far from any patch of driveway that she didn't consider hers. Truly a no-man's-land. After her third swing-and-miss, we stood there, face to face. I yelled. She circled me, swinging her head sideways to keep one eye on my face. I circled along with her, not willing to let her get behind me. Then, like a switch went off, she turned and trotted back to her driveway. I backed up to my truck and climbed into the driver's side. For the first time in my life, I was grateful for vinyl seats. The dog had disappeared. I caught my breath, put the truck in gear and drove across town to get a dry pair of pants.

It wasn't the last time I'd need to change pants in the middle of the day, but it was the last time I'd forget to bring a tool with me when stepping out of the truck. And it was the last time I'd fully trust a wagging tail.

30. The Price of the Work

If I had a nickel for every time I heard, "I could never do your job!" I wouldn't have needed a job. Heck, I would have had enough nickels to run for public office. But I never really knew how to respond. What do you say to someone who thinks your job is terrible and you're a terrible person for doing it? This was the job that made my life worth living, the work that helped me sleep at night and woke me in the morning again, always ready for more. What did they mean when they said that? Of course, there were bad moments, harsh lessons. But I thought often about the black dog in the river under the Shawtown bridge. I was learning to use the tools I needed to make a difference for animals in harm's way, to make their lives better. How could anybody not want that? Maybe they thought we just didn't care about the outcome of the animal. Some thought we liked killing dogs and cats.

"No," I would say. "It's not like that."

But those words weren't enough to explain how important this work was to the animals I loved. I had no words to explain to them how it filled my heart every day. I didn't know then, but I and the people I worked with in those first years were part of a fundamental change in animal control. The harsh animal control officers I met in the beginning were disappearing fast, either fired, retired or forced to comply with new policies, new programs, and new principles demanded by a caring public who were becoming better informed every single day.

I was young, fresh, and committed to a purpose that began

with roots deep in my heart. I felt all the feels. I believed that my dedication and hard work were shaping a kinder, more thoughtful future for animals and people who loved them. Everyone I worked with, all the "new" people to this old business, did so with courage and charisma, creativity and kindness. Our work was sincere and compassionate, even if not always perfect. Finally, after decades of being the one career choice worse than the trash collector, animal control was becoming a true public service in more ways than just its name implied. But change never comes easily, and still, not everyone agreed that we could be the good guys.

31. Sometimes You Just Gotta Laugh

In my brown city uniform and short blond hair, I didn't look like the trash collector or the old guy with a limp and a scowl, sent to "the pound" to work the remaining years of a city tenure to collect full retirement. I worked hard to defy the dogcatcher stereotype of Disney movies and Saturday cartoons. It wasn't easy work.

There was a lot of humor, some of it not everyone would understand but some of it universal, like the day I was trying to get ahead of a loose dog in the wrong backyard. Rounding a corner of the house, I slipped and fell in mud. Getting up, I surveyed my wet and muddy uniform, and then I smelled myself. I had slipped in the mud of an overflowing septic system. It was on the same day I was scheduled to speak at a luncheon for the women of the local Ladies Auxiliary. I had been worried about not wearing a dress with pumps, or at least dressy sensible shoes, but the story, along with a clean uniform, helped me make a memorable impression.

There were days when, trying to put some perspective on a particularly heinous day, I would wonder about children suffering and starving in our city, living lives of poverty I couldn't imagine. It was impossible to balance the tragedies we encountered as animal officers with the harsh realities of a world that was also cruel to children. I'm not sure it was ever helpful, or even if thinking those things somehow made things worse over the years, knowing there was so much suffering beyond that of the animals we encountered.

But it did help me realize that the job I was doing, the one that not many people thought they were capable of doing, had real value, was making a difference, and was more than meaningful to me. The job I did helped animals and people and that was what kept me coming back, day after day. If I missed a day of work, who would take my place? Who would help the animals that were waiting for me to find them that day? I couldn't miss even one day.

32. Wolfie

With only two animal control officers, we traded on-call duties, the overnight responsibility for police-dispatched animal control calls, for a full week, every other week. It was mid-spring in northern Arkansas, a time of the year when seasons bounce off each other like hail on the sidewalks. It had been a glorious day, dandelions smiling on the fresh lawns around town, college students on bikes, the very air celebrating the newness of spring in the Ozarks. But in spring, especially in the south, the weather can be bipolar, and so it was this day, with clouds forming in late afternoon and the wind bringing a chilled edge that made me reach for my coat. Serious storms were in the forecast, and when they arrived, they fulfilled the promises made by the meteorologists.

My pager went off around 3 a.m., and I phoned into police dispatch. Lightning and thunder, wind and driving rain had arrived along with cold temperatures. It was a miserable night. MK, my favorite dispatcher, filled me in.

"I have a lady who says her kitten is stuck in a tree," she said. "She's worried about the rain."

"The kitten is still in a tree?" I asked.

"I guess so," she said. She gave me the caller's phone number. "Geez," she said. "Good luck. Don't go climbing any trees in this lightning."

"Don't worry about that," I said, and we hung up.

When I dialed the caller, her breath came in tears. Her family's kitten had been stuck in a tree for a few days. She had called the shelter that first day but had been told that he would come down eventually. She hadn't worried much but had kept an eye on Wolfie, their 5-month-old red tabby, for the past two days. The whole family tried to talk him down out of the tree, but the kitten hadn't been convinced. After listening to her, I assured her that cats wouldn't die in a tree; they had the tools and sense to come down when they could find the courage.

"But what about the rain?" she asked me.

"As long as he knows where home is, he'll come down," I told her. "Besides, have you ever seen a cat skeleton in a tree?"

That seemed to resonate with her, and we hung up after my promise to come to her address the very first thing in the morning. I slid back under my blankets, but now my head was awake, and with every crash of thunder, lash of wind and splash of lightning across my walls, I worried for Wolfie.

Unlike television and in movies, there is no magic fire department truck standing ready to pull foolish cats out of trees. Most of the time, the scenario is more like the Steve Martin movie where he advises the family to put a can of tuna under the tree for the cat, and down it comes. That's how it usually works. But a couple of things were at play that would prevent Wolfie from finding the courage to leave his perch in the tree. I knew I couldn't call our fire department out at 3 a.m. for a cat in a tree. They were good guys, and they had used their ladder truck once or twice to rescue terrified cats in trees, but the storm changed all that. I knew I couldn't go out there myself with an aluminum ladder. I might have tried it except for the lightning and wind. Spring storms in the south are nothing to fool around with; they were rarely good sleeping weather. As I listened to the cold storm pounding away and watched the minutes tick by on the clock, I realized that Wolfie was in trouble.

I finally rose at 6:45 a.m., got dressed in my brown ACO uniform and black boots, and donned the only raincoat I had, a black police jacket with my city badge pinned to the front. Getting in the animal control truck, the one with black letters designating it as "animal rescue and transport," I headed to Wolfie's address. I had no idea how I would get the kitten out of the tree. The lightning was gone but it was still raining, and many of the streets were partially flooded. It was cold enough to see my breath.

As I pulled up at the address, I scanned the trees near their house. In the gray light I could make out what looked like a cat, about 25 feet up an old mulberry tree. The branch he was on was long and thick and jutted out over the wooden fence that divided his yard from the neighbors. From where he was perched, he had a bird's-eye view of the neighbor's yard, whose two large dogs just then came barreling out of the back door, barking at the stranger nearby. Wolfie was dead, his legs hanging over both sides of the branch keeping his still body wedged there, his red tabby fur plastered smooth by cold rain.

Maybe he didn't understand why his people were calling him to come down into a yard full of dogs. Maybe teenage kittens just don't understand the principles of engineering, physics, and math, not comprehending that by walking back the opposite way on the branch, he could quickly come down and the fence dividing the yards would keep him safe. All he could see below him was the yard where dogs lived, and so he chose to stay. He couldn't anticipate the weather, and no one, including me, considered hypothermia.

It's hard not to get lost in the torment of "what if" and let guilt carry these memories. I needed to make the choice to step away from guilt and refuse to let it be my guide, when wrenching guilt was all I felt that morning, when my choices, as well as his family's, cost Wolfie his life. I had to believe that I could work harder, do better, be smarter the next time there was an animal in need. I would have that opportunity because in this work, there is always a next time. And for those times, I would carry Peaches, Seymour, Wolfie and every single animal I had failed with me so they could be my path forward.

The losses were lessons. The consequences of my failures

were often crushing, but I knew I wanted to keep trying. I knew it with every breath I took. There would be a day when all the failures of all the years would return, taunting me, but until then, I learned all I could about how to do the right thing for animals in need.

In 1987, my partner and I left Arkansas for an opportunity in Massachusetts, leaving the animal control job to support our relationship. Once settled in a new city, I quickly found work as a temporary vacation-relief package delivery driver in Worcester. Before long I found a full-time job managing a large horse farm. But we both missed our roots, hers in the South, mine in the Midwest. Arkansas had been a happy medium, and we both wanted to go home. In November 1990, just two months after Mom's death, we packed up and left Massachusetts, heading back to Arkansas.

33. A Birthday Gift

I walked through woods as a kid in the quiet noise of the trees and leaves, alone but not alone. Winter, spring, summer, fall; I loved all the seasons of the woods, no matter how the trees were dressed or how the dirt disguised itself. I also got to know the animals who lived there, and the more I knew about them, the more I knew their comforts. But the real woods were not a fairytale. In the woods I knew, life and death were everywhere. My human form, with all its noise and foreign scents, surely set off alarms for every creature there, even though every time I visited, I steadied my breath and slowed my heartbeat, my way of offering a soft, open greeting as all good friends do.

At first, their answer was silence. I stuck with it, staying quiet, staying still. I knew they were watching me; I had seen their tracks, their feathers, their homes. And then one day the quietness cracked, just a little, and I saw them; a deer and her fawn playing tag, leaping, spinning, joyful, something I never knew deer could be.

Another day soon after, I heard the shooshing of a Great Horned Owl dropping down from his oak tree perch, rising on powerful wings up to the next, settling soundlessly to watch me, watching him. Their offer of trust overwhelmed me. To them, I was danger, maybe even death, yet here they were, visible, vulnerable, beautiful. I felt a peace I had never known, my awkward-girl self now surrounded by friends. The woods and the wild things there combined to become a long-distance love affair. It would influence my very core, as all first loves do.

I fell in love first with the birds, for they were bravest, I thought. So many colors and then so many songs, I heard and saw them first. I saw the stories of life and death under the trees and along the banks of the creek. Here and there in the leaves and dirt were bits and pieces of secrets; scattered, broken feathers, lost and forgotten fur, animal footprints in the mud that suddenly stopped. With the glassy crack of a beaver's tail on a pond only it could know, my heart would nearly burst. All loves face the test of time, life brings changes and age finds us all, but I've kept the woods, and the world within them, safe in my heart.

There are days when I listen, eyes closed to my memory of the bright "chip-chip-chip" of a cardinal or the wistful melody of the pretty sparrow singing "Oh-Canada-Canada-Canada." Those visits to the woods and the lives I discovered there were the beginning of my story, but I couldn't have known it then. I wasn't a storyteller or an adventurer. At the end of the day, I went home and became my parent's only daughter again, not pink with ruffles but clad in hand-me-down blue jeans and smelling of fresh dirt and brown leaves.

Years later, on a day in Massachusetts, I was waiting outside on a patch of grass for a shared ride home from work. It was a sweet fall day, the sun not yet giving up the day and still warm as summer, when I looked a few yards out from my side. There sat a tiny gray mouse with enormous ears, looking at me, close enough that I could see its whiskers vibrating. What the heck. In an instant, I was back in my childhood woods, waiting for my friends there to come out. I held my hand out towards the little mouse, and it crept towards me, then took a few hops in the grass without hesitating. All the way to my hand it traveled, then it stopped right at the tip of my fingers. I don't remember any noise from the traffic around me or from the other people there on the patch of grass; it was just the two of us, maybe each comparing the size of the other's ears. In a quiet instant, the mouse licked my finger. I couldn't even breathe. Then it turned and ran.

It was my 29th birthday, the gift from the mouse a reminder that no matter how far I traveled or how old I became, I could never ignore my long-distance love affair with wild things.

34. The Interview

Even though I had been away from animal shelters for a couple years, I had learned enough about the job to feel confident applying for a supervisor's job in a small Arkansas town, a community close to several of the state's largest cities. Within a week of mailing my application, I received a call from the city manager's secretary to arrange an interview for the upcoming Friday afternoon, in just two days' time. I was instantly nervous. I really needed a job.

It was January 1991, President George H.W. Bush had declared war in Iraq. The world had gone crazy, and news of the war was all we heard. That Friday, while waiting in the secretary's office for my turn to interview, I heard men behind the door laughing together. The interview before me was clearly a chummy get-together of pals. They sounded like old friends sitting around their favorite bar. When the door opened, the three men shook hands goodbye, still chuckling.

"Talk to you soon," one said to the man leaving. I willed myself to stay positive.

As I made eye contact with one of the men, he asked, "Sandy?" I nodded. "Come on in."

He introduced himself as the city manager, and to his left was Ronald, the supervisor of the Public Works Department.

"Nice to meet you," I said.

We shook hands, then sat down. Interview questions are usually predictable, falling within the range of "need to know" and "wish we knew," but there were a couple questions during my interview that have always made me wonder.

"Can you lift 50 pounds?" the city manager asked.

I stifled a smile. Clearly my years throwing hay bales and feed bags didn't show through the flowered blouse and tan dress pants I wore, but I was pretty sure I could arm wrestle this guy and win.

"Yes, sir," I replied. "I'm used to working on a farm, and I've been a package delivery driver." His eyebrows arched as he looked at me over the rim of his glasses. I met his gaze, not blinking.

"Hmmm," he said, leaning back in his chair. "What about computers?" He laced his fingers across an ample belly. "Do you have any problems with computers?"

"No problem at all," I responded.

"Great," he replied. We concluded the short interview with a few more benign-sounding questions, then wrapped it up. "Well, thanks for coming in. We'll be in touch." He said.

We stood and shook hands, and I thanked them for their time. There were no companionable jokes.

For the last question, I had been honest in my reply if not entirely forthcoming. I didn't have any trouble with computers because I didn't even know how to turn one on, much less use the things. The little white lie had come quickly, easily, not even a slip of the tongue. I wanted this job, and I knew I could do the job well. I could figure out what a computer was, how hard could it be? In January 1991, electronic mail was still not universal; in fact, e-mail was still a news story that made many people suspicious. Ferris Bueller and his chirping modem were the closest I had been to the World Wide Web.

The following Monday morning I woke early, hoping against hope that I had gotten the job. I got dressed, made some toast and coffee, and turned on the news. An hour passed. My heart was heavy. Now what do I do? Then, just before nine, the phone rang. I pounced on it.

"Hello?" Then, "Is Sandy there?" said the male voice on the line.

"This is Sandy," I said. My heart was hammering. "This is Ronald from the city. If you still want the job, it's yours."

"Yes!" I practically shouted.

"How soon can you get here?" he asked.

I got the job. In less than an hour, I was walking through the door of my new life.

35. My Own Shelter

My learning curve was steep and filled with new people, new responsibilities, and challenges big and small. As I sat at my very own supervisor's desk on that first day, I called my old boss and friend, Lib, the tiny woman who had trusted me with my first volunteer job in this field, and then hired me as a rookie animal control officer. She offered some wise words.

"First off," she said, "you can do this. Secondly, when you can hire staff, never be afraid to hire someone smarter than you. You're their boss, and if you stay their boss, they'll make your job easier and make you look like a star. That's their job, and that's your job. Thirdly, in this business, never be afraid to make someone mad. If a day goes by that someone, somewhere isn't mad at you for doing what's right, then you're not doing your job for the animals. Buckle up."

I called Lib many times for advice and encouragement, but those first words gave me the strength I needed to believe that yes, I could do this job.

As the days came and went, I waffled between being bored to death and busy as hell. I had no staff yet, so the work was all mine when there was work to do. The phone rarely rang in those first weeks. The few hours we were open to the public, painted on a large sign at the end of the road, functioned more as a deterrent than an invitation. The sign may as well have read, "Don't bother us."

One afternoon I woke up with my head on the desk, a tiny bit of drool on my cheek and a stiff neck. I had fallen asleep on the job. I was horrified. This wasn't what I had signed up for when I applied for the job. I knew there was work to be done, but it looked like I would have to find it myself. So, rather than sit and wait for the world to come to me, I went looking. I started by driving through town every day, then getting out and walking the park and neighborhood sidewalks and playgrounds, talking with citizens, meeting their dogs, and learning what they liked and didn't like about their animal shelter.

Their faces told me stories about the employees who had my job before me. I got used to seeing people see me, the new dogcatcher, then grab up their dogs to turn and go the other direction. Rather than get discouraged, I accepted the challenge. Lib had always told me that people were the key to success in our work, and these people were the ones I needed to meet. As I learned my way around the small community, population 4500, it was clear that the people here did not trust this animal control department. I eventually learned that their reasons were as obscure as they were specific. Walt Disney couldn't have painted a bleaker picture of my new-to-me shelter and animal control program.

So, I began handing out free ice cream cone coupons, redeemable at the local hamburger drive-through. Pet owners, at least the ones who didn't run the other way when they saw me coming, were shocked to be handed one of those coupons as a thank you for having their dogs safely on a leash. Free ice cream was the perfect way to open the door to more conversation. With each person I met, I learned their dog's names, sometimes their kid's names, and most of the time we ended up laughing together. It was a simple blueprint, but I hoped it would begin to turn the small department into a true community service. I had a lot of work to do.

One afternoon, a call came in from a real estate agent. "Hi Sandy, this is Ellen. We've got a house on the golf course finally coming on the market, and I think one of your animal cages is in the basement."

"Wow," I said. "I've been trying to collect all the equipment that's out there. Thank you for letting me know. What's the address, and I'll get it picked up today."

Ellen gave me the address and instructions on how to access the house with the hidden key. There was no inventory of the animal control equipment, so I had been building a new one with each piece of equipment I found around the shelter or out in the community. Before the day was over, I drove to the golf course house to collect the missing cage.

With no electric power in the vacant home, I turned on my flashlight and made my way down the steps to the crawl space. Shining the light around, I saw the cage in a corner. It was a live trap, a cage with a spring-door that closed behind an animal as it entered the trap for the food inside. Then I stopped breathing. There was something in the trap. I looked closer. It was the remains of a possum, now just a dried, flat pelt and dusty tail, its head stretched out, bony and long-dead nose poked as far into the corner of the trap door as possible. Its head was lying flat as if it had simply taken a nap, its chin resting on the skeletal front paws dried to the wire floor. As I looked down at the possum in the light of my flashlight, my heart broke.

How many days had it been trapped? I wondered angrily. Why did no human hear it struggling to escape? I now knew one of the reasons why the last animal control officer had not been well liked, but there was nothing to be done. Not anymore. I quietly picked up the trap and made my way back up the stairs.

36. Opossums Are Not from Ireland

Before the year was out, I was given permission from the city administration to hire an animal control officer. Once hired, it was hard to get used to having help, but with just the two of us, we quickly became a good team. It was fun to teach someone the things I had already learned, and, like Lib had promised, it was fun to learn new things from someone who knew more than I did. Philip loved snakes and was afraid of nothing, two things I couldn't lay claim to myself. Together we turned our little shelter into a hidden gem, keeping it spotless and providing comfort for every animal we handled. Philip was wonderful with the dogs and cats in our shelter, but his true passion was wildlife. For both of us, the wild animal calls were a fringe benefit, and the easiest wild animals to help were the possums.

Even though they ended up in harm's way all too often, I admired every possum I met. Many of the gentle, slow-moving marsupials met sad endings, either hit by cars, attacked by dogs or injured by people, but there were as many times when helping them was as easy as tipping over a trash can so the possum inside could scamper away, or encouraging a homeowner to clean up the scattered bird seed under their backyard bird feeders, or put away their backyard pet's food at night.

Their shape, color, pointy noses and naked tails did not endear them to many people. As a result, they were never far behind snakes when it came to being on the receiving end of danger at the hands of uneducated homeowners. They were our most often complained about nuisance animals, second only to barking dogs, and we did a lot of educating. If we failed to convince homeowners that they could, with a little work and some tolerance, live in peace with their homely, hissing wild animal neighbors, we'd have to humanely trap and then relocate them to other parts of town where there were more open spaces and less hazards. Relocating wild animals who were officially identified as "nuisance" was common, but I never knew how many survived in a new environment. Once moved, they would have to find new food sources, new safe shelters, and learn how to recognize new dangers to their lives. Wildlife professionals told me their survival rate could be as low as 25%. We always tried to educate first.

Without a doubt, the wild animal babies were charming. Baby skunks, baby birds, baby squirrels, baby turtles, even baby snakes. But the baby possums! Their tiny, beady eyes always hopeful, their silver fur always surprisingly soft, clean, and shiny. I laughed at their name, Opossum, as if they were from Ireland or Scotland or wherever the culture added an "O" to the front of last names. They are correctly called an Opossum, but true to form, our human trend to embrace colloquialisms has shortened it to possum. Easier to say, and just a tiny bit cuter. From the first time I met a possum in Arkansas, I loved them all, but Philip and I both agreed. We especially loved the babies.

My first spring there, I welcomed six little possums brought to the shelter. Carefully, I looked inside the cardboard box. It was the first time I had seen baby possums up close.

"I found their mother dead on the road," the finder said.

They were tiny, perfect little images of their parents, little pink noses pointing upward and sniffing. I met their tiny eyes. What did they see in my own?

"How did you know there were babies?" I asked.

"I didn't," the man said. "But my wife had met Philip one day when he was out picking up another dead one, and he showed her what he was doing. Kinda gross," he continued, "but pretty cool. Can you help 'em?"

"Absolutely," I said. "Thank you!"

Both Philip and I made a habit of checking the entire body of any deceased possum we were removing from the road. There was always a chance that if the animal was a mother, her babies had survived. It happened often.

It was Philip's day off, but I knew he'd be delighted to hear why these babies had been saved. I set them up in a wire hamster cage with plenty of clean warm bedding. The real work had just begun. With this little pack of six, just a bit bigger than "pinkies" as my rehab friend soon told me, I was surprised to learn how obsessively clean baby possums are, how they loved to groom their shiny coats and keep their paws and thumbs clean and dry. I suppose if you lived in a tight, furry pouch with plenty of other noisy siblings, and in that pouch is where you ate, slept, pooped and played, then clean needed to be non-negotiable.

As the days went by and the babies became accustomed to either Philip or me feeding them, we learned they are gentle, funny babies and we began to truly understand just how hard animal mothers work to raise their babies. They can't drive to the grocery store when the refrigerator is out of milk. They can't slap on a new diaper when the other one is dirty. They can't close and lock the door to the house for safety when night falls. Every bit of care needed by an animal baby comes from the bravery and dedication of an animal mom whose only resource is instinct. It had never occurred to me until I met those first baby possums.

As part of their learning process with a real mom, young possums gain strength in their legs and paws by riding on mom's back during her excursions for groceries. This practice serves several purposes. First, it gives the babies the strength they'll need to climb on their own once they leave the safety of mom. Secondly, they watch the scenery pass by as Momma travels around hunting for food. Once they know where food is located and how to find it, the path to food becomes a road map inked in memory. Later in my life, that memory would be why I gave up keeping chickens. Possums found my chicken nest boxes, and those became an institution in generations of possums in our country neighborhood. I may as well have hung a neon sign with a drive-through window. Thirdly, they learn to employ their "prehensile" tail, which is more tool than tail. It was our job to make sure that this baby-possum-six-pack could do everything they needed to survive on their own before turning them loose in the big mean world.

We could do this. Philip went out to the woods surrounding the shelter building, and brought a big, leafy tree branch into the office.

"Holy hell!" I said. "It's the size of a tree!"

With a little work, we secured it to the corner wall. When we were done, we stood back to admire our new forest. Philip laughed.

"Looks like it grew there," he said.

Since the babies were beyond the "pinkie" stage, old enough to cling and crawl and toddle around, it took both of us to keep them clean and fed. We were getting good at being possum moms, watching the little ones learn how to use the keys to their new kingdom.

We sat in an office chair in front of the branch, taking the possums one by one and gently swinging them, like tiny, furry clock pendulums, towards the branch. When the babies spotted the branches, they'd begin reaching out for a piece, and with a little timing we sent them softly airborne towards the branch. Their little legs and paws grabbed hold, and the climbing and playtime would begin. We called them the Velcro possums. When it was time for them to go out on their own, we knew they had the best start we could give them and wished them luck as they ventured forth into the wild of our small town's suburban woods.

37. A Skunk Story

In all the years I've handled skunks in all the different predicaments they landed in, I've only been sprayed once. It's fair to say that standing downwind played a significant role in that mistake, and like all the great learning moments, that one taught me why I will always love them for their gentle good nature, fair-minded early-warning system, and overall beauty.

Several were memorable, like the skunk who was chased into the open door of a luxury home early one morning by the owner's two dogs, who were let out to roam and do their business on other people's lawns. During the pursuit, the skunk saw the open door of the house and made a beeline, followed by the two dogs. Once cornered inside, the skunk began to defend itself as only a skunk can do. It defended itself in the entryway, in the kitchen, once again in the formal living room, down the hallway with dogs still in pursuit. Then into the master bedroom, under the bed and then into the huge master bedroom closet, where the dog's owner had stood just seconds before, choosing his day's wardrobe from the dozens of designer clothes and business suits hanging there. Until the moment I arrived in the driveway, I didn't know that skunk perfume, up close and this personal, can smell like burning rubber tires. The smell was astonishing in its power. Weeks later I learned that there had been a lot of conversation about insurance coverage for the extensive damage done by the perfume. Was it an "act of God" or not? I never learned either way, although I still have my own conclusion. God had everything to do with the events of that morning, but it was the act of the homeowner who created the damage.

Then there were the four tiny beauties discovered under a backyard doghouse. When I lifted the doghouse to see them, I figured I would soon smell a lot like burning tires, but there they were, eight tiny eyes peering up at me, snuggled together for safety. The dog who owned the doghouse had killed the mother, so these littles had to be saved. Gently setting a bath towel over them, I was able to scoop them all together up into my hands, then as I stood there, I rolled the bundle over so I could see them. There they were in my hands, snuggled into the safety of a towel. They never sprayed.

Some of my best problem-solving challenges were inspired by the predicaments skunks found themselves in, and some of those situations defied description. It was almost closing time when a battered pickup truck pulled into the parking lot in front of the shelter. I sighed. It had been a long day, and I was ready to go home. Even though it was five o'clock on the dot, the man got out of his truck and came inside. I should have locked the door, I thought to myself.

Instead, I said, "Can I help you?" He looked at me, deadpan.

"I've got a skunk in my truck," he said. "I'm pretty sure it's in the glove box."

I laughed. "Are you kidding me? Did Michael send you?"

Michael was a good friend who managed another shelter in a nearby town. He had a great sense of humor, and we often played jokes on one another. This was a good one. The man stood there, not smiling.

"Not kidding," he said.

Realizing he was serious, I came out from behind the counter.

"Let's go take a look," I said.

He drove an older model truck, the kind with one big bench seat, all vinyl but with a patterned fabric seat cover. The metal dashboard had a big glove compartment with a good-size door and a small silver button in the middle.

"How did it get in there?" I asked. He shrugged.

"Coupla guys playing a joke on me? I dunno."

I still didn't believe him, but he looked serious. I pushed the button and cracked open the glove compartment door, just a sliver. There it was. A tiny bit of black hair gave it away. I shut the glove box door as quickly and gently as I could. This would have been a great joke, but it wasn't. There was a skunk in his glove box. There was nothing to be done but get it out, and I would have to pick it up. Skunks have impressive, cat-like teeth, so I grabbed my heavy welder's gloves from the patrol truck. As I stood in the door of the truck staring at the glove box, I tried to come up with a plan that wouldn't leave me without friends for a month. I was hoping against hope that teeth would be my biggest problem. I took a deep breath, then blew it out slowly.

One, two, three, I counted. On three, I opened the little compartment door, scooped up the skunk in both hands and dropped it on the driveway in one smooth motion. Then I turned and ran. At about a 20-yard distance, I stopped to turn and look. There sat the skunk, a tiny young adult. It looked around, getting its bearings. What must it have been like for this little gentle animal to find itself trapped in a metal box, then feel the motion of the vehicle moving, then to be suddenly snatched up by a human and dropped into a totally unfamiliar area? I watched it work to figure out a next move. The skunk sat there a minute, then turned and quietly walked away. My faith in the easygoing nature of one of nature's most misunderstood creatures had been reinforced. Bon voyage, Pepe le Pew, I thought to myself.

In many discussions about the neighborly behaviors of skunks, I have often said that I would cheerfully walk through an airport carrying a skunk in a pet carrier. I am just that confident in the honesty and fairness of one of my favorite wild animals. Not that I've ever done it, but there's a right way and a wrong way to do such a stunt, and in handling any wild animal, the meek yet mighty skunk has always reminded me to treat all animals with respect. It didn't matter whether it was my favorite dog, a neighborhood stray, a possum stuck in a trash bin, a fish on a hook or a feral cat in a live trap, dignity and compassion should be non-negotiable. If every animal we meet could spray like the skunk when they were frightened or harassed, wouldn't we meet them differently?

38. The Face of the Public

By now I was pretty good at reading dog body language, anticipating which way they would run, correctly guessing most of the time which way I needed to lean, turn, or walk to gain the trust of a scared, lost dog. I had gotten familiar with the chronic strays, those who just wouldn't be caught, and our repeat offenders, those dogs whose owners couldn't be bothered with being responsible. They were all unique in their response to my truck and pocket of treats, but none of them were so clever as the two I worked to catch early one morning.

It promised to be a hot day. The two dogs were skilled at dodging traffic, but I knew one day their luck would run out. I was hoping that day wasn't today. These two buddies, a Dalmatian and a Dachshund, knew the streets as well as we did. I had already radioed the shelter; the owner had been called, and she was on her way back home from work to help catch the dogs. The little Dachshund was already safe in my arms. Using him to settle the nervous Dalmatian, I hoped to convince his spotted pal to jump in the passenger seat of my animal control truck. The door was open, an invitation that almost always worked for nervous family pets on the run. Standing next to the street with my truck door open and small dog in my arms, I begged the Dalmatian. "Load up!"

But the dog was having none of that. Commuter traffic had slowed, moving into the other lane as the cars passed by, making a space for me to work. Then, one car drove closer to me. I watched the driver roll down her window as she slowed almost to a stop in front of me. I was suddenly conscious of my sweaty uniform.

Then she leaned out, looked me square in the eye, and spat, "You should be ashamed of yourself!"

I looked at her, speechless. Clearly, she meant what she said.

People are strange animals, but rather than let her words deter me, they have been a useful reminder to never feel ashamed of the work I did. It was never work to me; it was life, and that day, two more dogs were able to keep theirs, with grateful thanks from their owner.

39. Owls and Ducks

As an animal control officer, I had almost daily opportunities to meet Arkansas' wild animals. Birds and mammals of every size and species are no strangers to danger, and many found themselves in need of a human helping hand. The orphaned babies were the hardest, so much work to help them live, so much time to get them back into their own habitat successfully, but it was impossible to turn them away. With the help, oversight and knowledge of licensed wildlife rehab friends, I learned what it takes to help wild animal babies and countless other injured wild animals and birds.

I have never forgotten the first Barred Owl I ever met. It was found in a warehouse parking lot by a truck driver, dangling upside down, tangled in the webbing of the tied-down load on his 18-wheeler. He had no idea how long the bird had been hanging there during his trip, but it was still alive. After a veterinary exam to rule out broken bones and weeks of rehabilitative care, we released the owl, healthy again, with a prayer and a spoken wish for luck. We had no idea where it had originated, the truck had traveled through multiple states on its overnight journey, but we held out hope that this bird was resilient enough to re-establish a territory in a new environment.

One spring, a fluffy wood duck hatchling was brought to the shelter, found walking alone down a residential street, blocks from any water source. There was no mother duck nearby, nor were there any siblings in sight, the finder said. It was no more than a day or two old. As the weeks went by, "Sarah" the duck became a temporary mascot for our shelter until the day we released her. To save Sarah, we needed to learn quickly how to feed a baby duck who learns to eat only by imitating a parent. As "diving ducks," most of their food sources are found under water. It would not be an easy trick to raise a baby woodie, our rehab friends told me. In rehab, almost all of them die in the first five days.

Despite the warnings, Sarah thrived. We taught her to swim in the shelter's oversize stainless-steel tub, following our hands under water as we moved them up and down in the tub. She was a marvel with her tiny wings tucked tight, feet stretched far behind her, kicking for speed, her lithe body flying faster underwater than we thought possible. We found ways to float her food on top of the water in the tub, baby parrot food, learning how to cook it carefully so it would hold together just long enough for Sarah to find it and eat it after it sunk underwater.

When she began to test her wings for flight, it was time to get her into some real water, and we spent days introducing her to the pond in front of the shelter. She needed to learn how to find her own food in the dark, wild water of the pond. Time after time she panicked, refusing to touch the water she couldn't see through, until one day she spotted a bug skimming along on the surface. Instinct took over, and her panic disappeared as quickly as the bug. From that point, she became increasingly comfortable playing in the depths of the pond every day, finding her own food and learning how to be a wild duck.

As she became familiar with the real environment of the pond, we didn't know what to expect. Would she leave? Would she hear other ducks of her own kind and know to fly to them? Would they accept her? But, as most animal babies do, she left gradually. Each day she flew higher, her playful circles over our heads becoming purposeful. She stayed away from the shelter longer every day, only returning late in the afternoon for some corn snacks and a safe blanket in her plastic carrier, the only home she had known since the day she had arrived.

Then came the day we had worked so hard for. Pausing before I locked the door for the night, Sarah didn't appear. She had always appeared just in time, but that night there was no sign of her. I lingered a little while longer, scanning the pond, straining to hear her squeaky voice overhead telling me to "Wait!! Wait a minute!" But she didn't come for her snacks and bedtime that night. We didn't think we would ever see her again.

The next year, a mother wood duck showed up at our door, pacing back and forth like Sarah used to do. Behind her on the bank of the pond, the same pond where Sarah learned to become a wild duck again, were 12 tiny ducklings, and just beyond the baby ducks, a male wood duck, standing nervously near the water's edge. I threw some corn out on the driveway, just like we used to do for Sarah. The female duck flew off a few yards when the corn bounced off the driveway, then went to the babies on the bank. We watched from the window as the family slipped away through the water, swimming across the pond, the smooth V-shape in the water reminding me that soon this family would be in the wind, making another kind of V as they migrated. It was the one and only time we saw Sarah again.

40. Spiders and Snakes

In the parking lot of the shelter one morning while chatting with one of the local police officers, we began comparing our calls and joking back and forth over which department received the craziest requests for help. Dogs, people, cats, snakes, teenagers, dangerous dogs, drunk drivers, car accidents. Everything was fair game in our conversation, and for public servants, often laughter was the only way to get through some of the difficult scenes we experienced. As we stood there, I had my hand on the hood of our white animal control truck. It was comfortable to the touch, lending a little sun-warmed energy to my hand. As we talked back and forth, I noticed a tiny black speck on the hood, right there, near my hand. I looked closer. It was a spider. So small I had to squint, but there it stood, legs spread, motionless. All it needed was a tiny sign saying, GET OFF MY LAWN!

"Look!" I said to the officer. "A real bad guy!"

He looked at me as I leaned closer, "What is it?" he asked.

"A spider!" I said.

Instead of coming closer, he took several steps back, and even put his hand on his holstered gun, an instinctive reaction to an adrenaline rush, I suppose.

"I hate spiders!" he said.

But his curiosity kicked in, and he stepped forward a bit. Together, we leaned into the hood of the truck and stared at the little dot, perched there on eight legs over the invisible line drawn in the dust on the truck hood. I tapped my finger on the hood. One, two, three. We laughed to see it dance in response, all eight legs in unison, one, two, three, jumping up and down in place. I tapped again, and we leaned closer, our heads nearly touching. One, two, three... one, two, three. I moved my hand closer to the spider. One, two, BAM! It jumped straight at our faces as if its hair had been lit on fire. Faster than a speeding bullet, my cop friend disappeared into the shelter. As for me, I found myself a half-dozen feet from the truck, and my heart was pounding.

The spider looked much bigger now than it had a few seconds ago, the tiny triumphant owner of the truck hood. I've always wondered if the cop remembered that kind of courage as he went about his job. He was a great cop. I always told him I could never do his job, and I always thanked him for the job he and his fellow officers performed every day and night. But I do hope he never had to face down a spider again. They don't make bullets that small.

Second to spiders, I'm not sure there's anything more hated in the animal world than snakes. Yes, there are a lot of folks who champion them, help educate the public about the benefits and habits of snakes, but they fight an uphill battle. For some people, the sight of a spider or snake is enough to create a runaway, irrational panic. For people with true phobias about spiders and snakes, these are the only times that size really doesn't matter.

As for me, I had to figure out how to be the expert when a snake call came in. I had to respond with a cool head, comfortable manner, and the right tools to educate, safely handle and usually relocate all manner of snakes. If I were to believe our callers, all snakes were venomous criminals, hunting their children or pets. The reality was that most of the time, snakes were either sunning themselves peacefully or trying like hell to get out of the way of a human with a garden tool. I had a lot to learn about snakes, but I vowed to treat them like all the other wild animals we encountered, believing that all of them had a purpose here and it was my responsibility to help them survive. But the truth of the matter was that I had to fight back squeamish willies with every snake I helped. I could have gotten an Oscar for most of my snake-catching performances.

Before leaving for work one morning, I walked to the barn to feed and water the horses. My partner and I had built a small house in the middle of five acres of woods, and the barn and pasture sat in a small clearing just below the house. Still half asleep, I picked up a bucket from the feed room and walked to the water hydrant. As I leaned down to set the bucket under the spigot, I shrieked. My full-on 12-year-old girl returned. I had barely seen them, but there were two adult copperhead snakes quietly snoozing under the water hydrant. Not aggressive, but clearly disturbed by the shrieking human. Even my composure had run screaming.

My first thought was *Call Animal Control!* My second thought was *IDIOT! You ARE animal control.* I remember feeling disappointed, and maybe even a little panicked.

There was no one to call. No one was coming to save me. As I stood there in my uniform, I realized it was time to buckle up. Summoning my best inner actress, I looked around and spied a broken broom stick. Would it be long enough? It better be, I thought. Sliding the broom handle under its body, I lifted the first snake carefully and then slowly stepped to the doorway of the barn. True to form, the snake hung there, balanced, as all the snakes did, every time, at other people's homes. Well, what do you know? I thought. I'm animal control! Then I tossed it into the air towards the field next to the barn. I didn't expect snake number two to still be there when I went back to the water hydrant, but there it was. "Fly ME!" it seemed to say. And fly it did. In a tribute to my cool-headed success that morning and possession of at least one rational thought, I did not light the barn on fire.

There were hard days, heartbreaking days, when there was simply no solution for animals in need of help. One morning, there was a kitten in a cardboard box at our door. Her body mostly burned, maggots crawling everywhere. The kitten looked up at me when I opened the box. As I looked at the extent of its injuries, I offered a quiet, "Well hello, teeny tiny." As I euthanized the tiny cat, it responded with a soft meow and a purr.

I will always remember the German Shepherd with two broken legs and likely a shattered pelvis, the victim of a midnight car crash. His owner, the driver, was killed, and the dog had been thrown from the vehicle. With permission from the veterinarian, I was getting ready to euthanize the dog. I was in the ditch with him. It was raining. As I slipped the needle into his vein, he wagged his tail.

Every animal control officer has stories like this, and they all have wonderful stories, too. While many of the days were heartbreaking, there were just as many that brought joy and good friendships, laughter and camaraderie between co-workers and the citizens we served. What made the difference were the people. It was important to me to always remember that while I was an animal control professional, my job must first be about helping people. People were the key to success. Animals didn't create their own problems and predicaments; people did. Animals couldn't resolve their own problems, only people could. As an animal control officer, I had to be a "people person" first. I was rarely impressed with the job applicants who told me they loved animals during their interviews.

Instead, I was more impressed with the applicant who expressed an interest in helping people. To me, those were the problem solvers the animals needed. People were often the hardest animals we had to deal with. One day I would learn this truth in the most painful way possible, but in the meantime, none were harder to help than the residents of our little town who, one dry summer, were invaded by an army.

41. Armadillos

Some days I can remember 30 years ago better than 30 minutes ago, but the summer of the armadillo will always be unforgettable. As a northern girl, my learning curve was as steep as it got when it came to southern wildlife, and now I served a community of people who expected me to be an expert. Until my move to Arkansas, I had never seen a live armadillo. The truth of the matter was I had only seen one or two, and those were upside down alongside the road, their stiff feet pointing to the sky. But from the first time I saw a real live one with its tiny eyes, pointy nose and little cloven feet, I was charmed to my core.

It was late in the summer when rain was scarce, creek beds dried up and wildlife took chances they would normally avoid. At the shelter, we were swamped with demands from people to do something about the armadillo invasion. Lawns and flower beds were being decimated every night. The armadillos had moved in. Nobody cared anymore about the feral hogs on the outskirts of town.

For those who lived in or near the golf course neighborhoods, especially those with expensive irrigated lawns and flower beds, the general feeling was that the entire world was coming to an end. Many lawns were brown; trees were shedding their leaves early. But the irrigated lawns and flower beds in the yards of the homes around the golf course soon became a flashpoint. As I drove through the neighborhoods, I could see that every lush, green lawn had some sort of damage. Most of them looked like rodeo arenas. Dirt and wads of grass lay in piles around the holes dug everywhere. The armadillos were having parties. Every night, more lawns were being destroyed. Flower beds full of beautiful blooms were being uprooted, years of work gone in just a few dark hours. But the dry, brown yards where the lawns had already turned to dust? Perfect. Not so much as a footprint.

I tried to be empathetic to the homeowners, but I was secretly rooting for the armadillos. Every time I saw the destruction wrought upon one of those perfect lawns by an overnight armadillo invasion, I had to stifle a smile. I never understood the need to water, fertilize, water some more, and then mow in between all the water and fertilizer applications. To me, the brown grass was a welcome arrival. I could stash my lawn mower and put my feet up in the shade while the neighbors were busy mowing. I was happy to let Mother Nature manage the life and death of my lawn. Every spring it returned, green and vibrant, and in the harsh heat of the late summer it predictably turned brown, gratefully falling dormant. Southern lawns left to their own lifecycle are decently low maintenance.

But my job required me to respond, so I set live traps in response to the complaints. The wire box traps were designed to catch nuisance animals without harming them. Once caught, we would cover the trap with a sheet or towel and transport the animal to another location where it could live without ruining human habitat. A few weeks went by, and it was still armadillos 1, Sandy 0. Even the golf course managers were calling me now. Something needed to be done.

42. Worms

On a whim, I reached out to a state parks wildlife specialist, and when he heard my dilemma, he began rattling off advice. One tip sounded like an instant winner. Worms.

"Armadillos don't have great eyesight," he said, "so you'll need to set up long wings with two by fours or some sort of lumber on either side of your traps to help funnel them into the entrance."

"Right," I said. "Wings. Check."

"Next," he said, "go buy a couple tubs of earthworms from the bait store. Armadillos dig because they're looking for grubs and worms underground. That's why they're so common around lawns with irrigation systems. Bugs and grubs need water, too. You'll want to give the armadillos a free meal."

"Earthworms," I said. "Check. How do I keep the worms inside the trap?"

"Well," he said, "here's the sketchy part. Do you have a blender?" Now I was paying attention.

"Yes," I said.

And he proceeded to give me instructions on how to make an earthworm stay in the trap.

"First," he said, "add the tub of worms to your blender, dirt and all. Then add some water, just enough to help mix it all. Then cover the blender and turn it on. Pulse setting works best."

I was horrified.

"When it's a nice consistency," he continued, "pour your mix into a glass jar, cover it with a cloth and rubber band, and set the jar in a warm dark place for about a week. And whatever you do, DO NOT sniff this mix when you go to use it."

My silence must have provided punctuation. How bad could it smell? I mean, I routinely picked up dead animals alongside the road and cleaned dog and cat cages every day. I was used to bad smells. I waited to see if he was joking with me. Worms in a blender, he had said. My head was spinning. Did even worms stink when they died? Weren't they just dirt in a worm suit? He waited too. Maybe he'd told this story a time or two before me. Ok then. Figuring that I was still on board, he continued.

"When you get ready to use your bait, set your trap where you want it, and be sure to stake it down on all four corners. This stuff is so potent, you'll get armadillos coming from miles away fighting each other to get inside."

I imagined that scene, armadillo warriors with their built-in armor, all fighting to be the first inside my traps. Sometimes my imagination scared me a little bit. It still does. And so, my plan was in place. I bought the worms. I did not share with them their impending fate. At the shelter, I put them in a blender with a little water. I turned my head and closed my eyes, then hit the pulse button. My imagination heard a thousand tiny screams as the worms were blended into soupy bits. I tried humming loudly to drown out the screams. When it was soup, I poured it all into a glass jar and covered it as instructed. With the jar safely stashed in the storage shed behind the shelter, I prayed for forgiveness. I still do this today. Worms haunt me.

But a week went by, and I had to see it work. So, I went to the little shed and grabbed my jar of sins. Of course, the first thing I did was remove the cloth cover and take a giant sniff. I thought my head would explode. My nose slammed shut, and my eyes felt like they were bleeding. The worm juice was worse than any smell I had ever smelled, ever. It was a hot, nasty, green cloud of black toxins that made its way to my brain, lodging there for all of time. The smell was equivalent to getting zapped by an electric fence, something I had already learned and could never forget. Odd how that happens.

As our little town grew in population, I shuddered at the marketing ploys the real estate developers used to entice metro families to come enjoy the "country life." Images of browsing deer, playful raccoons and chubby, smiling squirrels encouraged future residents to consider living among the wild animal neighbors in our little community. I cringed at these signs because I knew the price the wildlife paid for the new homes and roads being built. I was the one who had live-trapped the red fox family to prevent their den from being bulldozed by a developer. When we met face-to-face, the developer coldly informed me that his financial timeline was his only concern. With that said, I knew the new fox kits would not have enough time to mature enough to be on their own. Wave enough money in front of some faces and soon that's all those faces can see.

With the help of my wildlife rehab friends, the foxes were successfully relocated, but it was hard to cause so much upheaval in the lives of animals which many people rarely even saw. As a result of this "progress," as everyone called it, I trapped, caught and relocated beavers, mink, opossums, snakes, squirrels by the hundreds, rehabilitated countless songbirds whose nests had fallen with the trees that were cut down or bulldozed and more than a few birds of prey. And in defiance of state regulations, I caught and secretly released more skunks than I can even remember. It was a tough balance to strike, doing the job I was required to do while at the same time being an advocate for the wild animal population and the benefits they provided to our community. Not everybody wanted to hear me.

But now it was time to use the worm juice. A triumph over the invasion of these ferocious diggers was mine to claim. I loaded my traps into the truck, grabbed my jar of magic-park-ranger-potion and headed to the first address on my list of complainants, expectations high.

43. The VIP

And so, I arrived at the home of a city councilperson, one of the most vocal armadillo complainants. She had built a grand home on a section of the river with stunning views and perfect sunset vistas. The berms and slopes of their landscaping had been professionally installed and then maintained every week throughout the year. From the first day of the groundbreaking at their property, she was a routine caller to our office. I tried to share some tips to co-exist with the wild animals that she wanted displaced, but to no avail. After they moved in, a beaver easily clipped off a Japanese maple tree in their yard. She insisted I set traps in the river itself, as "that is where they are coming from, and that tree cost me $500!"

Without missing a beat, I said that it would be illegal for me to trap a beaver out of season and without a state permit. We stood there, squared off. Her eyes narrowed. I could see her re-writing our animal ordinance in her head.

I said, "Let's try this," offering up several methods of beaver deterrent, which included wrapping the remaining trees with special tape, building decorative but sturdy fencing around the base of the trees, and so forth. She wasn't happy, but the law was the law, I gently said. While my voice stayed friendly and calm and my smile looked genuine and sincere, inside I was screaming. And now she had armadillos.

I climbed out of the truck and knocked at her door.

"I'm glad to see you!" she said, turning her back instantly and walking away briskly, her high heels clipping in rhythm on the smooth marble floor. "Follow me to the back. You won't believe what is happening I've spent $20,000 on grass this year alone and I need you to get rid of these things what in the world would do THAT!?" and she pointed at the grass in the backyard, her breath coming fast and hard through her nose.

The tiny rodeo bulls had found her. What's worse, they had indeed held a party there the night before. I sighed.

"Armadillos," I said.

"Well, I want them GONE!" her nose said. "Surely you don't need a state permit for them!"

"Well," I said, "they're not easy to trap, but I'm learning. I've talked to a state park ranger, and he's given me some tips on how to trap them. I have some new bait and a few traps on the truck. Is it ok if I set them up?"

"By all means," she said. "Make yourself at home."

So, I got busy. From the bay of my truck, I grabbed two armadillo-sized traps, each with trigger-doors at both ends, known as a double-sided trap. Setting them down in the yard where the most damage was, I returned to the truck and grabbed the wooden "wings" the ranger had recommended, eight 6-foot long 2x6 boards, two for each entrance of the two traps. I had packed a set of metal tent stakes as well, some for the wings and some for the traps, as recommended by the park ranger, in anticipation of the armadillo festival I hoped would happen that very night. Once the traps were set and secured, I surveyed my work.

Dang, that looks perfect, I thought.

Now for the bait. I grabbed the jar of worm juice from the cab of the truck and walked to the traps. Carefully, I dribbled the liquid into the base of the traps, around them, in little paths leading up to the doors along the inside edges of the wings, and especially on the trip-pan the armadillos would have to step on to trigger the doors. I sprinkled torn grass and dirt on top of the wire trap floor to make for a more familiar pathway as the armadillos worked their way into my traps. As an added flourish, I swirled a few s's on the lawn near the traps, just to empty the last of the juice. I'd stop and buy more earthworms on the way back to the shelter. I was super excited, but I had no idea what I had just done.

The next morning, I took a detour on my way into the shelter. I needed to stop by the riverfront mansion and check the armadillo traps. I already knew where I would relocate them, a quiet spot with good water sources, safe from roaming dogs and bulldozers, with plenty of acreage and creek banks to raise armadillo families. As I pulled up to her driveway, I could hardly contain my excitement. Parking at the curb, I walked quickly to the fence and then stood on my tiptoes to see over. The traps were empty, the doors still propped open. I sagged with disappointment. Back at the shelter, I called my new friend, the park ranger. He pondered the dilemma. We laughed a bit about my predictable behavior with the jar of worm juice, and he gave me a few more suggestions. He thought that maybe the armadillos had eaten all the bugs and grubs available in that section of her yard.

"Try resetting the traps in a part of the yard without damage," he suggested.

I went back to square one, calling the homeowner and letting her know what the plan was. I said a little prayer to the earthworm gods, closing my eyes as I hit the blender button. Once again, I poured the worm juice into the glass jar, covered it and set it aside. This time I was not tempted to smell it. My eyes had barely recovered from the first time. In a few days I set out for the mansion, worm juice at the ready, intent on setting the best traps I could. Except for the location, I did everything the same, up to the signature "S" flourish when I got to the bottom of the jar. This time I set the traps on the most beautiful section of the lawn. The grass was deep green and luxurious, the soil underneath was soft, rich, and inviting. It looked and felt every bit of a $20,000 lawn. I'm sure their neighbors suffered from lawn envy, but that would soon change.

Everything was set. The next morning, I eagerly drove to the riverfront house, sure I would be successful that day. But with every passing day, I grew more disappointed. Four days had gone by with the traps in the new location, and it was clear that the new techniques had been a failure. I left the traps in place one more day to be sure. For good measure, I dribbled a few more pints of worm juice around the yard and left.

44. Not What I Expected

Armadillos are wonderful creatures, unique in many ways from other mammal species. For their size, they are some of the strongest and fastest diggers on the planet, making sense that their preferred diet of grubs, worms, and roots are all under the ground we walk on. They typically give birth to identical quadruplets, formed from the same fertilized egg which divides into four at after fertilization. They aren't recognized as swimmers, but I've seen them. They are fast, confident and skillful swimmers, but they do make a curious picture as they cut a path through the water on their way to the other side. They also provide an amazing benefit to our landscapes, whether cultured or wild. In their hunt for grubs and underground insects, they provide soil and thatch aeration, as do skunks, helping plants to thrive and, in many cases, germinate. I've been told that they also love fire ants.

But to so many, these benefits were distant and unimportant. My complainants wanted their green lawns safe. As the days went by without catching any armadillos, our late summer weather became increasingly dry, and the armadillos became increasingly bold. The damp lawns and flower beds, nurtured by lawn sprinkler systems, were the perfect places to find easy meals, and the complaints about armadillo damage were pouring in. A few weeks into my experiment with the worm juice, I admitted defeat but promised all the complainants I would continue my research. The day I went to collect the traps from the councilperson's yard, I was not prepared for what I found. Clearly, she had not ventured a foot into her yard either.

The first thing I saw were the large brown s's near the traps. My s's. My head began to hurt. As I looked closely, I could see every inch of where I had poured the worm juice. Every blade of grass that had been touched by the juice was dead, burned brown and crispy by the sun and by the high-powered liquid fertilizer I had poured in lovely designs everywhere. And then it struck me. While I don't know much about the chemical composition of earthworm juice, I had clearly created a disaster of phosphor-etic proportions. As the councilperson joined me on her now multi-colored lawn, she was speechless, which was more terrifying than her outbursts. There was nothing I could do.

I gulped a brief but sincere apology, adding that I would call soon with next steps. I did my best to offer assurances that I would do all I could to find a solution. I drove off, hoping I hadn't just lost my job, but determined to figure out the problem for the benefit of everyone, including the armadillos. Experience had shown me that if I couldn't find a solution to someone's wild animal problem, they would take matters into their own hands, and I had seen some of those results. They weren't pretty and they sure weren't humane.

45. The Grass is Always Greener

I decided to abandon the park ranger, thinking he had probably enjoyed his fun with the dogcatcher. Next, I called a wildlife relocation expert, a guy who had forgotten more about our wild animal friends than I would ever know. He had his own small business providing wildlife solutions to homeowners. His solutions worked for both animals and people. He was honest, effective, and compassionate, and his business was booming. I had enjoyed working together with him to solve problems, learning a lot from him in the few years we had known each other.

Why hadn't I thought of him first? He was the one who taught me how to use a glue board to remove snakes from tight spaces, and how to get that snake, and other animals, safely and humanely off the glue board using cooking spray and gentle handling, a technique I've used many times over. He taught me how to safely live trap and correctly relocate beavers. As an expert on waterfowl, he taught me how to identify dozens of different types of migrating ducks. For the years we worked together, we loved watching the winter migration of ducks on the pond in front of the shelter.

In a great televised rescue, he helped me get a pet cat out of a 40-foot-tall pine tree using multiple pool-cleaning poles, duct tape and tree climber's spikes. For that adventure, he listened to me as I taught him how to safely use the loop on the control pole so the cat could be lowered to the ground without injury. It was a happy ending in the public eye. We were a good team, and the respect we had for each other was priceless.

I dialed his number. As we talked, I learned about some of the armadillo's eccentricities, and its greatest weakness.

"What do armadillos eat?" he asked me.

I listed off all the things I knew, adding lots of things I had been told, including my park ranger earthworm fiasco. By the time my story ended, he was choking with laughter. He knew the guy, he said, and told me he was a joker, not in the literal sense but in the sense that most people, including the guy's mother, wondered how he kept a job. Of course, I thought. Just like me to fall for that foolishness.

"Do armadillos eat ants?" he asked.

"Yes," I said.

"Do ants like sugar?" he pressed.

"Ummm, yes," I said.

"What is jelly made of?" and off went the light bulb.

"Grape jelly," he said. "The flavor doesn't really matter," he added. "Jelly is jelly is jelly, but grape, for whatever reason, is always the cheapest. Set the traps along a wall or fence line. Never mind about avoiding previous damage, they'll go back to where they found bugs because they know the bugs will be back." He continued, "Use the wings just like you've been doing, because while their eyesight isn't great, they can smell an ant at a hundred yards. Then, drop a spoonful of grape jelly on the trip pan of the trap, enough to last a zillion ants at least one or two nights. The armadillos will come for the ants."

And come they did.

46. Mistakes That Last Forever

I relished telling the people how we were catching so many armadillos.

"Grape jelly," I would say, then smile, leaving them to wonder how it was that their dogcatcher had lost her mind so quickly.

I do love an occasional mystery, and I had earned this one. Eventually the seasons changed, rain returned and with the rain, the armadillos disappeared back into their trees and creek banks, safely invisible once again. The brown burned grass where I had drooled all the worm juice blended as usual with the brown of winter. At the shelter, I threw away the blender. It would never make a decent daiquiri again. Then March arrived, bringing an Ozark spring, blooming redbud trees and glorious white dogwoods competing for attention. The grass began to come to life.

I happened to stop near that same house one bright and pretty day. The grass along her driveway was already green, and I couldn't resist peeking over the fence. I don't know why. I surely could have lived just fine without seeing what I saw next. There, as large as life from the day I had written them, were the large s's I had swirled onto the grass. No longer brown and dead, no. Now the letters were beautifully dark green, much darker than the other areas of lawn and easy to spot from a window, a neighbor's yard, or from my perch as I stared in horror over the fence. The fertilizer of the fermented worm juice had done its job, and it would continue doing that job for who knew how long. With luck and the good grace of the councilperson, I continued doing my job, too. She understood that my efforts, while misguided were well intentioned.

I've never been able to look at earthworms the same, but as the next years went by, I learned. My knowledge expanded so quickly I couldn't seem to keep up, which makes no sense at all, but that's how it felt. I wanted more, wanted to be more, wanted to see more, wanted to do more. I became bored and itchy with the need for new challenges. Some people would call that ambition, but what I knew was that I wanted to do better, every day. I dreamed of building a bigger shelter with all sorts of natural features. Sunlight, fresh air, running water, a wetland boardwalk nature park. It would be a facility for all people, and all animals that came there would get a fair chance at a new and better start in life. It was an ambitious vision and a bit too big to be real, then. I still dreamed of a bigger, more challenging job managing a larger city's animal population and programs. I became irritable in my relationship with my partner even though we built a house on our own acreage, where I loved coming home each night. A few horses, chickens and a garden followed, but I couldn't shake the restlessness.

47. Tigers and Tornadoes

On the last day of February 1997, I received a phone call from the veterinarian for a wildlife zoo and safari park located a few counties north of my shelter. She needed to borrow a dart gun. I had to ask why. Quietly and quickly, she told me she had just gotten a panicked call from one of the workers at the safari park. The owner of the park was out of town, and when the worker came in that morning to feed the animals, she was ambushed by a pair of escaped Siberian tigers. Without knowing they were on the loose, she had pulled into the compound through a set of ten-foot-high wooden gates with a tall load of boxed, frozen chicken parts in the bed of her small pickup truck. Getting out to close the gates behind her, she turned and was greeted by the sight of both tigers on top of the load of chicken, staring at her. Keeping her cool, she closed the gates and retreated to the safety of a building a few hundred feet away while the tigers got busy ripping into the boxes of meat.

From there, she called the vet, describing a scene of destruction. The tigers had been loose for hours, it looked like. Dead animals were everywhere. Raccoons, kangaroos, geese and goats all lay scattered. Some were missing limbs, all were dead, likely killed for fun, as cats will do. The bear and mountain lion cages were still intact, she told the vet, those animals still safely behind their locked doors.

The business was known to me, and I also knew that it was not well-respected. But in a state where such things were still legal, they stayed in business selling "safari" tickets to busloads of schoolchildren and visitors. The veterinarian, while not condoning the business, nonetheless knew that the animals deserved good veterinary care, and she had always done her best for them. She knew these tigers and knew they would be difficult.

There are those who will say that God works in mysterious ways, and this day was pure proof. I had spent the previous several months preparing to host a remote tranquilizer, or "dart gun" certification class for Arkansas's animal control officers. This type of training was hard to come by, but it was essential education for an animal control officer. Dart guns aren't the first tool to reach for in any given scenario, but when needed, it's the only tool that will work. Those times were rare, but they happened, and when they did, animal control officers needed to know how to operate the equipment safely and correctly.

The class was in its second day of instruction, and the training room at city hall was packed with ACOs from across the state. The company providing the instruction was well known, and the instructor had brought with him virtually every type of tranquilizer projector, the "gun," then available on the market. The timing couldn't have been more perfect. Thinking quickly and with the blessing from the city attorney, the company providing the class, and the owner of the safari park who the vet had reached by phone, we transferred class a few dozen miles up the highway to the compound of the safari park.

Working together, the instructor of the class and the veterinarian put together a plan. With the vet's expertise in tranquilizer drugs, knowledge of the health status of both big cats, and the instructor's skill with the tranquilizer projector itself, both tigers, once located, were safely sedated within an hour. As quickly as we could, we loaded the slumbering cats into the bed of a pickup truck and back into secure cages.

I had never touched a tiger. Their feet were as large as a five-gallon bucket, heavy and built to destroy things, their claws like curved knives. Up close, their teeth were thick, dense, and powerful. Their whiskers looked as strong as fiberglass fishing poles. Touching the striped fur, I was shocked to feel the softness. I had imagined a coarse texture, but this fur felt the same as my cat's, only thicker. No wonder people killed them for their fur. I was awestruck.

48. Tornado Number One

The next day, March 1, 1997, parts of Arkansas were struck by a devastating F3 tornado. Twenty people were killed in a swath of damage that swept away much of the tiny town of Arkadelphia, 50 or so miles to the south of our city and further still from the safari park. Within days, the Red Cross and state disaster response services were requesting help managing the animal aspect of the disaster. Our little shelter sent staff and equipment to help capture, house and care for displaced and injured animals. It was my first exposure to a storm of such magnitude, and my first experience as an official responder to a disaster.

Growing up in Wisconsin, our thunderstorms brought what we called "good sleeping weather." When storms were forecast, we'd crack open the windows, close the garage door and go to bed early. Rarely did we worry. But it was different in the south, especially Arkansas and Oklahoma. Storms here were strong and could kill people. Even thunderstorms. As the disaster response efforts got underway in Arkadelphia, I rotated shifts between our community's regular duties and the needs of the animals and people of Arkadelphia. The skills I was learning would be needed again, much sooner than I could even dream.

And life carried on. Our small animal control department was growing as our city, situated near two larger metropolitan areas, became a popular small-city destination for families wishing for a quieter life while still being close to the metro areas. I worked to update our animal ordinance, and I requested and received an increased budget to expand our small facility and add another animal control officer.

Through donations and public support, we became the state's first shelter-based spay-neuter and wellness veterinary clinic for shelter animals. We outfitted a small surgery room in our shelter, which allowed for a veterinarian to perform as many spay or neuter surgeries as they had time for. My animal officers and I provided the technician support, prepping the animals for their surgeries, tending to them in recovery. Other shelters in the state soon followed our lead with their own in-house programs.

Meeting some initial resistance from the local veterinary community, I gained their support by proving to them that clean, healthy, recently adopted and spayed or neutered pets would come to them for a lifetime of full-service support. With each adoption I offered a free wellness visit to the participating vet of the adopter's choice, paid for by a program funded by our new volunteer group "Friends of the Animals." The vets were happy; they were getting a steady source of new clients and income, all without spending a nickel. The adopters were happy; they were getting healthy new pets with free initial veterinary care. Additionally, adopters got access to a free training program offered by a local trainer, a new part of our city's Parks and Recreation curriculum. City administrators were happy, the adoption program had gotten a lot of attention in the media for successful innovations in adoption programs, high adoption numbers and low euthanasia statistics, and growing public support. I smiled every time visitors to our shelter walked in and their faces changed from unpleasant expectation to wonder.

"It smells so good in here!" they often exclaimed. "It's so clean!"

We worked hard to keep our shelter clean so our animals would be healthy as well as happy. Our standards became the model for other shelters across the state. But all was not sunshine and roses, as any aspect of being a public servant will eventually guarantee.

In 1998, Arkansas's animal control professionals banded together in a coalition to introduce mandatory spay-neuter legislation to the legislative session. With a freshman legislator as its sponsor, the legislation didn't get much traction until ACOs from across the state began to show up to speak on its behalf. As an introductory and somewhat controversial piece of animal law, it was written sparsely. Requiring mandatory spay or neuter of every shelter animal being adopted from a shelter in a county of 500,000 people or more, it affected our shelter and our programs. I had lobbied in person for its passage, and it passed. I, along with the entire animal control community in Arkansas, cheered.

49. Anti-Social Media

One new law didn't change our intake numbers though, and we still faced the usual peak seasons, in particular puppy and kitten season. One spring day, as I was beginning to close the shelter for the night and our last visitor of the day was still visiting the adoptable animals, a car pulled up to the shelter. The driver stepped out, then reached back inside and pulled out a large cardboard box. I groaned. We were full. Every available cage had an occupant; some cages had more than one. Inside the box were four beautiful half-grown tabby kittens, clean and fluffy, frightened but curious. They looked highly adoptable if I could only find one more cage for them.

Just then, the adoption shopper came back into the office. "I found a cat I'd like to adopt," she said with an excited smile. She handed me the cage card.

"Wonderful!" I replied. "One of our favorites!"

She had chosen a beautiful calico cat with a gentle personality and a huge purr. As the new cats were being processed in by the officer, I processed the adoption. It would be a quick swap. The new cats could have the cage vacated by the adopted cat; all we'd have to do was clean the cage. I explained the new spay-neuter law to the adopter, a local woman. I also explained what her adoption fee covered, which included a free first vet visit and the spay surgery. She was delighted to learn how much money she would save and thrilled with the free veterinary exam and follow-up vaccinations provided by a local vet.

"Usually," I told her, "adopted animals stay here until after the spay surgery, then the adopter comes to pick it up. Because we're so full and I don't want to euthanize any animals for space reasons, you can take your new kitty home tonight and bring her back on Tuesday. We'll get her spayed, and you can pick her up that afternoon."

"Sounds perfect," she said.

Tuesday came and went with no sign of the adopter or her new cat. I called her, and we rescheduled the appointment for the following week. She didn't show up for that appointment either. Nor did she show for the next. Three weeks had transpired. Then, she returned one of my frustrated phone calls to inform me the cat was now pregnant and her mother was against abortion. She wouldn't be returning the cat. She stopped answering my phone calls. More than four weeks into the standoff, I received a call from one of my favorite police sergeants, David.

"Sandy!" he said.

"Hey David!" I smiled through the phone.

"I have a lady who wants to file harassment charges against you. What's going on?"

When I learned that the complainant was my cat adopter who was refusing to have her adopted cat spayed, I filled him in, including the new state law.

"Ah," he said. "I'll call her back. Don't worry."

A few hours passed, and then a phone call came for which I was totally unprepared. The state's largest newspaper had received a tip about a problem with a cat adoption. The reporter, who sounded young and a little too sincere, told me that one of our city residents, who had recently adopted a cat, told her that I was demanding that she return the cat because it wasn't spayed, and that when she brought her new kitty back to the shelter it would probably be euthanized. She paused, then asked if I had any comment. By this time, I was plenty angry and frustrated with the adopter. First a phony claim of harassment, now a call to the state newspaper claiming that the "shelter woman" wanted her to return her pregnant cat to be euthanized.

I didn't know then what I have learned since. Messaging the public about issues and policies is a tricky and delicate thing. Secondly, less is more, especially when the message concerns animals. Humans aren't as smart as we'd like to think, either in the delivery of such messages or in the receiving of them, and I was 100% human. Between the two of us, my message of "your cat needs to be spayed per the state law" and her message of "my cat is pregnant, my mom doesn't believe in abortion, and I'm not bringing the cat back for an abortion" had reached an impasse. I spilled my heart out to the reporter, using words like overpopulation, crowded shelters, and euthanasia. Then my biggest mistake, the spoken sentence with the most power.

"We have to kill cats every day to make room for more."

It was the perfect sound bite that every reporter dreams about. I had meant to explain to the reporter how important spay surgery was to limit the problem of animal overpopulation. I had hoped to help her understand that in the matter of pregnancy for cats, it's about procreation, not recreation. As a last resort, I hoped she would understand that to spay a cat in the early stages of pregnancy did not equate to a human abortion, something she had told me the adopter had shared with her as one of her beliefs. I urged her to look up the new state law, and then we said goodbye. She was polite, almost cheerful in her tone. By the weekend, I would know why.

The Sunday paper was once the favorite news source for most people I knew. Thick, colorful, with world news, local news, editorials, advertisements, classifieds, a society section, sports and comics, it was a sort of prehistoric social media in paper format. Grandpa on the farm took an entire week to make his way through the Sunday paper, carefully re-folding the sections read, then reaching for the stack of sections waiting to be read. I still miss the Sunday newspaper, but that Sunday I had no idea what was in store for me.

As I picked up the newspaper on the sidewalk and unlocked the door to the shelter, I heard the phone ringing non-stop.

What the heck, I thought. It was Sunday, for Pete's sake. I had come in to clean and take care of the shelter animals. Even though we were closed, the animals still required care, and it was my weekend on duty. Setting the paper down on my desk and listening to the phone ringing, I wondered what was going on. Then I heard some of the messages left on our answering machine. The answering machine was full; there was no room for any more messages, but the phone kept ringing.

Up to that moment, I hadn't thought of all the ways a human being could deliver hate to another human being, all without landing one physical blow. But hate poured from those messages, some so full of dark venom that there remains, today, simply no words I can find to describe them. The messages were mostly from people with phone numbers outside our own state. Some threatened to "…come kill you and see how you like it!" Some threatened to get me fired, one even called me "The Mad Butcher." It was nearly more than I could bear. On the advice of the city manager, I unplugged the phone.

Inside the paper, situated in the prominent City section, was a half-page full-color photo of a mother cat grinning up at the camera as her four tiny kittens were stretched out at the milk bar, nursing furiously. I don't remember the headline, but it could have read "Local Animal Shelter Supervisor Vows to Kill Mother Cat and Kittens to Fulfill State Spay Neuter Law." It was unimaginably ridiculous, but that was the gist of the article. The story made its way to the Associated Press network, and it spread from there across the country.

There are dumpster fires in everyone's life at one time or another, and as everyone will say, the flames either burn you down or build your character; the choice is yours. While I grieved for years over the hatred directed at me that day and in the coming weeks, eventually, as all news stories do, my cat story cycled out of circulation. The cat and her kittens were all spayed and neutered, and life went on. What happened the following Monday, however, was that I met, over the phone, the person I had been searching for all my life. Lou was a regional representative of one of the country's largest non-profit animal welfare agencies. She had gotten calls complaining about the cat-killer in Arkansas and called to get my side of the story. She introduced herself and said she was from the regional office in Dallas.

"What happened?" she asked.

50. Lou

I didn't remember then, but I had met Lou a year or so before, at a conference on managing feral cats, held at a hotel in Little Rock. I was a scheduled speaker, and she was a representative of the agency she worked for, a primary sponsor of the conference. I was asked to speak about feral dogs, and I was cranky about the assignment. Who wants to listen to a presentation on dogs when you're attending a conference on cats?

Regardless, my presentation was brilliant. I was comfortable in the large crowd, and in no time had them fully engaged with my stories from the field, animal population statistics, humane handling and trapping techniques, and community programming. I found a way to spin the presentation so that the information related to both dogs and cats, and along the way I told a few jokes. I had them laughing, paying attention and asking questions. Lou was in the crowd. When the presentation wrapped up, most of the attendees stepped outside for a break. Lou found me there and introduced herself, complimenting me on the presentation.

"Nice to meet you," I said.

We talked for a few minutes, then I left. I needed to get back to work. The next time I saw her would be in my shelter lobby after the worst week of my entire life.

A week after the pregnant cat story broke, I received a call from a representative of the same organization that had sponsored the feral cat conference. When I answered and heard, "Hi, I'm Lou and we met a while back at a cat conference."

I remembered meeting her, and I literally exploded with the pregnant cat story, telling it from start to finish with such speed I'm not sure I even took a breath between sentences. I don't remember what she said when I stopped talking, but the words of understanding were enough to help me catch my breath and see a glimmer of hope.

She offered to come to Arkansas to tour our shelter and see the programs in action. I told her about our surgery clinic, our dog park, our Friends of the Animals group, our new ordinance and our adoption numbers. Did she believe enough of what I told her? Maybe, maybe not. But we scheduled a day for her to come to the shelter. I would meet Lou again.

51. Tornado Number Two

In May, 1999, one of the most devastating tornadoes in our country's history pummeled parts of Oklahoma, most notably Moore, Oklahoma and parts of southern Oklahoma City. Nearly 40 people were killed, hundreds were injured. Over one billion dollars in damage occurred because of the F5 tornado, which measured a world-record wind speed of 321 miles per hour.

Lou had been tasked by her agency with spearheading the animal rescue response. Using the Oklahoma City Animal Control building as a headquarters, Lou organized city and county animal control personnel and volunteers from across the country. Again, my small staff and I, with previous experience from Arkadelphia, rearranged our schedule to allow one person a week to travel to OKC to volunteer in any way they needed. After his week-long shift, one of my ACOs came back home and told me he had been working to capture a few frightened dogs. When he looked up at a stripped, nearly limb-less tree, there hung the carcass of a horse, dropped by the storm.

When my turn came to head to Oklahoma City, I found ways to spend time working with Lou. She was in charge, she had solid plans of action, she dispatched the animal control crews and kennel staff every morning with tasks and instructions that they understood. She solved problems on the run and through it all, through all the dysfunction we saw in the shelter procedures, for all the terrible images thrown at all of us every day, she saw the bigger picture. She saw the help needed by the city's animal control staff. She saw the gaping holes in the programs, policies, and procedures that even before the tornado, offered little comfort to the impounded animals, and even less service to the taxpayers who needed a better program. I watched her work with dozens of people at all social levels and through every interaction I saw her impart her vision for a better job done, a better outcome pursued, a better way of doing things. I saw her inspire, lead, coach, comfort, and care about everyone and every animal.

By the time I went home to Arkansas, I had been swept away by an entirely different tornado, but one that was just as powerful. I had hoped for a future with someone with whom I could soak my dentures. She would soon become my "we."

52. Ruby

She came to me in a tiny box, her weightless beauty resting on a small cloud of cotton. The man said he heard a quiet thump at his window and upon investigating, discovered her under the window, bright green feathers an anomaly even among the plant foliage. Clearly, she couldn't fly.

"A female Ruby-Throated Hummingbird," I said, and I thanked him for bringing her in.

My friends at the wildlife rehab center listened as I explained her symptoms: alert but unable to maintain a perching position, wings attempting to fly but she was not able to gain meaningful flight. They diagnosed what may have been a traumatic brain injury from the window collision and gave me permission to attempt to rehabilitate her. They warned me that chances of success would be slim.

She quickly learned to sip the sugar and protein water from the end of a syringe while resting in the palm of my hand. Each day I counted her progress in bubbles, the ones that traveled up the syringe as she sipped the mixture from the syringe tip. Four, eight, twelve at a time, I was sure she was getting better. Even though she still couldn't perch, I hoped. Too often I would go to her little cage and find her upside down, her beautiful wings spread out under her, her shiny eyes meeting mine as I gently set her right-side up again.

One day, after I'd counted a good number of bubbles, she stepped forward onto my thumb and perched. She looked around at our small yard, the flowers, the trees surrounding the deck. I imagined she was scouting a flight path to freedom. My breath stopped. I was transfixed. As I watched this tiny miracle standing sure and free on my hand, the hum of the world around us quieted. We were alone, just me and little Ruby, and in that moment, all I was aware of was this little bird and my hope.

And then she fell backwards into my palm. Putting my tears behind a brave, practical face, I called my friends at the rehab center.

"It's been too long. She can't survive on sugar water, and she'll need to migrate soon. If she can't orient herself to perch and fly, she'll never make it."

We discussed the dilemma a bit more, enough to help me come to terms with reality.

As a supervisor of an animal shelter, I had legal access to the drugs I needed to help animals out of whatever misery they had fallen into. Injury, illness, disease or just the crime of being unwanted. It was my job to give the animals in my care an appropriate outcome to alleviate suffering. Euthanasia is the term for "kind death," and I had trained to become an expert. I can't imagine the kind of misery it is for a bird known as "The Acrobat of the Skies" to be trapped inside the hand of a human, but that day I released my little friend, not into the sky as I had hoped, but into another realm where I imagined she could fly forever.

Every morning, I hold my coffee, left hand raising the cup on demand, right hand sliding the computer mouse back and forth and side to side, navigating the blue screen of my morning ritual. But my hands have held much more, things that are momentarily forgotten but return, unexpected, in memories. Throughout our lives, we all hold things. In our hands, in respect, in awe, sometimes in contempt, sometimes in regret. But to have and to hold, those all-too-common words, is one of our greatest gifts. Like the baby skunks I once held in awe, and the feel of the iron grip from the talons of a Barred Owl, each of these creatures and hundreds more through the years left the care of my hands to continue their journeys, either in life or in death.

I look for Ruby in every hummingbird I see, remembering the feeling of her tiny bird feet gripping my thumb, the sparkle in her shiny bird eyes. I hear Sarah's voice in every wood duck flying overhead. I remember the skunks from those days every time their smell comes on the breeze. I am rich in these memories I can still feel, here in the palm of my hand. To have, and then to hold.

53. One Last Miracle

As the only girl in a house full of boys, Mom worked hard to teach me all the "girl things." Dresses, makeup, etiquette around strangers, how to wear pink anything as she tried in vain to deflect the tomboy identity I wore so easily. In many ways, she was never able to reach the pretty pink princess she hoped I'd become. But through the years, her ability to work miracles left me in awe, even today, more than 30 years after her death.

She never found her own miracle in her fight with cancer, but in those last few weeks with her, I recognized the silver lining in cancer, the bit of time it gives people to say goodbye. She didn't want to die in a hospital bed, so Dad set up the living room with everything she needed to be comfortable. As Dad and I counted days, Mom became weaker and more dependent on pain medication. Dad and I took turns being her nurse.

As she lay on her favorite couch, each passing day becoming weaker, we had the time to laugh together over memories like the wand and the pheasant chicks, our red horse, Sunny, and so many of our adventures together.

"Don't be sad when I go," she said one day. "I don't know how I could have lived if this was one of you kids instead of me."

Watching someone you love die, slipping away over the course of weeks as I did with Mom as her final caretaker, might be too hard for some people to comprehend, but is a tragedy easier? When a life is taken without a chance for goodbye, a sudden accident taking someone you love, shattering your heart without warning? Unsaid words, unresolved anger, unshared memories, laughter not laughed, tears not shed? I still remember our last hug as she lay on the couch. Hugging had always been her best dance move, and that day, even as she lay on the couch, was one of her finest.

"Are you happy in your life?" she asked one afternoon without warning.

I was sitting next to her, reading a book as she slept. I looked over at her, and she was looking back at me, her head on the pillow, hands quietly folded on the blanket. Her blue eyes were brilliant blue that day, crystalline and clear and as deep as Lake Superior. She looked worried. I sensed that she had thought long and hard about asking this question. I hesitated. A few years before her diagnosis, I had stopped dating my boyfriend. Both my parents loved him and were hoping we would marry.

Instead, I had discovered a close community of women. The new world of close friends had consumed much of my time and had brought me the greatest joy I had known. In that community, I had grown more comfortable each year as I learned and understood more about who I was born to be. But I also knew that without a man in my future, my parents might not accept me. I couldn't bear to lose them, so I hadn't spent much time with them at all, letting our relationship with each other rest on the strength of our history. But she had seen that my friends brought me joy, and she had tried hard to understand this new version of her only daughter.

When her diagnosis was revealed to me, it came as a shock. She had always been strong, always the person with the solution to a problem, always with a laugh or a hug or a word of encouragement. What would I do without her? That afternoon as she waited for my reply, maybe she knew she had one more miracle up her sleeve. Then again, maybe she didn't, and maybe for her, miracles were just what moms did without a lot of fuss or noise. But her question hung in the air.

"Yes," I said quietly. "I am."

"I'm happy for you, then," she said. She lifted a hand, and I leaned close, taking it into mine. We smiled together.

"Thank you for always being my miracle," I told her.
"And thank you for always being my angel," she replied.

PART THREE, TEXAS

"There are no ordinary lives." Ken Burns

54. The Wild West

My relationship in Arkansas had been crumbling while a new relationship in Texas beckoned. There are some who would call this cheating, and maybe they would be right, seen in that singular light. For me, I craved freedom from the constant oversight that had become the baseline of the previous 13 years. I had let constraints and routine define my life. I wanted to stand in front of metaphorical grocery store doors, the kind that open when its sensor detects movement, and know they would open because it was ME, walking in with a self-assured gait such as I'd never had. Those doors would see me and tremble. How many times had I waited humbly for someone to walk in and make those doors open on my behalf? It was time to take charge of my own life. I wanted to be more than nearly famous. Open, Sesame.

It wasn't easy, breaking someone else's heart in favor of my own. But I knew I had finally chosen to leave behind my lifelong habit of being an easy doormat for others. I thought at long last I was putting that version of me away, in its place a person with a stronger sense of self and clarity on my own ideas and dreams. I knew it was right, but I still felt selfish. Was this what being a grown-up was like?

I was born with the ability to feel guilty about literally everything, and those painful, exciting days of change brought guilt by the gallon. Even with that, I found a side of myself I had never met. The person in the mirror smiled again. It was exhilarating, filled with the promise of new hope, new adventures, and new opportunities. Two sides of the same coin. As the chapters in Arkansas came to an end, I felt the guilt and responsibility for other's emotions, behaviors which had managed so many of my choices for so many years, begin to fade. When that door finally opened, it was yet another threshold, and this one would be the biggest of my life.

55. Ode to Oscar

New Year's Eve, 1999. The end of my first year in Texas, a new beginning. We had spent that last day of the year waiting for the world to come to an end, as had been predicted. We watched football, made popcorn, ate black-eyed peas for good luck, and kept a nice fire burning in the fireplace all day. By 10:00 PM we were amused to still be alive despite all the dire Y2K predictions. We shared a piece of cheesecake by the fireplace, then turned off Dick Clark's Rocking New Year's Eve television broadcast.

"Enjoy the crowd, Dick," I said to the TV. "I'm too old for the noise." Nope, I wasn't going to party with Prince tonight.

Just as we turned the lights off, the dogs came alive, barking at the window facing the driveway. Shushing them, I looked out the window. "It's Joni," I said to Lou. Joni, an investigator from the local humane society, lived nearby and was probably on her way home. But why was she stopping here so late at night? I went out to meet her, my pajamas thin against the cold night.

"I brought you a present!" she said, laughing. With Joni you never knew what she would run across. Goat? Pony? Chickens? Puppies? "How many?" I asked.

"Just one," she answered with a grin. She slid the side door of the white van open. "I'm not sure it's still alive, but I thought if anybody could save it, you guys could," she said. In the rear of the van was an empty 100-gallon fish tank, aquarium filter odds and ends and a 5-gallon bucket full of dark water. "It's been abandoned," she said. "Looks like a Red Tiger Oscar fish, pretty good size but just about dead. Think you guys can give it a chance?"

By now, Lou had joined us outside. We looked at each other, then laughed. "Sure," Lou said. "Why not?"

Except for the fact that it wasn't floating belly-up in the bucket, the fish looked dead. Working quickly, we cleaned the tank, set it in the living room on its stand and began to fill it with water. It seemed like forever before there was enough water in the tank for the fish to float. The water would be too cold for hours yet, but we eased him in. It must have been a shock to the fish, to wake up in water it could breathe. Watching it acclimate to clean water, I saw again the pike and the trout from my childhood, felt them leaving my hands, watched them linger in confusion just under the surface of their home, felt again the sharp loss as they disappeared in the dark water. Watching the fish struggle, I remembered how my grandparents and I had celebrated the lives of those fish so many years ago.

He was a big fish for a tropical species, close to 14 inches long. Watching the fish begin to swim, I heard Grandpa's voice marveling with me, a secret whisper from the bridge on the slough. I heard Grandma beside me on the bank of the trout pond, telling me about the brown trout in my hands, showing me the egg sac on her belly, standing with me as I let her go back into the quiet world of the pond. I was young again, and everything was a wonder.

For hours throughout the night, as the water warmed and the filter worked, Lou and I took turns gently maneuvering the fish through the clean water to encourage flow over the gills. We were hopeful. We had, after all, just survived Y2K, the world's worst fake disaster. Hope was afloat. In small bursts, he began to swim on his own, his eyes began to glimmer with focus and his gills were again moving with purpose. By morning he was still alive and swimming on his own. It had been one of the longest New Year's nights for either of us, and we didn't touch a drop of champagne or blow one kazoo. Armageddon, for us and for the fish, had come and gone. We had welcomed another new year, but it was the years that had come before, all the years of childhood, that I celebrated as we worked to save the life of a fish.

We added a new filter, new filter media and new tank decorations to make his home more appealing. The tank and the stand took up an entire wall of our living room. One hundred gallons is a lot of water. As the months went by, the sound of his filter, like a small waterfall, became part of our household noises, a background of calming, bubbling life. He built a nest of aquarium gravel and plastic plants, a corner where he'd spend most of his time watching the activities of our home and, I imagined, some of the television shows we watched in the evenings. He was recovering and even thriving. I suppose there are ways to determine the gender of an Oscar fish, but to us he was a he. Cleverly, we named him Oscar, and soon learned he was nearly 14 years old. Oscar had become part of the family.

As he healed, we noticed a distinct personality. He was a particular eater, watching pricey snacks like shrimp and other goodies drop to the floor of the tank but always gobbling up the cheaper flaked fish food and occasional vitamin pellets. Children were enemies, and Oscar seemed to have a personal mission to rid the world of them all, deliberately charging at them when they walked past. Flinging his fins forward and with bright tiger colors flaring, he would crash nose-first into the sides of the tank, threatening all small humans like a frothing, snarling dog. We briefly thought of a tiny sign for his tank, but "Beware of Fish" seemed silly. He also enjoyed music, something no one believed until they saw him swimming in rhythm with music. It was true. He had his favorites, and we watched as he floated gently, fins folded, moving purposely in time with songs from Alison Krauss and others. What did he feel or hear, we wondered? His movements were not sporadic. When the songs were over, he'd return to his bed, gently fluttering now-healthy gills.

There were a few moments of panic over the years Oscar lived with us. When the lid to the top of his tank was left open, he seemed to know, taking aim on several occasions to break his own glass ceiling, never remembering that "free" landed him on the hardwood floor of the living room, literally a fish out of water. We kept a few towels close by for these times, dipping them into his tank and then wrapping him in the wet towel for transfer back to the tank.

Then, almost overnight, he was old. Days would pass without a nibble, occasionally eating a few bites only to return to his chosen corner, resting there for days on end. He didn't dance much anymore, even music wasn't enough to stir him. Sensing the inevitable but not knowing much about the lifespan of aquarium fish, we began to research humane euthanasia options for pet fish. We didn't want Oscar to starve to death. But the dilemma was in the process. If Oscar didn't pass away in his own time, how do you humanely end the life of a fish? We didn't want him to die, but we didn't want him to suffer, either. We wanted to give him the same compassion and consideration, just like we'd always given to our dogs, cats, horses, chickens, and goats. But how to comfort a dying fish? Surely, he deserved comfort, too.

Our options, according to veterinarians and tropical fish experts, were to let him just die on his own time. From what we were seeing, that meant a slow death from starvation, which some said could be painful. Other options mentioned in the online fish forums were to "flush" him down the toilet into our country septic system. Another was to net him from the tank, wrap him in a towel and put him in the freezer while he suffocated. Perhaps the quickest method recommended by fish hobbyists was to remove him from the tank and club him with a baseball bat. We were horrified.

Through the years he was with us, we came to know Oscar as family, a creature who responded appreciatively to music, disliked children and had a tremendous sense of humor and passion for life, even though it was a different type of life than we could ever understand.

Eventually, and after nearly two full weeks of refusing any

kind of food, we knew it was time to end his suffering. His once-vibrant red tiger stripes were dull and pale, and he was not moving from his corner to forage, float or exercise. Research gave us an option we thought kindest. On a pre-arranged day, Oscar's tank was drained of most of the water while his favorite music played. A fish tranquilizer drug, the same kind used to tranquilize and safely transport young fish from fish farms to new, natural environments, would work if we dosed it to cause an overdose. All we needed to do was measure the powder, mix it with baking soda and water to buffer the pH level, and pour it into the water in his tank. With his music playing, we added the drug. In seconds, his color faded, and he went still, rising lifeless to the surface. We buried him in the yard, in the company of cats and dogs, chickens, pocket pets, even one hermit crab. All had gone before him; all had shared our home and hearts.

Fishing on Lake Superior as a kid with Grandpa in town, a man fond of fried-fish lunches, I never thought of a fish as a companion animal, a pet. Fish, like the German brown trout in the farm pond, were there for me to catch, and I spent hours in the northern sun trying every kind of bait I could think of to fill my hooks. We watched Grandma on the farm expertly prepare the smelt we caught, preserving and cooking them for family food. I watched the bait minnows in Grandpa's town garage dart in panic to avoid the tiny net that caught them easily. Then, I'd thread a hook through their backs like both grandparents had taught me, hoping to catch a larger fish in the depths of the lake or pond or even the monster trout that lurked in the dark curve of Whittlesey Creek.

I never understood that fish might have the ability to feel pain. While they fascinated me, I knew them as sport and food. Catching them from the lake was an enjoyable pastime, and eating them was just another lunch for Grandpa. Then I met Oscar. He helped me connect with a part of nature that I couldn't hold in my hand, the unreachable and un-seeable wild animals of underwater worlds. In a way, Oscar gave my heart a bridge, one which I would stand on in later years as I tried to understand both the fishermen and the fish, the hunted and the hunters.

56. Bright Lights, Big Cities

There was a lot about Texas that changed me, and so much that happened in the years since I had arrived it would fill another book. But in the beginning, much was familiar. In the first year there, I wrangled work riding young horses for anyone who needed one ridden. With a saddle and a sack lunch, I drove to farms and ranches, ready to ride anyone's horse for $10 a ride. I had a business card that called me a horse trainer, so it must have been true. I loved it even though it was hard, dusty, and often dangerous work, but it wasn't long before I admitted that this approach would never be a sustainable career.

I posted a few flyers and within a year had collected a handful of dependable clients who agreed to bring their horses to the farm I now shared with Lou. No more driving 100 miles a day for $10 a ride. With seven good stalls to fill, it wasn't long until I had a waiting list of customers who appreciated an honest approach to how their horses were progressing. But then I was jolted back to reality on the day I was dropped into the dirt, coming off a small, agile young horse, not on purpose. She didn't ask first; she just jumped left and then right when I wasn't looking. Horses are like that, and I had become complacent, forgetting how quick and strong they can be. In less than ten seconds, I was out of a job. The resulting broken bones reminded me harshly that horse training was a take-no-prisoners career. I was lucky.

As my bones began to heal, I interviewed with a national animal welfare company and accepted a position as a liaison for a spay/neuter and animal wellness outreach program, a pilot program between the organization and a veterinary college. The intended demographics were Native American communities in the western United States. It was the most interesting job I had ever had, but at the time I was profoundly ignorant of the fact. I loved the work and loved the adventure, but it didn't pay much. There were no benefits, and the travel demands were tough, issues that convinced me to accept a local opportunity as a kennel supervisor, returning to animal shelter work at one of the largest municipal animal control departments in Texas.

I had no idea what I was about to face.

In weeks, I found the new job horrifying. I had no idea how to navigate the politics or culture of a highly charged big city, and being middle management gave me even fewer tools than had been advertised. This agency had its own political playwrights along with an abundance of animal tragedies and travesties. I was shocked at what I saw. Never had it been clearer to me that I was still an idealistic country girl. I had landed on an alien planet. The shock wouldn't wear off and, combined with too many animals, not enough staff, low pay rates and even lower employee morale, I realized that these were challenges I was not prepared to manage.

It came to a head one morning when the daily lunch truck arrived at 10:15, its regular time. The crew leader in the kennels hollered the announcement, and every single worker dropped their tasks at-hand and made their way to the break room. With only four paid city staff for a kennel that held over 400 dogs, the daily cleaning was done by a group of city-jail parolees earning their community service hours, marking another day off their adjudicated sentences. From my first day there, I and their crew leader, another city employee, clashed. He was efficient, he knew the system, and he was bilingual, a skill the city valued. He was also cruel, but he wasn't going anywhere.

The cleaning procedures the crew leader had put in place hadn't been approved by anyone in leadership. He had no training on disinfectants, detergents, or proper animal handling. Instead, he was left to his own devices. When the break announcement came, hoses, still running full blast and without spray-head handles, were dropped in aisles. Dogs and puppies, removed from their kennels for cleaning, were left to sit or stand where they were, either tied to kennel gates, jammed into wire crates on the floor or in rolling plastic trash dollies. Into that scene I walked to see no work being done and dozens of dogs, tied with nylon slip leads, standing in the aisles. To my horror, a blasting water hose was spraying forcefully into the tied and choking face of a young dog who clearly had never been tied before.

The timbre of my furious and horrified voice stopped all voices in the cavernous facility, both dog and human. In the resulting silence, I rushed to shut off the hose and rescue the choking dog. I bellowed again for the crew leader. As we faced off in the soaking aisle, I had no temper left to save. He received the full brunt of my anger and shock at not just the choking pup but everything. The glut of roaches in the quarantine kennels. The filthy drains behind each kennel. The terrified cats handled improperly on control poles by orange-jump-suited parolees. I did not stop. I cursed, waved my arms and blew furious snot at the man I blamed for everything.

And then the morning break was over. The crew leader sidled away and began directing the returning workers back to their stations. I turned and walked back to the offices, then sat down and cried into my hands. This job was bigger than the skills I had brought.

Within a few weeks I left for a brief job as a veterinary technician, and then in a few more months, accepted a position as animal shelter superintendent at a smaller city close to home. It felt like I had barely escaped.

The new position was in a tight-knit small town, where a brand-new, state-of-the-art animal shelter had just been completed but remained empty, the old shelter still home base for the current staff of one plus a few volunteers. Leadership in the department was needed to get new programs introduced and put in place and complete the move to the new building. It was a good fit for me, but after a year of hard work and positive change for the city, I fell victim to my ego and accepted another supervisor position with the neighboring city, again a large metropolitan agency. It promised easy work with solid work procedures and policies in place, a full staff, and a good reputation in the animal welfare community.

In a few weeks at the new job, I was bored and restless. With all the procedures in place and functioning, all there was to do was babysit well-trained staff, submit a daily euthanasia list so there were always enough empty kennels for the next day's animal intake, and review paperwork for errors. I realized I should have never left the small, friendly city.

57. Over the Cliff

With all the moves I had made from one job to another, my integrity as an employee, at least on paper, was beginning to fade. After leaving the last big city supervisor job, I found an odd job or two but chafed at being out of the animal welfare community. In 2006, I found a job opening at the local private Humane Society as a kennel attendant, and just like that, I had completed the circle. Twenty years had passed, and I was back to minimum wage, cleaning kennels, and making comfort happen for animals in need.

The Humane Society turned out to be a good fit for me. As the economy faltered due to the housing crash of 2007, the resulting recession created an animal problem. Along with increasing numbers of unwanted companion animals, the Humane Society became the go-to drop-off point for unwanted horses and assorted small livestock animals. Without someone on staff familiar with horses, goats, sheep and chickens, animals the non-profit agency had not routinely handled throughout its hundred-year history, I became their default expert.

As the intake numbers were climbing, the cases of neglect began pouring in. People who once had jobs and ready cash to pay their bills and care for their animals were now struggling to find enough money to buy groceries. Horses and cattle began to starve, dogs and cats were discarded or worse.

Without any formality, a tight-knit team of just a few of us responded to the need. Slowly, one case at a time, our work together formed the nucleus of what was to become one of the best humane investigations team the organization had ever seen. We worked hard, and not just for the animals in harm's way but for people. The stories of the animals we helped were on the news on a regular basis. We made friends in law enforcement and at all levels in the community, as well as many smaller communities in Texas. Donors were taking note, and with more dollars we were able to help more animals. We were making a difference.

It was hard, emotionally tough work, but none of us knew what was in store for us. 2009 would bring a storm of giant animal cruelty cases, cascading in on us, one right after the other. We didn't know it, but some of them became the largest in Texas history.

In February, a mammoth horse and livestock case involving participation from multiple county sheriff's offices: 247 livestock animals, all in various stages of starvation and neglect. On the day we served the search warrant, we counted dozens of carcasses on the 80-acre ranch. One sorrel horse, unable to stand but not yet dead, raised its head repeatedly as we stood nearby. It was fighting to live. Legally, we weren't allowed to touch the horse. The owner's veterinarian, present for the search, did not share our concern for the horse's welfare. When we returned the next morning with the seizure warrant, the horse was dead. The case brought not only animal cruelty charges, but attempted capital murder charges against the defendant. On the day of the seizure, with trucks, trailers, staff and volunteers staged safely up the highway, we waited for sheriff's deputies to serve the seizure warrant and secure the property, a process that can be tricky.

In response to the presence of so many law enforcement personnel, the animal's owner ran deep onto the property, hiding in a large stand of brush and trees where he began to shoot at the deputies searching for him. No injuries occurred, and he was arrested and transported to jail to await charges. The next three weeks seemed like a lifetime, but on the day of the custody hearing, a legal process to determine permanent ownership of the animals, a county judge awarded full custody of all animals to the Humane Society along with damages in the form of documented costs.

April, a local animal feed and pet store: 3000 souls rescued from horrible conditions. All manner of pocket pets and pet-store animals were living in filth out of the view of shoppers. Rats, living in flooded cupboard-like stacked compartments, swam for days to stay alive as their tiny plastic boxes flooded time and again from a faulty watering system. Guinea pigs lived in overcrowded and filthy livestock water tanks. The offenses filled pages for the municipal court's consideration. In weeks, custody of all animals was awarded to the Humane Society.

June, a puppy mill case in a nearby county: 497 dogs and puppies, most of them neglected and filthy. On the day of the seizure, several were sent directly to emergency veterinary care, dozens more would require immediate veterinary care to alleviate wounds and address horrible body condition. This case brought together the business community, the media, other shelters, breed rescue groups and individual adopters in ways we never expected.

July, the Arabian horse case in another county: 77 starving Egyptian Arabian horses, many of which were drinking urine in their stalls to stay alive. 33 stallions, 43 mares and one senior gelding represented a collection of some of the finest Egyptian Arabian bloodlines in the entire world. The case attracted international attention. In three months, all the horses, by then on the road to full health, were placed in homes while several went on to homes in countries outside the United States.

August, another case in yet another county: 44 feral quarter horses, none of which had ever been handled by a human in any meaningful way, were gently corralled and transported to a large, rented facility. There, using an ingenious system of corrals and gates we were able to handle each horse quietly, then evaluate them for eventual placement. It's hard to find real homes for horses that have never been handled and would rather not be, especially in a country reeling from recession. Eventually, all were placed safely.

But the year wasn't over.

Late October: Our organization joined with a local animal control shelter, another local, large non-profit animal welfare organization, and a national not-for-profit animal rights group. The national group had culminated a year-long undercover investigation of a local business, an animal broker, shipper and wholesaler of exotic animals for the pet store industry. The final tally of the number of animals saved in that tremendous, record-breaking operation was 30,000, making it the largest cruelty case in the United States at the time.

Saving these animals, from horses to hissing cockroaches, guinea pigs to geckos, turtles to tarantulas and snakes to sloths was one thing, and that was big enough. But they all needed homes and, for the exotic animals, nearly all of which were wild animals, appropriate placement. It was 2009, and everyone, everywhere, was affected by the financial disaster affecting the country. There was no blueprint, no procedure manual, no precedent to follow as we began the work to review, then qualify the credentials of all adopters and caretakers interested. Not everyone is qualified to provide proper housing and nutrition for a sloth, or a pink-toed tarantula.

The task of caring for so many, performed by a team of so many professionals, was daunting but placing them safely and correctly was a job on another level. For safe and appropriate placement, which had become known as re-homing, we were dependent upon our own values, instincts, and judgments of the intentions and capabilities of other people, including each other. We were each forced to look deep within our own selves, evaluate our own biases, ignore or indulge our prejudices, but keep working. Some days, the impetus to keep placing these animals was simply for financial reasons. There are not many animal welfare organizations with the infrastructure or financial base to feed and care for thousands at a time. Even though I was there, I still don't know how we did it, but we did. Every one of us welcomed the end of that year.

58. Turn Signals

By 2011, I had seen enough. My patience was thinner than I realized, and I needed to get out of humane investigations and back inside a shelter, delivering care, or so I thought. After leaving the Humane Society, I accepted another position as supervisor for another municipal animal control agency, and crossed my fingers that what I had been told about the programs and people there were right. I was looking forward to a straightforward, uncomplicated job as kennel supervisor for an expensive, newly built big-city shelter. My job would be to keep it clean and manage a well-organized intake and adoption program, working together with a large, vocal volunteer program and a full city staff. I should have known better.

In just a few months, the manager who had hired me quit, taking an early retirement after a disagreement with his supervisor. Shortly after that, the staff veterinarian quit, leaving the shelter and the spay, neuter and wellness program in limbo. I accepted the role of interim manager and took on the responsibilities of two jobs, shelter supervisor and department manager, while trying to find solutions for the veterinary program, which our adoption program depended on. To add to the challenge, the volunteer groups were not much more than warring, tribal factions vying for donor dollars while fighting to "save every one" of our sheltered animals. In weeks, most of the field officers quit when they realized I was not going to play the "walking-wounded-can't-come-to-work-today" game. They quit before my careful documentation necessitated firing them. The remaining staff gave me a chance to prove myself, and together we dug in.

For a fresh, energetic soul this might have been an exciting challenge, a chance to make a difference and put one's own mark on the world of what was now recognized as animal services. Our work was no longer just about control, the work had evolved, correctly and at long last, as a service to animals and the people who loved them. I recognized the opportunity. But for me, those final months, one day after another, became an emotional cascade.

Maybe it was the cats that did it. The shelter's computer inventory showed 300 cats in the building, but only 175 could be counted. Where were the rest? My questions revealed that the balance of the cat inventory was stashed in a few rental homes owned by one of the key volunteers for the cat adoption program. A good idea gone horribly awry. Over the course of a few weeks, the volunteers began to return the cats they had in the rental homes. In no time, every cat cage was full, and a huge adoption event had been planned. Then the cats began to die mysteriously, first one, then two or three a day, healthy one day and dead the next. Multiple tests confirmed feline panleukopenia, highly contagious and often deadly. It was a death sentence for my cats.

After consulting with the shelter's advising veterinarian and getting permission from the city's legal department, all the cats were euthanized, one by one, on a quiet Sunday morning.

As cat after cat took their last breath and joined the growing pile at our feet, it became impossible to fight back the emotion of what we were doing. But the three of us kept on, talking quietly to each other, talking quietly to each cat, working through what we needed to do, work that would protect the lives of all the cats that would need us in the future, the cats not yet born, cats that would find themselves in harm's way, cats that would need a precious second chance at life while waiting in a shelter that was safe. The rationale and available veterinary guidance of that time made sense, but it was an impossible task.

A few months later, on the way in to work, I wondered how hard it would be to drive my truck into a wall. As I drove, I imagined the scenario and the impact that mess would have on my family. I had read somewhere once that as we age, we lose the vivid imagination we enjoy as children. That has never been true for me. The scene in my mind was colorful and violent. But that kind of escape didn't seem fair, plus there was the guilt, already eating away at me, and all I had done was think about it. So, I chucked that idea to the curb and kept sipping my coffee while driving. Then this popped into my head. If I were given a diagnosis that very day of a terminal illness, then I would have something to look forward to. As I turned the thought over in my head, I realized I was numb to the shock I should have felt.

It was time to make a change.

59. On Silence

As we discussed the implications of leaving my career, Lou and I worked through the logistics of the loss of income and loss of routine. We put together a plan that would allow me to step away from a job that paid a lot of bills and helped us live a comfortable lifestyle. What I didn't plan for was the loss of all the other things that disappear when you leave not just a job, but a part of your life.

I knew the exact moment Mom died, on that September evening in 1990, even though I wasn't even in the same room with her when her breathing stopped. I was in the kitchen talking to Dad, and we both heard it; the stillness that arrives the moment a life ends. It's the deeper quiet, like when the electricity goes out and all the gadgets that make up the life of a home, stop. Ceiling fans stop twirling, the fridge stops humming, the background silence which isn't silent at all is gone and you're left with a stillness that makes no sense and offers no comfort. It's how you can hear a pin drop. It's the moment in your life when you hear yourself swallow and you hear the ringing in your ears, the echo of a life always surrounded by constant noise. Give it a minute and the echo fades, leaving nothing in its place. There is no deeper silence. When Mom died, the silence was deafening, the stillness, extraordinary. Her electricity wasn't going to return and everywhere outside, the world kept turning, oblivious that here, kneeling next to my dead mother, everything in my own life had stopped.

Then the electric co-op guys get the problem fixed and,

without blinking, you settle back in with the noise, the constant hum that defines a home alive and vibrant. An electric current of living. Leaving my job in December 2012, even though I needed to, was a new kind of death I had to experience to stay alive. I didn't expect that. When the silence came, it overwhelmed me. I had no idea what I was going to do.

When we find ourselves adrift, either physically or emotionally, sometimes the only thing we can do is grab onto something familiar and hang on until help arrives. Caught in the current, every living creature fights to find something to hang onto. In a flood, ants hang on to each other, their solidarity of purpose creating floating ant-islands of survival and perseverance. The rest of us find floating things to grab. I have witnessed the struggle to live, in ways I can't measure and over days I can't count. Some lives left this world peacefully, glad to be rid of whatever pain haunted them. Some fought fiercely, regardless of the pain, their will to keep fighting more powerful than the call of death. We are all different like this, who we will be at the exact moment of death is something none of us know until that moment is at the door. But as I packed up my desk and drove home for the final time from a shelter that should have been the pinnacle of a glorious career not yet complete, it felt like death.

In that moment, I remembered the black dog in the winter river so many years ago. Now I was that dog, straining to hear a voice giving me encouragement to keep swimming. I spun in circles searching for something to hang onto. Even though I was adrift now, my fight was real. I heard the whistle from the railing of the winter bridge. I wanted to feel joy again. I wasn't done. It was then I turned to my own dogs and saw them waiting. Just-Dave, Sticklet, Amelia. What took so long, they seemed to say. How had I missed these small friends, a constant in my home, for so many years? How had I not seen the joy they offered?

At the urging of an old friend, I started some dog sports as a raw beginner with Dave. He wasn't a young dog anymore, but neither was I. We began learning new skills together, and the joy he found in the companionship of our time together began to rub off on me. Some sort of work still had to be at least part of the answer after I left my career, so I returned to driving a school bus. I loved the job when I drove during college years, made some good friends along the way, and I even credited driving school bus with helping me define the feelings and questions I had grown up with, but never understood as gay. Now, I studied for the commercial driver's license test and with effort, passed. I had a new job.

"How can you stand all the kids?" some people asked, shaking their heads.

The truth was that the kids were the best part of the job, even though some of them could be challenging. Like any other job, I quickly learned that in any endeavor, you get back what you put in, and I poured my heart into the kids on my bus routes.

60. Turtle Ninjas and a Mom with an Umbrella

Mid-spring in Texas is when the state is at its finest. Mild temperatures and spring rains bring forth a beauty that is hard to beat anywhere else in the country. The violent pre-summer storms were still a few weeks off while wildflowers, fully living up to the wild in their names, converged in vibrant hues along Texas roads and highways, drawing the eyes of drivers. Blue, orange, pink, then yellow, I have learned to tick off the days of the season by the color of the flowers. It's also when there is far too much squashed wildlife on the roads. Here in Texas, strawberry season and pink wildflower season is also dead turtle season. Shy Red-Eared Sliders, all sizes of snapping turtles and beautiful box turtles begin to come forth, taking dangerous chances on their pre-destined path to procreate. It's particularly difficult to see the turtle carcasses because they are non-offensive to, well, pretty much everybody. I don't know anyone who has ever said they hate turtles.

My entire route was less than 25 miles, and that included the back-and-forth between schools, following the same roads for all three routes. I knew every single crack and pothole. This time of year, there was a new turtle tragedy nearly every day. I struggled to not look at the gruesome remains. One day, there were seven. I often wondered how that happened exactly. It's not like they dashed out in front of 60-mile-per-hour wheels at the last second, flashing a middle finger as their last words.

No, it's a safe bet that most turtle tragedies are the result of poor human driving. I say *most* because I hit a turtle once on a state highway. Directly in my lane and with a long line of oncoming vehicles on my left, my choices were to hit the turtle or drive into the ditch. I should have hit the brakes instead, but like most of my human friends, my brain doesn't work that fast, and I grimaced as my tires did the quick "bump-bump" of the impact. In the rearview mirror, I saw the turtle's body spinning across the highway. Why did I even look?

I've been told turtles cross the road because they are driven to do so by their prehistoric DNA. They instinctively follow pre-destined pathways, traveling far from the comfort and safety of their ponds and woodlands to lay a once-yearly clutch of fertilized eggs. They do this so the eggs incubate in an area that won't flood, giving them a better chance of hatching. I like this theory, so I'll stick to it.

So, there I was that spring day, driving the last six students to each of their stops, when I saw a telltale spot in the road. Was it alive? Was it dead already? Was it a turtle or was it trash? As we got closer, I could see it was a turtle, very much alive. The wet trail behind it showed me which direction it had come from. It was about 9,700 miles from the other side of the road. I stopped the bus. The turtle stopped too.

A stopped school bus in the middle of a busy road has an instant effect on traffic flow. Everybody else stopped, too. And then waited. Of course, the only drivers who knew why we were waiting were me and the lady driving the car first in line in the oncoming lane. Her brake lights had stopped the car behind her, and now there was a long line of cars behind her, waiting.

Times like this always made me wonder how people get their driver's licenses. The tests I took for my license required me to understand most of the laws of the road, particularly when it's legal to pass a stopped school bus. Flashing yellow bus lights mean slow down, the red lights are next, and then you must stop. Hazard warning lights, or four-way lights, mean just that;

proceed with caution. With just my four-way hazard lights on, it turned out to be a good thing that the driver in the oncoming lane didn't know the rules. The cars behind the bus stopped as well, and nobody but two of us knew why. Bring on the horn section.

The rule at this school district was that the driver cannot exit the bus at any time unless on school grounds, there are no children on the bus, the bus is parked, and the key is in the driver's hand. Another rule is that students, once on board the bus, couldn't exit the bus unless they were being dropped at their designated bus stop or they were on school grounds. None of this was true now. So, there we were, seven humans stuck on a bus, staring at a wet turtle in the road who was staring back at us.

The line of cars began to lengthen. The students, all in the fifth or sixth grade, were now clamoring to be let off the bus to help the turtle. They couldn't have been louder than my own head and heart, all the years of animal welfare work had sent me on countless rescue missions just like this, except now I was the needy one and there was no me to come scoot the turtle to safety. It had been a long time since I had been without a solution to an animal crisis. I wasn't about to move the bus. I couldn't step off the bus and move the turtle. The students could not possibly be sent to save the turtle, that would be precisely when some driver would give in to their impatience and tragedy would happen. I could count about 20 cars in the lane in front of us. I had no idea how many were waiting behind.

And then the lady in the first car in line eased up a few notches and rolled her window down. I opened my side window, and we made eye contact.

"He's under your tire," she said, looking up at me and pointing to the front tire.

I told her I was not allowed to exit the bus, nor were the students.

"Do you have anything I can use to push it out of the way?" she asked.

I looked around for a tool, anything that might work.

"What about an umbrella?"

She put her car in park and came around to the passenger door on the bus. Opening the door, I handed her my umbrella. The only animal control tool I carry on a school bus, of course. Leaning down and looking under the bus, she called out.

"Forward a few inches!" I eased the bus forward.

"Stop!" she shouted, holding her hand up over her head as she leaned down.

I put the bus in park and snapped on the emergency brake. Now on her hands and knees at the front wheels of the bus, she slid the umbrella towards the turtle and smoothly slid it out from under the wheel.

How many moms smiled cheerfully when their children brought reptiles into the house to share their prize? I think this mom would have been one of those. Without wincing, she scooped it up in both hands and carried it to the grassy safety of the opposite ditch. Once in the grass, the turtle powered forward and quickly disappeared. As she rounded the front of the bus to return the umbrella, cheers, applause, and a chorus of "thank you!" from the students greeted her. We smiled together. As she pulled away, several drivers in the waiting line rolled their windows down and flashed "thumbs up" as they drove past.

Turtle victory. A small thing, but the day was a shade brighter with one less deceased turtle and a few cheering students. And to the mom who stopped and rescued a small turtle using a school bus driver's umbrella on a sunny afternoon, may you forever have a smile in your pocket, remembering the day you crawled under a school bus to save one tiny life.

61. Other People's Children

I was living in yet another full-circle moment, trading the years of animal welfare work for days behind the windshield of a school bus. What had I done? But then there were moments like puzzle pieces, all scattered on a tabletop, then finding their partners in color and shape, the fit that begins to make a whole. Not every day, but often, I could feel my heart healing a piece at a time. At a friend's home one day we laughed as their new kitten fiercely and proudly swung from the curtains, then, as its tiny claws slipped, fell to the floor. With a bottle-brush tail, arched back, and all four legs working as one singular kitten-driving-piston, the tiny orange ball shot across the kitchen floor and disappeared around the corner. The kitten's I meant to do that! sign was clear. Our laughter was as spontaneous as the kitten. When had I forgotten how joyful kittens were? For too many years kittens were dirty litter boxes, runny eyes and noses, dried diarrhea on stainless steel cage walls and don't get attached because you might have to euthanize it later. But to other people, kittens were joy. I had to learn that all over again.

I didn't have a basket of kittens at home, but I had dogs. I started to see them with fresh eyes. They looked back at me as if saying Are you home for real this time? Once I really looked, the hope in their expressions was unmistakable. It was time to meet my own dogs. Slowly, I learned to let go of the inner motor that had been driving me for so long, the same kind carried by so many people I had known. These new days took on a steady rhythm, a tempo that included enough time in the day, something I had forgotten was even possible. My decision to leave began to feel right. Gradually, I remembered why I had left animal shelters, and I remembered why I had loved driving bus.

As the weeks and months went by, I settled into a new routine.

The high school students generally all stayed mute, their pre-adult mannerisms tested out for durability, earbuds glued in, their faces always turned to the bus windows or dipped down to phone screens. There were the middle and intermediate school kids, their shiny new hormones shouting for attention, vulnerabilities worn high and loud and no question left unasked. But for all the taciturn high schoolers and frustrating new teenagers, the elementary littles made up the difference in spades.

As a group, these tiny human elements were always all noise and joy and exuberance. Pure, fresh life. It can make for a wild bus ride, sometimes at speeds of 65 miles per hour, all while making sure Perfect-Haircut-Boy, for the 18th time, doesn't punch Boy-Who-Won't-Shut-Up. It was a simple thing, the bus driving gig, but safety was sometimes elusive and always a bit tricky.

On the last day of school, the littles, all between the ages of five and nine years old, boarded the bus stoked full of cupcake sugar and carrying paper bags of popcorn, which I had prepared for. It was Friday. All the fourth-grade girls and a few of the fourth-grade boys, after a full week of celebrating their last year in elementary school, were crying. I hadn't seen that coming.

All, that is, except one. She always sat in the second seat back from the front on the passenger side, seat number four of 24, a spot where I could always see the top of her brunette head in my rear-view interior mirror. From the minute she sat down until she stepped off at her driveway, that's all I ever saw. It was clear she was one of the shy kids, avoiding the other girls her age who always traveled together in packs of three except for the days when one of them offended another. On those days, the pack of three would scatter loudly and demand an adult mediation, drawing some measure of power from sharing their drama, throwing insults and tears and vowing "never again!" until the next day when the pack-of-three-rule was reinstated, and all was forgiven, or at the very least, forgotten. My quiet friend steered clear of the drama, and I remembered what that was like.

I wished then that the world wasn't so cruel and singular, and that it wasn't against the rules to hug a kid, or to wipe a tear, or to share a joke, or to ask a kid about their world, their life, their hopes, their dreams. As "just drivers," we were only allowed to deal with the moment, and then only within pre-scribed boundaries, just in case someone sees on the video recording something other than monotone rule enforcement or momentary awkward and false comfort. It's a harsh world we've come to when a sincere human response to a child's need for adult support in the absence of their parents must be stifled. And that's where my shy young friend found herself every day. Today's kids are alone until they get to a place where comfort is approved. That place is not the school bus.

But still, I shared small gifts with the kids on special occa-sions. At Christmas, 50 red fabric stockings with candy and a few small things to make them smile. On Valentine's Day, I'd hand out suckers or packages of taffy since chocolates are out-lawed along with peanuts in most schools these days. In return, I received a few cards from parents, some boxes of cookies and a gift card or two with their thanks.

As we pulled up to her driveway on the Friday of her last fourth-grade Christmas vacation, I received a handmade con-struction-paper card from Seat-Number-Four, folded once and decorated in colorful marker. As soon as the bus rolled to a stop she stood up, swung her backpack on, ducked her head to her chest as always and handed me the card quickly, but not until the door was opened and she could hand it off as she was getting off the bus. I thanked her with a big smile and waited a second, hoping she would turn, but instead she waved her hand behind her and hurried up the drive. I hated our rules then, more than most days. I took a moment and opened the card, right there in the road, idling at the end of her driveway, red school bus lights still flashing. Maybe she would see me reading her card.

On the inside, a handwritten Merry Christmas message and "I'm glad you're my bus driver, Love, J." They were the only words we had shared for the whole semester.

And this was the last day of the school year. With Christmas a distant memory, sugar vibrations rattled the bus windows, and popcorn glitter covered the vinyl bus floor. Maybe this day my Seat-Number-Four friend and all the graduating fourth graders finally understood that their world had just gotten a bit bigger. After they had all boarded the bus and found their favorite seats in their little packs of three, I got out of my seat and faced the kids, standing in the aisle near the front, close to the second seat. I was focused on the fourth graders' tears, wanting to help them find their smiles on their last day of little-kids school. I searched for words that would help, and which wouldn't be interpreted as inappropriate.

"Congratulations on graduating! You're going to love fifth grade!" I said lamely, hoping my smile covered how awkward that sounded. "You'll have new adventures and make great new friends!"

From the mid-section of the bus there were sobs and more tears, but from my silent friend in the seat next to me, words. They were the first she had spoken out loud over the course of the entire year.

"I don't have any friends anyway," Seat-Number-Four said.

When I looked over at her, truly the first real look I had ever shared with her, I saw a sweetly pretty girl with straight brown hair and squared-off glasses framing sharply intelligent eyes. No tears. Clearly, she would become a beautiful young lady, something her father already knew. He always smiled big and waved at me on the days he was home when his daughter arrived. He would be intensely proud when he pinned her first prom corsage, or watched her sign her first driver's license, or watched her receive a diploma on the stage of higher learning. And one day, if fate allowed, he would walk her down an aisle and give her away to another, his job complete, his love giving her wings.

From the first day of school that year, I felt a connection with her dad, knowing intuitively he provided everything my little friend needed. But I knew he couldn't provide the camaraderie of friends her age. I believed though, that he understood what was missing in her life. He knew that she would be fine, she would grow and come to learn that not all packs of pals are friends, and that the status granted to loud fourth graders wouldn't translate to the same status as an adult. He was there for her.

Maybe today she understands that she is worthy as a friend, even though she's undoubtedly met some who are not worth having. But she's survived the growing pains just fine, and the comfort of being alone has molded the strong person she's become. I remember what that's like, too.

I gave good-luck cards to my bus kids on the last day that year, but I saved two special cards with messages from me. One was for the bright and imaginative second-grade boy who struggled with a form of autism and cruel rejection by his peers simply for being different, or maybe also for having two dads. I wrote him a thank you for always working hard to find a "try", even though he didn't always succeed. I handed him a roll of lifesavers. Throughout his life, he'll undoubtedly face more cruelty, but I'll always hope he remembers it's worth his effort to keep trying.

The other card was to the quiet little girl in the second seat. I couldn't tell her I had been a lonely and awkward kid too. I couldn't tell her she'd grow to be a confident and smart kid, her dad would be sure of it, and the memory of the silly girls in the back of the bus would become her strength, sooner than she knew.

Instead, I wrote, "Have a great summer. I'm glad you rode my bus. Fifth grade will be awesome!"

I hoped she could read between the lines.

62. Murder, She Rode

Imagine a middle-aged woman on a yellow riding mower, riding full throttle around a pasture, leaning forward into the wind, zigging and then zagging in random circles. Who cuts grass in jagged zigs and zags, you wonder? And then you see it. A small brown rat, jumping and leaping in the path of the mower, barely staying ahead of the tires and the spinning mower blades. It's a funny picture, but somehow you don't laugh.

That was me on the mower, and I wasn't laughing. As I drove, never taking my eyes off the rat, I had several opportunities to make contact, rubber to rat. Instead, I began a mental check. Who was I? It had been three years since I left animal welfare. I hadn't expected to grieve, but as the weeks and months passed, grief washed over me in waves that were suffocating.

I had begun to feel a change, brief glimmers of the return of real laughter and some joy. Working through these revelations, accepting the reality of the loss of the voices from my animal welfare family, I felt myself healing. But on this day, I forgot I had spent a lifetime protecting animals and helping people. Here I was on a lawnmower, murderously running down one small rat in broad daylight. It was time for a second thought.

On the Rock Falls farm I once saved a tiny brown bat who had fallen into the water tank. By the time I found it, the bat was exhausted and chilled, nearly dead. I didn't think twice as I scooped it out and placed it inside an empty black rubber bucket, making it a tiny nest with some cotton fabric from Mom's sewing closet. I faced the bucket into the sun, hoping the bat would recover before the barn cats found it. A few hours later it was gone, the little cotton nest where it had recovered still warm. Maybe it lived, maybe the cats discovered it, but at least it had a chance.

That farm was my magic kingdom. I loved its woods, the animals, the birds, the beaver pond, and the barn. I loved the sound of partridge drumming on the hill in the woods where I sat for hours, waiting for a glimpse of the beaver family below. I loved winter and the cold, loved when spring returned and then yielded its chill to summer softness again. I suppose it's possible that this love, uncluttered by reason and as pure as it was simple, helped me find an easy confidence and camaraderie of my own that I had never found with my peers. It became a part of me, to be re-discovered years later in the company of people. On the farm, though, I was happiest in the silence of being alone, even on the furthest reaches of our acreage. Those quiet hours were my reset as I faced each awkward day of adolescence.

We all do things for love, and for my first true love I had no second thoughts about breaking the law to protect the lives of the animals in the woods. I didn't hesitate to steal beaver traps set in the pond of my beaver friends, but I did pay the price for that, learning that I would have to get smarter if I wanted to make animal lives better. From where I sat, there weren't a lot of people who cared as much about the lives of animals as I did.

More than forty years later, I've put away two dozen years of helping animals and people as a professional animal control officer, shelter manager and animal advocate. I've watched myself walk away from the horse industry with its own forms of deep and glossy abuse of the quiet, gentle, and easily frightened animals. I've struggled to define words like abuse, neglect, ignorance, intent, and compassion. Through it all, the politics of helping were hard to learn, even harder to practice. With all of this, I still find it impossible to define the word "suffer." I don't know anyone who can.

The question was posed to us as cruelty investigators while

participating in a class with forensic pathologists. We were there to understand their science better, and they were there to understand our motivation for sending them the types of cases we did.

"What is cruelty?" they asked, and our answer was something long and rambling and related to the law. The scientists were not satisfied, and we struggled on, looking inward for more descriptive terms.

"We prevent suffering," we finally said.

"What is suffering?" they replied. An hour later, we were out of time and had yet to answer that question.

As a child, I understood suffering completely, although I didn't know it. It was the skunk, baking in the summer sun with its half-chewed off leg still hanging in a steel trap. It was a drowning bat, nearly dead from hypothermia. It was me as a young adult, seeing a black dog spinning in frantic circles in the winter current of a Wisconsin river, unable to do anything to save it. As I found my place in the world, suffering was a blind cat, spinning in terror on a garage floor with no familiar comfort to save him. It was dozens, then hundreds, and then thousands of unwanted animals waiting in lonely cages for the soft and quiet hand of a human to tell them it would all be ok. It would be decades before it all came together for me, and by then, suffering had become personal.

Fast forward to the middle-aged woman on a lawn mower, driving hot after a running rat. I debated whether running the rat over would be quick and decided no, it would only injure it and create a further dilemma. I played a movie in my head, where I was armed with a pistol and from the bumpy seat of my twelve mile-an-hour lawn mower I could shoot and instantly kill as many rats as I had seen in the previous forty-five minutes, which was dozens. But I wasn't a good shot. I didn't even have a gun. Not to mention the neighbors. Surely, they would be horrified. Poison was out of the question, non-negotiable and simply a non-starter. I stopped the mower and watched the rat disappear into a burrow.

The reality was that we had been overrun by rats. Pipeline construction on the next-door property had tragically altered hundreds of acres of previously deep woods and mature hardwood trees, and the wildlife had all been making their ways elsewhere, one species at a time. Barred owls, red-shouldered hawks, coyotes, foxes, squirrels, all the creatures that make up a healthy ecosystem were searching for new territories, including the rats. There was no longer enough room for all. Now the rats were in our pastures, the livestock shelters, chicken coop, barn, in the garage and in the attic of our home. I even removed a half-built nest from the engine of one of our cars. I needed humane solutions.

Friends who admire the ingenuity of rats as much as I do offered opposite perspectives and options for co-existing with the rodents. But no amount of discussion could sway them to see my point of view. In their minds, rats were wonderful. But these weren't my little friend Madeline, the Hooded rat who accompanied me on education presentations for elementary schools so many years ago. Madeline made children laugh and teachers shriek just through the simple act of sitting on my hand and holding her own cookie while she nibbled. Madeline and I had some fun. No, these wild rats were clever and multiplying quickly.

My sins were exposed even as I crossed my heart and hoped to die, then stuck my finger in the eye of a wild rat who didn't read my tiny "no trespassing" signs. I was confounded as I grieved the death of two small rabbits, found dead in our pool, my fault for not checking the pool more routinely. At the same time, I plotted and planned how best to trap and kill the rats in the field, under the house, in the attic and in the goat shelter and horse barn. I was further confounded when I remembered how my heart hurt at discovering a different rat shivering and soaked on the pool float, an item designed to save toads and frogs from drowning in the cement pond they don't understand. I rescued the rat and relocated it to a patch of woods a few miles up the road. I celebrated each animal saved by the ingenious float.

I have friends who are avid hunters, combining passion for their sport with a love for the environment and the creatures supported by it. To them, one form of suffering would be deer dying of starvation due to overpopulation. I have many friends who vehemently oppose hunting in any form and to them, suffering is the same deer who runs in terror from the hordes of seasonal hunters, sometimes dying slow deaths from a poor shot. Or geese, who mostly mate for life, spending the remainder of their life grieving the loss of their mate from a hunter's bullet. I have dear friends who are vegetarian and vegan, their form of protest over their perception of the suffering of animals farmed solely to produce meat. I have friends who condemn the horse racing industry, and I have friends who are part of the horse racing industry. I have nieces and nephews who are avid hunters and fishermen like my grandfather. In our own ways, we all share a love for our environment and the role animals play. We all have these things in common; we have come to cherish our own lifetime love affair with the natural world. But there is no single definition of suffering. We all see things differently.

Why didn't I celebrate the circumstances of the rat? How is it I could plan to kill them, yet never dismiss an opportunity to save them?

Maybe it is the years I had to practice my sins of the heart, a path as easy and familiar as the wooded paths I walked as a child, cat on my shoulder and favorite dog following close behind. Maybe it is the years of loving and saving as many troubled animals as I could, but then becoming an expert in fitting those same animals in the heavy black plastic body bags we used after their euthanasia. I've spent far too much time trying to unravel the paradox of my years working in animal welfare. Maybe someday I will find the words that make sense.

Then again, maybe I'm fooling myself. Maybe somehow my heart has reminded me how to be that lonely and awkward girl again, the one without sin.

63. Adios, Amigos

And so, without the use of poisons, I managed to reduce our rat population to an invisible level. With a running editorial commentary and no apologies, here's the full list of techniques I used to declare this likely temporary victory:

Snap traps. Not just any snap trap, but the chunky black plastic ones, because those antiquated wooden ones were simply a sightseeing trip for the rat families and their children. They worked for a while but then the familiarity of them caused failure. I needed solutions with a long term application.

Live traps. Yes, the wire-box "humane" live traps, touted by all souls compassionate near and far as the next best thing to bringing the rats indoors, like long-lost relatives, to share bathroom space, Netflix, and pay half the utilities. My rodent communities added these to their "must-see" tour list when they planned the family vacation. So, because my live traps were never, ever successful, I've added them to this list as Failed Attempt #781 to give Mother Nature the benefit of the doubt.

"The Nooski." An interesting tube-like device billed as one of the most effective and humane ways to rid one's home of mice and rats. Kind of like the "banding" device used to castrate young male livestock animals like calves and goats or sheep. It's the same concept, and uses the very same thick, tiny green rubber bands, stretched around a plastic tube and rigged with a trigger behind which one places the tasty bait. After trying these things, I wondered why they hadn't been on a "Live From New York It's Saturday Night!" skit as The Ronco Rat-O-Matic. It was a complete failure.

Then, there was the elegant, exotic, CO2-powered, guaranteed-humane "A-24" from the national forests of New Zealand. This device featured its own social media page of testimonial action videos, all showing the eerie, green-tinted night-vision recorded scenarios of rats, mice and a bizarre creature the Kiwis call "stoats" meeting their fast and undeniably humane demise. With an action like a captive bolt hammer, this machine looked too good to be true, its testimonials satisfied my need for a humane method of rodent dispatch. It had become clear that my attempts at live removal as a control method would never succeed, at least not for my rodent community, and I was still adamantly opposed to any type of poison. So of course, I robbed a bank and ordered one.

This cool contraption also proved to be a bust. Over the summer I tallied three deceased rats. One in the garden, where my tomatoes and cucumbers had totally succumbed to the rat onslaught, and two out by the goat shelter. The motion-activated counter told me that I had dispatched three to four rats per week, but without the little bodies to prove it, I suspected the rats were messing with me.

"Here, hold my beer." These were, after all, Texas rats.

Then there was the "Raticator," a fun name for one of the most efficient rat traps I've ever used, and the clear winner. I paid $50 for this red plastic submarine-shaped thing with some very cool graphics and a slot for four "D" batteries. With a handful of sunflower seeds placed in the rear of the contraption, it began to make a dent. It worked on battery-powered electricity, and not many rodents lived to tell their friends what not to do when trying to outsmart this thing. The Raticator drew them in by offering a tempting dark tunnel with the bait placed at the far end. When the rat was all the way inside and all four feet were on the metal floor plate, the batteries sent a jolt of electricity, and the rat ceased to live. Brutal and quick, but I did spend some time erasing some scenes from *The Green Mile* from my brain. With a nod to Mr. Jingles, I breathed a sigh of relief.

Throughout my trapping adventures I repaired, patched, hauled away, collected, and burned whatever piles of old wood, brush, fencing supplies, and random stuff I could find around the farm. It wasn't much, but apparently it was enough. I built wire hardware-cloth barriers around every tiny hole and vent in our house foundation, garage walls, and roof soffits. I removed our bird feeders and relocated our wild-bird water spots to secure and elevated locations. I re-homed our beloved flock of 22 hens and one proud rooster with a good friend who promised to care for them like family. I applied to adopt two feral barn cats, and upon delivery spent several careful weeks acclimating them to our feeding routine and noises around the farm.

The feral cat lady told me to get a donkey and put used kitty litter in the holes and burrows of the rats. We had already tried a donkey, but as a deterrent for coyotes. I'm not sure how she figured a donkey could be a rat hunter, but those were the days before I learned to ask questions instead of making up my own answers, so who knows? I did try the used kitty litter idea and was impressed. Nowhere had I read or heard of this idea, not even on social media, but it's worth five stars.

I learned that Castor oil is one of the ingredients in the "all-natural rodent repellent" pellets sold at big box stores, so I did the idea one better; I purchased two full gallons of Castor oil, then poured the stuff into every rat gathering location I could find. While it worked for a little bit, I did eventually see rat activity back in the same spots as I had poured the oil. Another fail, and another $50 down the drain.

I put out a call for snakes to the animal control agencies in the area and was lucky enough to receive two very nice city snakes in need of a safe country relocation, a green water snake and a cranky, beautiful, and very large black rat snake. I saw the tail end of this guy dangling out from under the damaged wall in our garage one day and silently cheered him on in his endeavors.

It took me a few days of work, but I tore out a large section of drywall on a wall in the garage, the same wall where The Raticator had dispatched a good number of rats and where the snakes could be found from time to time. I removed all the stinky, ratty old insulation and added new insulation, then cut more hardware cloth barriers to fit over all the entry holes and stapled them in place. I coupled this with expandable spray foam insulation, then topped it all off with new two-by-four supports and new sheet rock. It's the very same type of fix I would have recommended to any homeowner who requested advice from an animal control officer on how to manage a rodent problem. In this case, I simply asked myself, "What would a smart dogcatcher do?" and then applied my own answer to my own circumstances. I was surprised.

One morning as I walked into the goat shelter to feed the old lady goats there, I was greeted by five sleek gray rats, all waiting for breakfast as well. They almost waved at me. I called a friend who arrived shortly with a twenty-two rifle and a pocketful of rat-shot ammunition. I didn't even know they made such a thing. Five rats were humanely dispatched within an hour.

After all this, it seemed my rat adventure, and the community they had built around our farm and home had become a rat ghost town. Trails of droppings began to accumulate dust. Burrows in the grass and under the water tanks showed signs of abandonment, as did the holes in the goat shelter. The underground trails and tunnels I could feel under my feet wherever I walked in our yard and pastures began to cave in, filling with solid dirt once again. There were no more tracks and fresh rat droppings in the attic. I took great comfort in my success without using poison, knowing that the barred owls and red-shouldered hawks could safely hunt for healthy rodents which hadn't been dangerously poisoned.

I cautiously declared victory.

For now, the plastic snap traps remain stowed and empty. I still make the rounds of the rat hiding places, inspecting each area for any signs of fresh activity. One day, another family of rats will move in. I finally know the truth in the saying, "Nature hates a vacuum." When I was a kid, this took me a while to understand that it wasn't about Hoovers. When I do see the rats again, they will be met with the most humane and effective no trespassing sign I can muster. With luck, they will move on to another location. If not, I will be satisfied that I have done everything I can to provide the best, safest, and most environmentally sound response I can. I love living in the country, and I love the animals that make my life here more complete. I hope I've found a happy medium.

Vaya con Dios, mi pequenos amigos.

64. What Cowboys Are Made Of

In the summer of 2016, we arranged for my 14-year-old niece, Emily, to spend time with friends in Quanah, a small north Texas ranching community. She would get to experience a few days of real cowboying during her annual visit to Texas from Wisconsin. Hoping to surprise her with cowboys, cow horses, and real Texas country, good friends Joey and Carrie enthusiastically agreed. Emily could ride Bo, one of their trusted ranch geldings and help gather cattle for the annual "doctoring" planned for their cattle herd. I was excited to tell Emily she'd be able to ride along on a real cowboy adventure. For her part, Emily said she'd be happy to help, but she already knew what real cowboys did. I learned to smile when she said things like that, knowing it was pointless to argue. She was, after all, related to me. She said she'd seen lots of wide-open prairies, ridden lots of cowboy horses, and seen lots of wild cattle, too.

"Of course," I nodded.

When I told Joey this, he laughed. He laughed because he knew kids almost as well as he knew horses and cattle, and he knew she would learn something whether she expected to or not. He knew he could show her how to spot the horizon on a deep Texas prairie; he knew he could show her how to avoid the hollers and washes where the rattlesnakes denned. He knew Bo, the horse she would ride, would take care of her like he had taken care of Joey's children, stepping carefully through the calici rocks, avoiding the prickly pear cactus and, most of the time, galloping wide around thorny mesquite branches. He laughed because he knew that once she saw it, she would never forget the land he loved and the life he lived.

"Send her up," he said.

Joey and Carrie shared a love for Texas, cattle, good horses, good neighbors, God, and family. He also liked beer; the colder and cheaper the better. I told him once on a visit to their ranch that I wasn't sure God would forgive him for the cheap beer.

"Seems like a sin," I said. "Cheap beer."

We laughed together, and he held out a cold can for me.

"I'd be willing to bet that God loves a cold, cheap beer every now and again," he said.

I took the beer. Sitting there on the tailgate of his truck, my legs swinging, boots dangling just above the dust on the driveway, I looked at the smiling, whiskered man sitting in front of me, his own boots up on the dash of his green four-wheeler, sweat-stained hat shading his brow. Bud, the blue heeler, was in his usual spot, riding shotgun. Joey met my gaze, then held his own beer up in the air, toasting our afternoon. It dawned on me then. It didn't matter how much it cost. Drinking a beer with Joey Dodson was just about the best beer you could have.

He worked hard, holding down a full-time job and working together with Carrie to manage their cattle, the ranch, help neighbors and tend to family. When he rode through his herd, he usually chose to ride his stout gray mare, Chic. She could be belligerent on a bad day or cranky on a good day, but he knew it was just her nature to be disagreeable, and her disagreeable nature totally agreed with him. He also knew that the mare knew cows, and he trusted her opinion on such things. When he swung his rope to move a cow or calf, Chic knew which one he needed, and she knew the next move Joey would make. They were a team.

The day I dropped Emily off in Quanah, Joey told me he needed to run out and repair a gap in a creek fence north of the ranch. Did I want to ride along? Heck yes. We left Emily with Carrie and Bo to get acquainted, and off I went with Joey. We didn't load the horses in a trailer, no, sir. Instead, we loaded the four-wheeler on a flatbed trailer then jumped in the truck and drove down the gravel county road, stopping at the wire gate entrance to an ocean of prairie grass stretching to the horizon. Once parked, Joey loosened the ratchet straps holding the four-wheeler on the trailer, then backed it down the trailer ramp amid dusty puffs of dirt. Somewhere out there were cattle, their grass-fat summer calves, and a broken gap in a creek fence.

I took Bud's spot on the four-wheeler, kicking rusty tools and random rope and wire bits out of the way with my boots. There were a few dented beer cans in the glovebox. We took off down the path, nothing more than a dusty cattle trail, and eventually the path disappeared, prairie grass and dust taking over as Joey navigated by memory. We rode along in silence for a few minutes.

"I had a good friend who almost died out here a few years back." Joey said, the noise of the four-wheeler settled now that we were driving along at a comfortable speed. I looked at him, waiting. "He was out on his horse, checking cattle. Dang cows can get stuck in the worst places. You never know. Anyway," he continued, "he didn't show up that night. We figured he probably got too far out, then decided to camp for the night rather than ride home in the dark."

I watched him there in the driver's seat, his eyes scanning the prairie ahead as the path rolled under and around the machine, white mustache whiskers parting slightly with the breeze as we drove.

"But somethin' didn't feel right," he said. "So, before light I got up and went lookin'. Still not sure how I found him, but I did."

There, in the middle of a thousand prairie acres, was his friend, battered, bloody and unconscious. He got his friend to the hospital, where he recovered from being dragged nearly to death after losing his balance in the saddle. After all the years that had passed since that night, his story was still powerful.

"Pretty sure he would have died out here," he said quietly. "Somethin' just told me to go lookin'."

He brushed off my admiration.

"He was my friend," Joey said. "That's what you do."

Driving along like this, I admired his easy conversation and laughter, this tall, whiskered man wearing a pistol, a favorite cowboy hat, toting a girl from the north who he'd always liked. Then we were there. He stopped the four-wheeler, grabbed the fence stretcher, a roll of wire and the fencing tool.

"Keep up," he told me.

Stepping out of the four-wheeler, all I could think of were snakes. But I kept up with Joey's long, easy stride and in a few minutes, we were standing at the top of a gully, striped by afternoon shade made by the bones of a county bridge, built to span the creek at the bottom of the gully. It was steep. Somewhere down there was the broken gate, the "gap" we were here to fix. He took his armful of supplies and found his way down the hill before I could decide which direction to go, even though I was following and didn't have to think at all. As he splashed through the creek at the bottom, he looked back at me.

"Watch out for the fish," he said as he dipped the brim of his hat towards the creek.

"Fish?"

Another Joey prank, I figured. I waded in. When I got to the middle of the creek, I stopped. There I stood in the middle of a creek in my Justin cowboy boots, the banks of the prairie gully rising around me, all of it like a John Wayne movie. I turned and looked up at the old bridge about 60 feet over my head, twisting away from the sun's rays to see its entire structure, trying to read the impossible graffiti painted there. Turning back, I watched Joey on the other side of the creek bank, my very own Texas cowboy friend, arranging fencing supplies on the bank, his tracks now swirling away in the creek's current.

I took a moment then, wanting to always remember that scene. Being there in that creek, under the blue of a sky that could have been Oklahoma or Texas, was probably as natural for him as passing gas after dinner. I watched the water slide just under the top of my boots, marveling that my feet were still dry.

Then I saw the fish. An alligator gar had come up behind me, and as I stood in the water it continued upstream, slipping past my Justins as calmly as if it saw boots every day. In one breath, I was a six-year-old cotton-top granddaughter again, tiny hands gripping the gunwale of an aluminum boat, lake water spray on my cheeks and my childhood, gone so many years in the rearview mirror, returned to me in one huge rush. As I watched the fish navigate the current and then disappear, Joey looked up at me as if to tell me to get a move on. Our eyes met, and we didn't speak, then we smiled. It was like he knew. I found my breath, then stepped through the water to the bank.

Joey died of cancer shortly after Thanksgiving, 2018. His wife and best friend, Carrie, misses him more than anyone, and probably more than she ever thought she could. There's no doubt his neighbors, friends, beer-drinking buddies and motorcycle pals, for sure, miss him. His cattle will miss him unless the next cowboys to doctor them were quiet and easy like Joey insisted. The cattle were always worked easy, and because of that, they were always easy to work. Made sense, Joey would say.

The bridge, the fish, the prairie grass and cattle, the afternoon sun slanting sideways into the creek with Joey looking up at me there, smiling. Even the fat bull snake that disappeared into the grass when he pulled the four-wheeler back onto the flatbed for the trip home is a masterpiece of memory I'll never part with, even as I've learned how to miss my friend. We shared a few cheap beers that afternoon with the neighbor, who stopped by on his tractor to share some gossip. Joey the cowboy, the husband, the neighbor, the cattleman, the horseman and friend. God loves a good cowboy, and it's a safe bet by now that He loves a cheap beer.

65. Fun with Furniture

Occasionally, events conspire to provide a lesson in life that is unexpected. For years leading up to my departure from animal welfare, and for years after, I lived with anger, frustration, unreasonable expectations of those around me, and a sense of martyrdom that were, quite simply, unattractive and overwhelming. While I blamed friends for abandoning me or taking my feelings too lightly, the real fault was mine. I had failed myself, and not until I walked away from the work did I begin to understand my own role in the loss of career and community. It would be more than a few years before I felt myself getting better and more like my younger, happier self. Once started, it became a physical feeling of gradual completeness, delivered in tiny increments, the puzzle pieces beginning to fit exactly there, there, and then there.

Like breath inhaled just before a sneeze, it went all the way down to my core. My life was beginning to get some color back in her cheeks. I was feeling a little less precarious, acutely aware of how close I had come to empty. But like laughter, tears, or any other extreme emotion, anger can have an upside too, and our adventure in early 2023 with one of the big box furniture companies provided an outlet for my unspent frustrations at the world and the sheer impossibility of how things sometimes just don't work.

Names have been changed to keep me out of jail.

In May 2022, we went shopping for a twin-size sleeper sofa. We needed one, we bought two. Reasons made sense then and still do, but while waiting for the saleslady to finish the trans-action, a red recliner, there on the sales floor, caught my eye. It felt good to sit down for a minute. It was a handsome chair, the color making it just feminine enough to be a good fit for Lou's home office, freshly re-painted and re-arranged. The red beauty would be perfect and dang. It was so comfortable. Impulsively, we added it to the delivery schedule. We didn't think to ask about a warranty. Who does? It wasn't a car; it was a chair.

It was delivered on June 14th. Who remembers the exact day they had furniture delivered? Well, we did, because two days later, on June 16th, Darling Wendy, the new puppy, decided that those wires under the chair, the ones that make the chair recline, leg support lift, and all the other stuff that chairs can do these days, needed to be shortened, and shorten she did. It looked like someone had taken side-cutter pliers and snipped those wires smoothly right next to the power box under the chair's private parts. The chair had been neutered. And so began my adventure with the customer service process at that big-box furniture store.

So I don't get sued, I'll call them Fill Your Rooms With Junk Furniture Company, or FYR. I'll cut to the chase a little bit here, and let you know that the red chair, which sat unused in the corner of Lou's office from June 14, 2022, to February 5, 2023, is now restored to a fully functioning four-way recliner with lumbar support. Fully un-neutered. Zoom-zoom. Which brings me back to the story of FYR and their customer service process.

You need to know that I followed FYR instructions, calling "The Number," setting an appointment for a repair guy to come take a look, waiting a few weeks for said repair guy, then waiting per his instructions for the part to be delivered to his contract repair company so he could then come back out and install the part. Weeks went by. The end of July had arrived, but not the parts accompanied by the repair guy. I called The Number. The person on the phone at the repair company was shocked at my ignorance. No repair was going to happen, at least not one that was free, because our chair was not covered by a warranty. You did not purchase chair insurance, she said.

I wasn't aware of a rash of chair accidents and nationwide recalls necessitating chair insurance, but nonetheless, there was nothing that they could do. The repair guy should have told us that, she added, with the tiniest bit of a mean smile in her voice.

And so, I asked. "What can I do to fix it?" Silence on the other end. Eventually, she provided the FYR customer service number and told me to call them to order whatever part I thought I might need. By the time I hung up, it was August.

In August, I started my conversations with FYR customer service people by talking to a young lady who verified that our chair was indeed without a warranty. The next person I talked to a few days later was a young lady named Adella. Adella asked for my information, phone number, address, name and order number so she could verify that some alien or criminal human wasn't attempting to repair my chair without permission. She then informed me that, due to the nature of the chair's injury, FYR was not liable for any repair reimbursement. I assured her that as the actual purchaser of the chair and not an alien or serial chair repairer with a criminal record, I simply needed to know how to order the part I would need to repair the chair myself. She was quick to remind me that the injury to our chair could not possibly be repaired by the FYR company. Again, I assured her I understood.

Had I known what was ahead, I would have asked Adella to pause and then pray with me to whatever higher power was relevant to her. I waited while she typed the form that proved the chair was wrecked by our own pet, fully proving that we did not, in fact, purchase life insurance for the chair and thus we were to be kicked to the FYR curb. She thanked me for my patience, gave me a phone number for a contract chair parts company, thanked me for choosing FYR and hung up.

The next day I called the contract chair parts company. As far as I could tell, the company was somewhere on the same continent. The woman heard my story of our Darling Wendy and the repair-guy-who-should-probably-be-fired. I explained that now I needed a part so I could fix the chair myself. She asked for my phone number, my name, my address, and the order number so she could verify that I was not one of those serial chair killers. I assured her I was not. I loved this chair, in fact, that was the whole problem. Had I hated the chair, I would have just put the thing in the ditch.

Here in Texas, there are a lot of good things one can find in ditches, even if you're not looking. Broken chairs, busted AC units, rolls of chain link fencing; it's like a giant Texas yard sale where everything is free once it's in your trunk. But we liked this chair. I spelled my email address seven times for her so she could send me the form to fill out and thus order the part I needed. Then she thanked me for choosing FYR and hung up. I checked my email, found the two-page form there and printed it so I could mail it to "Parts Department, Somewhere, FL, along with my check for $44, the cost for the part I needed. It was now the last week of August. I remembered her telling me that it might take up to 90 days to receive the part. I wrote that future date in my calendar.

A week prior to the expiration of the first 90 days, I called The Number. The lady who answered asked for my name, phone number, address, and the order number. She sounded bored, and quite frankly, completely disinterested in my quest to repair the chair. I did not ask her to repeat her name so I could understand it, as well as jot it down. I had not yet begun to assemble the Notebook on The Chair Repair Saga that I have today. She let me know that no parts had been shipped yet for our chair, in fact, the parts were likely coming from Vietnam, and so 90 days was entirely appropriate for that shipment. But it might be longer than that, she said. She suggested I check back later. I hung up. Vietnam.

It was almost Christmas when life gave me an opportunity to follow up on the ordered parts for our broken, brand-new-never-used red chair. I spoke with Brianna. She asked for my name, phone number, address, and order number, by this time I thought I should be on the red flag list for FYR, making the litany of credentials irrelevant. I mean, all I wanted to do was to repair the chair. Myself. She told me she could not see that any parts, from Vietnam or anywhere else, had been shipped. I reminded myself to breathe. It was on this call that I began to lose hope that FYR customer service would help me find a way to repair this chair myself, or do anything besides jump out a window in frustration. Happy to pay for the part, in fact I did pay for the part. My check for $44 had been cashed. She told me it might take up to 90 days to receive the part. I told her it had been 90 days.

"No," she said. "Another 90 days." Even though I'm not great at math, I did the math.

"So, you mean MARCH OF 2023, BRIANNA??"

"Yes," she said. Lots of words came to my head, but before I started shouting, I hung up.

The next day, I put together a new plan. I called The Number. I spoke with Brian who asked me the same identity questions. I provided the same answers. By now I had them memorized. I greeted Brian with what was to become my official FYR greeting; "Hello (insert representative's name and add my own name) this is my daily phone call to Fill Your Rooms With Junk." Then, while Brian took a moment to pull up my account and read the entries, which by now had become a few chapters, I waited. Upon Brian's return to the present, we discussed the additional 90-day shipping window for a part to repair my chair. I asked to speak to his supervisor. He informed me that would not be possible.

"Brian! Are you serious?" I was incredulous and at the same time, proud that I choked back a cuss word.

"There is no supervisor here," he replied.

"How do you clock in and out, Brian? I asked. How do you get paid for your work at FYR if you have no supervisor? More importantly, how can you resolve customer issues without the help of a supervisor who has more tools than you to effect solutions to complex broken-chair problems?"

That was a very long sentence to speak to Brian, and he simply responded that I would not be able to speak to a supervisor. Then Brian hung up. Holding the silent phone, I looked at my window, knowing that if I jumped out of it, it would be a short fall and thus, would fail to achieve my objective. Maybe I could just stab my own eyes out.

The next day I placed my Daily Call to FYR. I spoke with Rita. We went through the usual dance, including the March date for the arrival of my part. From Vietnam. I told her I could SWIM to Vietnam in 90 days. I don't think she was amused, and she probably wished I would swim to some other country, Vietnam or otherwise.

I asked to speak to her supervisor. She placed me on hold. And then there was a supervisor, Ms. Yolanda. Cue the singing angels. Someone needed to inform Brian. Yolanda and I went through the entire dance again. Name, rank, serial number. She placed me on hold. When she returned to the line, she had some surprising news. The part I had ordered was on backorder. Even more singing angels. It was like the sun came through the clouds. What a revelation! She explained that it would indeed take more time to arrive, but the order was active and to please continue to be patient. I thanked her for her information. Where was this woman six months ago?

On January 12th, 2023, we received the part from FYR via Vietnam. Our ship had come in. The box looked small, so without much hope, I opened it and discovered a $44 electric cord for the chair in question. The incorrect part. That same day I made my Daily FYR Call. I spoke to Ike. We did the identity dance, which by now had become less of a waltz and more like a death spiral from the top of the Grand Canyon while riding backwards on a motorcycle holding a burlap sack full of feral cats in my teeth. Such was my FYR customer service experience thus far.

After 30 minutes while I waited for him to review the novel my case file had now become, he promised he would get me a new order form from his supervisor so I could re-order another part, with luck this time, the correct part.

I had clearly explained the type of part I needed countless times, both on the first order form, on which I had drawn a lovely picture of the chair complete with colored arrows pointing to the private area where the part was attached and in conversation with virtually every customer service rep I spoke with thus far on this journey. Ike promised to get it right this time. I spelled my email address ten more times.

On January 17th, another part arrived in a box far too small to suggest any hope. This time it was the switch for the side of the chair. The little toggle thing that tells the chair motor what parts to move. There was nothing wrong with the existing switch, as had already been explained. By this time, I could have built another chair with the electric parts I had received. Thanks, Ike.

The very next day, I made my daily call. Did the dance. Spoke with Andy. We discussed the saga, he read the novel, and when he came back on the phone, asked me if I would send some photos of the part and the chair so he could be clear about what the issue was. I had pictures. I emailed them. I stayed on the line while he judged my photography skills. After seeing the pictures, he asked if he could have a day to speak with his supervisor.

I said sure. What did I have to lose? Any virtues I possessed as a rational human had been murdered sometime back in September of the previous year. Patience, tolerance, love for my fellow humans, empathy for another's lot in life, you get the picture. All those attributes were dead to me.

Well, he didn't return the call the next day, so I called again and asked to speak with him. I ended up leaving a message. He did return my call, and he had this information. The part I needed, he said, was called a "lumbar motor." My eyebrows raised. Those were new words. The total cost was $88, payable by check to FYR Parts Dept., same address as last time. He provided the actual part number. Who knew the parts had numbers? Then, he provided me with instructions for filling out the part order form. I did as he instructed, drew yet another picture complete with yellow-highlighted large arrows, and included a check for $88. Then I dared to dream.

For the record, this part is not available for purchase anywhere on the internet or anywhere from FYR. Anywhere. In desperation, we had ordered a similar part from Australia. It arrived in under two weeks. Clearly not on the same boat as the one that had gathered dust waiting in Vietnam. Sadly, it was just shy of being correct. But thank you, dear Aussie friends.

On February 4th, 2023, the part from Andy arrived. It was the part we needed. Hallah-freakin-youlah. With help from all the dogs except Darling Wendy, I was able to remove the broken piece and replace it with the new piece and a custom Wendy-barrier I fashioned from a piece of plywood and a few zip ties. After attaching all the correct wiring, I sat in the chair and hit a button. It worked. Thank you, Andy, for stepping outside the tiny box in which your company has you stuffed. While I didn't write down every date I called and every name of the customer service reps I spoke to on this journey, there were at least a dozen individuals who failed to resolve my issue. Andy, I think, was lucky number 13.

66. Fletcher

We met in 2022 at a sheep herding clinic, a two-day event with about ten other herding-breed dogs and their hopeful owners. Fletcher was there with his young Australian Shepherd, Liam. I was there with a friend and her young, untested border collie. We were curious to see how the border collie would respond to seeing sheep for the first time. While I huddled up with the other newbie herding-hopefuls and their dogs, Fletcher was one of the experienced handlers there, working to advance his team's skills with sheep. While we chatted getting to know each other, he told me he had turned 92 a few months earlier. I had my Nikon with me and asked him if I could get a few photos of the two of them. He looked at me appraisingly.

"Sure thing," he said. "I'd like a few to send to my family for when I die, so they can add it to my obituary and the rest of the story of my life. I want them to know this herding thing about me. And the dog is a good-looking guy, don't you think?" He smiled.

I smiled back. I liked this man.

As he and Liam entered the pen, Fletcher used his slim white herding cane to communicate with his dog. The fiberglass stick helped Liam understand when to stop, stay, down, come-by or away-to-me. As I watched them work, it was clear that Liam was young and Fletcher was not, but the age difference between the two made their dance with the sheep just that more beautiful.

I friended Fletcher on social media, hoping to forge a relationship that would allow me to share the awe and admiration I felt for this man. I'm guessing that there aren't many nearly-centenarians on social media and true, he wasn't on the platform much, but he did a fair job of stalking some of my posts over the year. I sent the set of pictures to the instructor so she could forward onto Fletcher's email. It was clear that he was a very special student to her.

One weekend we braved the February forecast and signed up for another herding clinic, this time with my young pup Parker. Despite the winter sun, the day was cold with a raw north wind tearing through our Texas coats and brightening our cheeks. Then, I recognized Fletcher's car. As he and Liam climbed out of the Cadillac sedan, his face looked like he had just come from a boxing match. Two black eyes, a large bandage on his forehead, and a swollen nose made quite a picture. Our trainer was aghast.

"What happened!?" she exclaimed.

"Squirrel," he said matter-of-factly. "Went to take Liam out to the yard yesterday and I face-planted. Got to meet my neighbors, though!" he smiled.

He said the neighbor guy had seen the whole thing and had come running to help him, just as the lady from across the street was leaving for work as a nurse. She drove into Fletcher's driveway instead, having seen the neighbor running towards Fletcher and Liam. With their help, he went to the ER where they diagnosed a broken nose and put a series of stitches in his forehead.

"I didn't count while the doc sewed, too many stitches for sure," he said. "My regular glasses broke too, so I have this old pair on today. Hoping I can see the sheep."

He said his doctor told him he should use a walking cane.

"I told that guy I already have a cane," he said. "For the sheep. And anyway, more than one is one too many."

He opened the trunk of his Caddy and grabbed his folding chair, then he and Liam joined the rest of us huddled on the hill near the sheep pens, braving the wind gusts. Fletcher's injured nose turned brighter red. Suddenly, the cold didn't seem that big of a deal to me.

The day was a full six hours of livestock work, with baby dogs taking turns learning how to control their baby-dog prey drive in a small pen with three savvy and "dog broke" sheep accompanied by our instructor, there to guide the young dogs and make sure the sheep stayed safe. The more advanced dogs, like Liam, took turns showing the rest of us how it was done, working a large group of sheep in a windswept pasture, turning them as a tight group around gates and obstacles as if they were at an advanced herding trial.

While Liam and Fletcher weren't perfect, they were a joy to behold, the dog tuned into Fletcher's herding cane and verbal commands most of the time but also testing his observation and handling skills at every step. Fletcher knew his dog and met those challenges with directions to the dog and corresponding quick steps left, right, or around the herd. The sheep obeyed the dog's pressure, their direction flowing as one unit towards the gates, dog behind the herd, Fletcher and his cane at the top of the herd, and the sheep quietly moving forward as the dog did as he was trained to do.

Whether I have 30 more years, 30 more days or 30 more minutes, I'll take every one of those moments and work to be more like Fletcher. With any luck, one cane is all I'll ever need, too.

67. One Dog to Lead Us

It would be impossible to ignore the contributions and influences of all the animals that came into our lives, the hundreds we saw each week in our work-for-a-dollar jobs and every animal who stayed with us beyond the usual stay of a few weeks. Some stayed forever, but most went onto other homes that promised forever. How many? I don't even know, but when all is said and done in the world of rescue, numbers shouldn't be what drives one's work and ignites your passion. I can safely say that we took in dozens of animals every year, mostly herding-breed-type dogs and more than a few cats. They all crossed our threshold not knowing that their lives were going to get better. As the years went by, it became hundreds. We lost count, learning that the count didn't matter. This one dog, whichever one it was and at whatever moment, mattered. And then the next one, and the next. Each one mattered.

Along the way, we took in a few parrots, too. Even though the birds were intimidating, they, too, went on to live better lives. I will always respect the power of a parrot's opinion, having learned the hard way.

We knew how to care for livestock and horses, and our barn and pastures had spare room, so goats, sheep, horses, chickens and a few cattle also came and went. Two fish surprised us, adding to our experience in ways we never expected, Oscar the Red Tiger Oscar fish and Taco the goldfish, a carnival prize for winning a ring-toss game. Taco came home in a plastic sandwich bag and left in a 50-gallon fish tank to continue growing in a friend's four-season water garden.

But it all started with one dog.

I was working at the small city shelter nearby, having completed the move into the brand-new building and fired and hired old and new staff. Shelter operations were running smoothly. One Saturday, as we emerged from the kennels to open the shelter after cleaning, we found a cardboard box sitting outside the front door. It was common for people to dump and run, sneaking up to shelters and leaving their animal problems in boxes and dented cages when no one was around to pose questions or inflict guilt. It's easy to run from judgment. But there are two ways to look at this. One, indict the droppers for not caring about their animals and leaving them for someone else to deal with. Pregnant cats, flea-infested puppies or kittens, broken or injured animals, sick animals, we saw these every day. Shelter workers still see this every day.

The other way to see it is the way I chose, almost always. I was glad the droppers had brought the animal to a shelter, even if they lacked the courage or time to face someone who might pass judgment on them. To me, I was grateful the animal was brought somewhere it could get help, instead of being abandoned where no one would find it, or find it in time. Our shelter doorstep was a place of hope; a ditch was a place to die. We found animals in both places nearly every day, but in ditches they weren't often still alive.

The puppy in the box on my shelter doorstep that Saturday was one of the lucky ones.

Being a small shelter in a city of less than 50,000 citizens meant that we also had a small, tight-knit staff. There were three of us. We were all there that Saturday morning, and each of us had broken a sweat scrubbing kennels and cleaning cat cages, getting ready for our usual busy Saturday, our best day for visitors hoping to adopt a new cat or dog. Neecee was the one who unlocked the door for the day and found the box. She set it on the reception counter and opened the folded top.

"Oh Mah GARSH!" she exclaimed. "It's just ATE UP WITH KEE-YUTE!"

Neecee was a delightful soul and a true country gal at heart. The people in our city loved her. Her easy smile and heavy country accent could unlock the coldest northern heart and put a beaming smile on the southernmost of drawling southerners. She was unique, and we adored her. But it was rare for her to be this excited over a puppy in a box.

What does that even mean, I muttered in my head as I moved closer to peek inside the box. Ate up with cute. Really. But as I looked inside, I saw what looked like a skunk with stand-up ears. A tiny black puppy with a white stripe running down the middle of its forehead. Round, liquid puppy eyes looked up at me, part humble, part fearful, part curious. Tiny brown eyebrows arched a question. The puppy was built like a dachshund, long and low with stubby legs at each corner, but square from front to back. His shape begged to be hugged. His ears, perched on top of his head like tiny camping tents, dominated the interior of the box. It was hard to believe the box had stayed closed with ears that tall on a puppy that small. Neecee lifted him out of the box and set him on a towel on the countertop. I had to agree. He was ate up with cute.

Throughout the day we all took turns getting to know the puppy. His little white feet were adorable too, complementing his skunk stripe and ears, pointed nose and long, wagging tail. We all thought he was likely a corgi mix, but mixed with what, exactly, none of us could guess. He was ridiculously cute.

It's important to get to know shelter animals. It's part of the job and provided several benefits. First, we needed to learn what kind of temperament each animal had, making for better adoption matches when the animal was ready for a new family. Second; it helped us understand what the animal might need in terms of behavior support or placement with a specialized rescue group, one with a solid reputation and sufficient resources to get the animal ready for adoption. Animal shelters had come a long way from the late 1980s when I had started as a green volunteer. As we all observed our Saturday pup, we reached the same conclusions. He was shy, easily frightened and lacked the confidence of a healthy, well-socialized puppy. He would not thrive in our kennels. As adorable as he looked, he would need more time to find the right family. I would need to find the right rescue group. He came home with me, just for the weekend. Where had I heard that phrase before?

We named him Houston, after the iconic NASA phrase, ... we have a problem. As the days went by, we worked hard to help him learn that our home was safe, and he could be a puppy all he wanted. He quickly trusted our Australian Cattle Dog, BillTheDog, who took him under his wing immediately. With Bill's support, Houston began to grow into a confident and affectionate puppy. Without warning, our family fell in love. As his puppy cuteness faded, an elegant but serious short dog emerged. Throughout his life he never discovered a decent sense of humor, the curmudgeon we suspected he was while evaluating him at the shelter was permanent, and so he stayed. With his prick ears and short legs, we decided he was most likely a cross between a corgi and Walter Matthau. Our rescue journey had begun.

The first commandment in rescue work, if one wants to do it right, is this: You can't keep them all. If I had just a nickel for every time someone said, "If I win the lottery, I'm building a giant shelter and taking them all home," I would be a millionaire. I'm not alone in saying that.

But taking them all home isn't a solution, it's a recipe for disaster. Working harder to find the best home is the solution. Not the perfect home, but the best home. The perfect home has only been discovered by the dogs and cats already in them. It will rarely, if ever, be discovered by shelter workers, as much as most will disagree. Perfect homes just don't happen by accident. But with knowledge, hard work and commitment, the right home will happen, the one that will become perfect with the right match between pet and people. So, with each new rescue dog or cat I brought home, we focused on those principles.

68. Leaving the Shelter Behind

There's a look in the eyes of a sheltered dog. Most especially in the eyes of the dog who has spent more than a few weeks waiting for relief from the noise, smell, wet cement, chaos and loneliness that swallows the courage of most animals in an animal shelter. As their days in cages wear on, hope is replaced by exhaustion, wariness, and caution. Their questions reflect up to the busy people with spray hoses, who squeeze through gates, disappear down aisleways and dump dry kibble twice a day into paper or metal bowls. The lucky dogs in a shelter system get blankets, maybe even a stuffed animal.

Then there are the animals dropped off at shelters with policies to never euthanize their sheltered animals, such is their belief that there's a perfect home, somewhere, for every dog or cat. They live months or even years there, sometimes in rooms designed to imitate a living room, a kitchen or even a bedroom. People feel better about this, and the waiting lists to bring in unwanted animals to no-kill shelters are long. But in any shelter, regardless of the specter of euthanasia, there is always one element missing. The element of home. Home brings the comfort of companionship and offers relief from anxiety. Home promises that a familiar human will return, bringing security to the relationship and balance in their life again. Home is where the pack is. For our pets, the person is the thing that completes their lives, solidifies the safety in a pack environment even if that pack is only one human and one dog. They are companion animals, and we made them this way. For our dogs and cats, the person is life itself, and nothing can replace that.

Before two weeks go by, 14 days for those who count, the look in a shelter dog's eyes change again. The noise and exhaustion declare victory. Resigned hopelessness and a growing understanding of their loss, of familiar places, people, and things, the world they knew before they came to a shelter, has a certain look, and shelter dogs wear it. For those dogs who didn't have a loving family to grieve, they grieved instead the loss of their freedom, freedom to choose where to sleep, when to sleep, and where and when to indulge their most basic individual needs. Even the dogs rescued from neglect eventually wore a haunted look. For those dogs and cats, it may take longer than a few weeks to sink in, but the separation from frequent and dependable human interaction chips away at the resilient nature of every shelter animal, day after long, loud day.

We recognized that look in every dog who came to us from a shelter. We worked hard to change it, from the minute we slipped on a leash and walked them down the aisle and out to our waiting car. The travel crate had soft, clean towels that smelled like home; laundry detergent, fresh air, even joy has a smell for a dog or cat. We fed them, medicated their illnesses, and for as long as they needed, gave them space and let them sleep. Shelter life is numbingly exhausting for animals. Silence, relief from stress and uninterrupted sleep was always the best medicine. But could we reignite their hope and return the brightness of confidence and joy to their eyes? We could and we did. More times than we could count.

69. Houston, You're Not a Problem

As he blended into our family more and more, it became clear that he would need a similar-sized friend to play with. His best pal had become a friend's Weimaraner, and Sullivan adored Houston with every fiber of his soul, as any Weimaraner will do. They are an "all-in" or "all-out" kind of dog. But the friendship, active and often overly energetic, put Houston's safety at risk due to the size difference between the two friends. It was time to get him an appropriately sized friend. So, Webster came into our lives, a quirky brindle Cardigan Corgi, the kind with a tail. He and Houston were perfect.

Because Cardigan Corgis were an uncommon breed, carefully managed by responsible and reputable breeders, there were no Cardigans waiting for homes in the shelters around us. So, we found a breeder with puppies and wrote a check for a pet-quality Cardigan. Houston's happiness at having a short dog friend was worth the looks we probably got from the animal shelter community for buying a dog. Oh well. We had vowed to offer rescue resources to any Cardigan Corgi in need, and we still planned to stand by that promise. All we needed were dogs in need.

Be careful what you wish for.

What we discovered was a lot of Pembroke Corgis in need. The kind without the tail. Most of the shelter agencies were not prepared to manage the unique needs of the "other" corgi, the one that was more popular. The "Queen's Dog" had become a regular animal shelter resident.

After Houston came Willie. He had been a holy terror in his first home, a common complaint with Pembroke puppies, but not for the reasons one might imagine. There are fewer things more adorable than a nine-week-old Pembroke Corgi puppy, and the breed was getting more popular each year. Not many new owners were prepared for the high-drive intensity of a short but determined, very vocal and often nippy herding dog, the original purpose of the small but serious working breed. Handsome Willie excelled at all of them. Young, high-energy corgis were showing up in shelters all over our combined metropolitan area, and there were no breed-specific corgi rescue groups to meet the needs. But there we were.

There really is no way to count the number of corgis and cattle dogs we brought into our home through the years of our rescue work. When they arrived, we began the work of "fixing them" in whatever ways they needed fixing. The last step was re-homing with new families, with thoughtfulness, care and compassion for both the dog and the potential family. We did what we had always found successful in the shelters we were familiar with; we learned about the dog itself, what their personality was like, what they preferred for human interaction, and what kind of home might be the best fit. That was a start. We paid for full vetting for each dog with our own money, preferring to make our own decisions, with our own veterinarians on veterinary care. Behavior evaluations, if more complicated than normal, were done with the help of a trained and certified local animal behaviorist, who was also a close friend. Temperament assessments took place every day of each dog's stay with us as they met all our animals here, experienced a farm, the outdoors, good family routines and learned good manners. They all blossomed.

When it came time for placement, we were not burdened with the often-ideological baggage of a rescue group. At the time, new rescue groups were popping up every day, and it was nearly impossible for the public to tell the difference between good groups and groups with selfish interests or lofty ambitions not based in reality. Many of those "groups" were not much more than just one or two people, like we were, and it would soon be common knowledge that many were using their rescued-dog stories to solicit funds to rescue more, while not standing by the promises they made to the animals they had already taken in. There was no regulation or oversight. It was a time when rescue group rules and etiquette were thrown away before they were even read, and it was several years before shelters universally began to require proof of legal non-profit status before releasing a sheltered dog into the care of a rescue organization. Rescuing shelter animals, for the unscrupulous "animal lover," was beginning to be a free-for-all, for-profit venture with the increasing use of social media, the high volume of needy dogs and cats and the rising popularity of the no-kill movement in communities. All of that, combined with the lack of accountability, created an honor system that couldn't last.

We continued to rescue what we could pay for ourselves, staying true to our own values, instincts and intuition. Adoption fees, if the adopter asked, were not required, but we recommended they send an adoption fee, the amount of their own choosing, to the shelter or rescue group with which they were most familiar, or to the shelter where their new corgi or cattle dog had come from. And just as soon as one corgi or cattle dog would leave our care, another would need a soft landing away from the rigors of a shelter. The local shelters had our number.

The sheer volume of herding dogs in shelters was soon overwhelming, and in 2009 we met a few brave members of a brand new, state-wide Australian Cattle Dog rescue group who were sensible, down-to-earth, and worked just as hard for the people who came to them in search of a dog, as they did for the dogs in search of new people. In exchange for considering referrals from us on sheltered cattle dogs in need, we offered to be a foster home for some of their hard-to-place dogs. For the years we worked together, we never regretted the relationship.

70. Bastille

It's nearly impossible to pick one foster dog to represent the dozens of animals who came into our lives over the years we did rescue work. But as Lou and I thought back on those years, names returned and the individual stories of the animals behind the names gained new life. One evening, with the television turned off and all our dogs soundly sleeping in their spots around the house, we took some time to remember some of the stories. Reminiscing together, one story returned to us both almost at the same moment, and we laughed.

"Great minds," Lou said, our shared phrase from the day we first met, recognizing then, that on many levels, our thoughts and hearts lived on the same wavelengths.

It was the story of Bastille.

It's been years since he left us for his final and perfect home with a family in another state. Bastille was a joyful and unassuming corgi who had had a tough go trying to find a family who would keep their promises. After his first home failed, two more homes failed, and he came back to us. We said he would never have to leave again.

His first owner had surrendered him to the shelter where I worked, sometime around 2007 or 2008. The reason?

"We don't want him anymore."

At the shelter, the man signed the papers and left. The corgi stood planted there in the lobby, shaking a bit, eyes wide with fear, staring at the closed door where the man had disappeared.

As the intake staff was completing the paperwork, the man returned.

"I need the collar," he said.

The dog on the floor jumped up on the man's pants, a look of joy beginning to shape the forgiving grin on his face. Then the man unbuckled the collar, brushed the dog off his pant leg and turned away. The door swallowed him up, and he was gone.

Even I could feel the crush. Being left behind was one thing, but somehow, losing his collar was a final blow. The dog stood still, staring at the closed door. The ruff of fur around his neck bore the shadow of the lost collar.

This wasn't a phenomenon; the need to keep the collar of a surrendered dog. It happened a lot. But it was always hard to comprehend how the previous owners seemed to value the collar more than the dog that wore it, and yet it happened often enough to prevent any of us from being surprised. That one small action burned a little hole in our hearts, just a little, but every time. We were the ones left holding our disposable leashes on unwanted pets, soon to be adrift in shelter systems overwhelmed with dogs who once wore collars.

So, Bastille, cute enough for the adoption kennels, was scheduled for the usual veterinary examinations and intake assessments. With any kind of luck, he would be adopted quickly.

But the news wasn't good. He was heartworm positive. Combined with a terrible coat, long toenails, dirty teeth and horrible breath, the vet team felt he would be better served in a rescue group, and so he would need a foster until an interested group came forward. If I had known how nearly impossible it was for this small dog to not be full of joy, his forlorn and frightened expression that day in the shelter lobby would have torn my heart in two. But he was a corgi, and he came home with me that night as a foster. Heartworm treatment would start the next week. When safely completed he would return to the shelter for adoption.

Once in the comfort of our home, Bastille began to shed the fear he had shown at the shelter. He quickly made friends with our own dogs and in moments was running through the yard like he had lived there his whole life. The resilience of dogs always stunned me. Just when you thought they had given up, here they came with their second wind.

But something was different about him. Corgis are notorious for their loud opinions on everything, and a corgi bark always announced their arrival, their departure, or anything that required an announcement. They had no need for any other kind of introduction because, as short-legged herding dogs of large livestock animals, their bark was how they managed their world. As we watched him run through the yard with our pack of corgis, we saw Bastille trying to bark, but the noise he made was like nothing we had ever heard. We realized he had been surgically de-barked.

But even that offense didn't steal the joy from this eternal optimist. He was a lemonade-from-lemons kind of guy. Even without a real voice, he just barked louder. He had a message for the world, and he insisted the world hear it. He was a dedicated messenger. We loved him for his outlook on life and, with all his health issues still looming, decided to take him on, giving us the extra time we would need to find a new home for him as a healthy dog.

There's really no need to waste words describing the first two families that came to adopt him. They made all the right promises but eventually returned him. It was always hard not to pass judgment, just like it's hard to not feel guilty that we might have done better in screening those families. So, we stayed content that he came back to us with his smile intact. In the end, Bastille's story could be about what we should have done, but instead it's about the strength of a discarded dog and how he kept his wounded heart shiny, perfect, and pure, believing that one day soon, his travels would bring him home.

After the second family returned him, grossly overweight and dirty, we agreed he would never have to leave again. That our home could forever be his, too. Third time's the charm, we told him.

But after a few months here, and with his new diet working well, I had a feeling, one I couldn't explain. One morning I grabbed my camera and while the corgis were playing in the yard together, took a few pictures, posting them on my social media page with a short story about his journey with us. In less than five minutes, a message from a woman, known to us only through our shared membership in the social media group "Corgi Nation," told me she had to have this dog. He was meant for them, she insisted in her message.

"What would it take to get him transported?" she asked.

Her home was more than 800 miles away. Bastille had finally settled with us, but he had been without a real family of his own, one that he didn't have to share with a pack, for much of his whole life.

I had posted the pictures, and I had had the "feeling." But I didn't know where it had come from or where it might lead. I balked.

How could she know this dog was "meant for them"? What kind of crazy is that? Yes, we were social media "friends," but that didn't mean we shared the same cheese dip and were ok with double dipping. And so, we talked a bit. A lot. A free ride on a rescue transport was offered, the same rescue transporter who had helped this family in the past, had been to their home, and who vouched for their integrity and diligence when it came to their pets. Their vet reference was so clean it could have been a paid infomercial. To this day, we don't really know where we found the faith to send our Bastille off with a stranger, to ride in a transport kennel for ten more hours to be delivered to yet another unfamiliar family, only this time in another state. We have no idea what led us to trust, except maybe it was her joy, so much like Bastille's, so pure and immediate. Maybe it was the joy. So vibrant you could feel it over the phone.

She said he was a perfect fit from the very first moment he arrived. He loved their girl corgi, just as he had instantly loved Sticklet, my corgi. He smooched all over their pre-teen daughter, who returned the smooches right back, unafraid of dog spit. And he slept on their beds that very first night. He barked until, well, until he was hoarse, is how I would normally say it, but of course his voice had been stolen years before. And so, his raspy, breathy, de-barked voice did everything it could to shout to the world that he was home.

Almost two years passed. During that time, Bastille's new family kept us updated. His hatred of vacuum cleaners had not changed one bit, but his everyday happiness had increased by a hundred. Everyone who met him loved him. He had finally found the perfect home, but no one anticipated what would come next. Without planning, a new human baby became an unexpected gift to the whole family. As much of a surprise as she was, the tight-knit family welcomed the new baby with love. But no one was more thrilled and excited than Bastille.

This is why Bastille was needed, this is why he was perfect from the beginning, and this is why sending him so far away had felt right, despite my doubts. He was born to love babies, and from the moment she arrived home, Bastille never left her side.

No, I wasn't clairvoyant, but we aren't supposed to know everything right away. We are supposed to trust it when faith leads us to something bigger than us. Bastille's purpose was invisible to me that day he stood shaking in fear in the shelter lobby. We just had to find it for him.

"He is beside her from the moment she wakes and lies down beside her until she closes her eyes. He loves this baby, and I wish we could make him live forever," she said.

"She" was mom to two beautiful girls, wife to a loving and supportive husband, and the keeper of Bastille's final promise.

Home. It's where joy lives.

71. Names

No story of rescuing dogs or cats could be complete without mentioning the name dilemma. So often when dogs are surrendered by owners to a shelter, the truth is hard to discern. Stories are told and egos are protected, and it never really mattered what they were trying to hide except for one thing. We almost never learned what sin they had committed which caused them to be surrendered to an animal shelter. Yes, sometimes they had committed no sin at all, and the shelter was truly a grieving family's last option. But, except for those instances, we almost never got the dog's real name. The name they were familiar with, the name they had answered to for however many years they had lived.

Was it worse for strays? Those lost dogs and cats who probably had names, but who landed in a shelter as a stray without even a sorry lie to hide their real name? I'm not sure. I've seen the emotion, though. The fear that overwhelmed, surrounded by stainless steel and strangers; the moment the dog heard a familiar voice, the explosion of joy and relief. Lost and found reunions were often causes for tear-jerking celebration, right there in the middle of the kennel aisle. They didn't happen often enough, especially for cats. Some of the most dramatic reunions were during the months of rescue work after the destruction of Hurricane Katrina. Those moments, the visual memories of owners reuniting with their pets or horses, their relief awash in tears of joy, have nurtured the collective consciousness of every single rescue professional or volunteer who helped during the course of those post-disaster days.

There can be no doubt that the joy of these reunions saved more than the lives of animals.

On the other side of the aisle, it was always a long and anxious wait for the animals who were never reclaimed. For them, it was the beginning of a new journey or the end of their current journey, depending. After losing their families or the comfort of things familiar, they also lost their names. Some would get new names and new lives, and some would get a last quiet word or soft caress under their chin as their life slipped away in the arms of a kind stranger.

What I am sure of is that we tried hard to find a name that at least sounded familiar to dogs who clearly used to have one. So many dogs knew the sit or stay or lay down words, obeying the commands as if they knew their life depended on it. They usually knew to stay when told, and they almost always walked like royalty on leash. So many stray cats used litterboxes faithfully, purred for a head scratch, squinted their eyes tight in comfort while being held. Surely, they had names once. So, when we brought them home from the shelter for their second chance with us, we sat with them and tried all the long vowels, all the short vowels, mixing and matching syllables and vowels and sometimes we got close and sometimes we gave up.

Animals are resilient, though, and they learn more quickly than we do. They also forgive more easily. Some of the names here came with the dog, or cat, or horse or bird or cow or goat, but not many. Most of the names were new bestowals. All the names and the animals behind them have their own story, but not all the names of all the animals we helped are here. Those names are lost in time and memory, but I see all their stories every time I look in the mirror. The endings to their stories were not always what I would have chosen for them, but the journey each had while they were with us was the best we could make it.

Bobby Earl. Lillie. Foxy. Faith. Sunny. Cookie. JustDave. Edie. Chaucer. Franki. Ollie. Echo. Daisy. Ritehand. Gordon Whitefoot. Peyton. Preacher Man. Mister. Happy. Maddie.

Freddie Mae. Whiskey. SLV. Cora. Tuffy. Bebop. Sari. Aiden. Dakota. Libby. Hani. Augustus. Henry. Wally. Timmie. Mr. Nubbins. Houston. Wilson. Noah. Biscuit.

Rocky. SpiderBite. BooBoo. Bold Ruler. Taquon. Alice. Raspberry. Prince Charles. Fudge. Reba. Brittany. Chip. Sally. Chili. Bastille. Boo. LowJoe. Spot. Honey Bear. Baxter. Cecil. Einstein. Kiwi. Diana. Brandy. NotFeralCarol. Rumor. Otter. Trotter. Silver. Levi. Mustang. Quick. Granny the goat. Granny the chicken. And yes, another Granny the goat.

Katie. Grady. Walter. Pepper. Mrs. Green. Peep. Little Red. Mrs. Frizzle. Broody=Trudy. Bardy. Little Blue. Roundy. Another Whisky. Winston. Sadie. KatKat. Bomber. Dixie. Willie. Penny the corgi. Penny the Russell Terrier. Pippi. Simon. Ruby the tortoise. Finnegan. Arya. Junebug. Goliath. Shorty. Otis. Dolly. Bubbles. Bruce. Lena Horn. Pete Peterson. Rio. Jake. Speedy. Hidy Ho. Roundy Cat.

We gave them names and healed their hearts. For dogcatchers, that's no small thing.

72. "If You Can Read This, I Will Lick You"

It was October 22nd, 2009. Becky, a good rescue friend, called just before bedtime. Seeing her name on the caller ID, I groaned inwardly. This late at night could mean only one thing.

"Hey Becky!" I answered brightly.

We both adored Becky and her husband, Phil so I was happy to hear from her, at least until I knew for sure what her call was about.

"Sandy!" she said. "I just got off the phone with the county shelter volunteer, and there's a corgi on the euthanasia list, scheduled for the morning. If I bring her to your office tomorrow, will you take her?"

She stopped to breathe, giving me an opportunity to respond. I hesitated.

"What's her story?" I asked, hoping to figure a way to find another option for the dog besides us. We were full, and that was no laughing matter. It was just Lou, me, our jobs, our own dogs, and a small country house. Full meant full.

Becky said she was going to the shelter to pick up a sheltie, the breed she had dedicated her life to. During the conversation with the volunteer, she learned it was "last call" for a small, skinny corgi who had become a favorite among the shelter staff. Metro shelters had a term for last call. They called it "Code Red." No more second chances. I sighed. It had been a year for the record books, literally. The cruelty cases had been exhausting, so many, so large, so many animals in need. Our own rescue promises had been hard to honor, so many dogs needed a helping hand, even for just a day or two. We hadn't said no yet, but we had come close. Lou and I both knew we needed to establish better boundaries, but we both knew that our no also meant euthanasia for a dog we would never meet. But Becky was persistent, and I gave in. Another unwanted corgi would be coming home tomorrow.

In 2009, there were a lot of "highly adoptable" dogs like corgis finding their way into shelters. At the same time, adoption rates were falling. The economy in the country was tough and many families were tightening their financial belts. Shelter agencies struggled, trying to find more space for more homeless dogs. Despite the best efforts of many shelters and rescue groups across the metroplex, the euthanasia rates were soaring.

In a few minutes, Becky emailed confirmation that the dog's identification number had been removed from the Code Red list. The corgi was safe. All that remained was pick-up and delivery. I thanked Becky and hung up the phone. Another corgi, I thought. Where would we put this one?

She arrived the next day at my office. I heard her before I saw her. I recognized a corgi voice, but this one was demanding to be heard. Her voice was impossible to ignore. My first thought when Becky led her into the room was that she wasn't very pretty. Then I saw how dirty she was. She would be hard to adopt and would take time.

"She's all yours, she barked the entire way!" Becky said. She was used to piercing, non-stop dog voices. I was getting used to sighing.

Her ribs were showing. Her coat was discolored and greasy. She smelled like motor oil and urine. Clusters of fleas crawled through the crevices on her ears, over her back and into a bleeding sore in the middle of her forehead. On her paws were dirty white markings, like ankle socks that had been worn too many times. A soiled white bib extended from her chin to under her chest, where it was clear she had just left a litter of puppies behind somewhere. Soap and water would go a long way, but at that moment, she wasn't pretty.

She weighed fifteen pounds that morning, even with what seemed like a pound of fleas and a half pound of motor oil. Surprisingly, she was clear of heartworms. She came home that night after some soap, water, flea prevention, and a good meal.

Through those first two weeks she ate, she slept, and she got to know our dog family. She showed little joy or interest in the world around her besides rest and food. We let her take her time. As I watched her walk slowly through the yard one afternoon, not lifting her head or communicating in any way, I wondered if she would ever be happy again. She must have heard me thinking, because the very next day she discovered the ugly yellow doghouse.

Her delight at finding the weird door and porch on this monstrosity of a doghouse was clear. She found it, she claimed it, and she reveled in her ownership of this thing we had purchased at a charity auction, built by a well-intentioned but ignorant architect. It had no value as a doghouse; our dogs were aghast at the prospect of dogs who lived anywhere but indoors with people. But once in it, this skinny, homely corgi discovered her smile again. Under the cantilevered roof, she was no longer adrift. We didn't know it then, but her smile was here to stay.

From that day, she made friends with everyone she met. Her sad wandering around the yard came to a stop, replaced with bright interest and energy. We tried names, finally settling on Vicky, or the longer version, Sticky Licky Vicky, for the way her shedding coat stuck to every surface she touched, and her joyful habit of licking every person's face who picked her up.

We even gave her a social media page of her own, where we "met" thousands of corgi friends around the world. I shared her daily adventures and photos for other corgi lovers, all of them members of the group we all called Corgi Nation. With our help as her typists, she found some fame as "SLV" in the Corgi

Nation community of personalities. SLV would never need to be adopted. She had claimed me, and she was home.

As we got to know her, she proved herself to be a gentle, funny extrovert, a kind heart to our two cats, an expert corgi "flopper," and a terrible car rider. She loved car rides, but the excitement always got the best of her. She became a dangerous distraction as she jumped from window to window, seat to seat in case she missed something. Riding in a safe crate in the car brought forth the voice.

SLV had no trouble convincing her new people friends that they were the greatest humans on the planet and completely perfect in every way. Her charm and joy were irresistible, her habit of licking, inescapable.

In the beginning, we guessed her age at around two years old. By around nine years old, she began to slow down. The slight limp that had plagued our walks for the previous two years had affected her exercise choices more and more. We noticed a lump that had no veterinary determination other than "not cancer." Like a true corgi, she had selective hearing but never missed mealtime. We hoped that as she aged, it would be easy for her.

When she was around ten years old, there was an occasional falter in her hind legs; a missed step up into the house, a shorter stride, sometimes even a stumble as she frapped, corgi-style, in happy-go-lucky circles around the yard during her "Frantic Random Acts of Play." She began to have less stamina in her outdoor excursions and after-work greeting frenzy with the rest of the pack. As the months went by, we watched the symptoms of what was looking more and more like degenerative myelopathy, or "DM," a spinal degenerative disease common in corgis, steadily progress. With no cure, we supported her needs and paid closer attention.

We talked about what her future would look like, knowing she would become more crippled with each day. We found a cart for her, a dog-wheelchair, but practice sessions quickly proved that she would never tolerate the loss of independence. Her ability to remember routines and familiar places and friends also began to fail, a frightening condition often called "dog dementia." She spent her days exhausted, sleeping upside down with two legs propped against the wall, her nights wandering the living room or turning circles in her crate in confusion. We worked hard to keep her routines simple and intuitive, knowing we weren't far from the heartbreak of losing her. Eventually, nothing we did could bring her comfort, and we knew it was time.

There's a cost to pay when we love a dog, whether it's a rescue dog or a dog from a good breeder. It's the cost of love that grows bigger through the years, like a high-risk investment in your own heart. The memories, moments, photos and friends, even tears and smiles all combine to bring value to our love beyond any we can imagine. With our dogs, we will always receive more than we can ever give. The risk proves its worth. Sticklet, with her soft, clean coat of pure gold, was the first dog in my life to show me that.

After her death in May 2021, delivered by a less-than-peaceful euthanasia journey in our own yard with a mobile veterinarian I didn't know, I struggled to navigate her loss. She brought a presence and an energy to our home that was impossible to fill, and now she was gone. It was months before I could think of her without fighting back a rush of tears.

I wasn't ready to miss her, but the next loss would be worse.

73. Coyote Songs

This morning before dawn, emergency vehicle sirens in town alerted the dogs and me to drama unfolding a few miles away. Even the air felt it.

Our older corgi Amelia, in her favorite feral-corgi response, began singing the song of her longer-legged ancestors. She's always the first to hear a siren, and always the first to begin the song. There are no human words to the song, but she knows all the lyrics and she has taught all the dogs in our house those secret, soulful stanzas. And so, they sang, our walls reverberating with the feral notes of seven dogs in that most sacred of almost-sleeping moments, the dark morning.

Through the din I heard other voices somewhere outside, higher pitched and with a different rhythm, wild like black chicory coffee. I went outside in my pajamas and stood on the porch, heard them just a few hundred yards to the south, invisible in the dark but so close I imagined I could smell their musky fur. Coyotes zealously celebrating a human tragedy heralded by a siren. I was glad my sheep were tucked away safely in the barn, snuggled into their pine shavings.

Then our dogs heard the wild things and on cue, fell silent, one at a time. The feral in their voices faded, perhaps so they could listen in and maybe learn those wild words, perhaps embarrassed at pretending.

74. The Magic of Birds

It's 2025 and I've made yet another full circle, as necessity convinced me it was time to go back to driving a school bus. Now, with our country and the entire world on fire, I guess I'm one of the lucky ones. With both a begrudging grumpiness about having my day managed by someone else's rules, and a relief that I can do something I enjoy and get paid for it, I get up in the pre-dawn dark to pilot a bus again.

For a bus driver there are a few perks that don't appear on a paycheck. The tiniest passengers provide them routinely if you take a minute to listen.

One little girl always needs a reminder about where her street is and where she needs to step off the bus.

I tell her, "It's the last stop, baby. You're always the last one on the bus."

She visibly relaxes when she sees the scruffy open field that collects all the windblown trash. It surrounds a man-made pond. It also collects birds.

She calls it the bird field.

One day, there were no herons or hawks like we've seen a few times already and which she looked for every afternoon. Twice we saw a Crested Cara Cara, its stunning size and black and white color standing stark against the backdrop of green, yellow, and orange wildflower weeds.

But the best find was a diving duck, floating alone on the pond one morning as my single passenger and I made our way to the next stop. As the bus got closer, I saw the duck's silhouette outlined in the reflection of the morning moon on the water, highlighted by the orange tint of the rising sun. What a beautiful picture, I thought, and slowed the bus, hoping to point it out to her.

Then it dove and disappeared. I stopped the bus.

"Look!" I whispered. She turned to me, sleepy-headed braids framing her face. "Look out the window!! There's going to be a DUCK!!" I kept my voice quiet to build the moment. This was the best part of driving a school bus. The imagination of the littles only needed a tiny seed and then it would grow by itself.

So far in her seven-year-old life she had seen three whole birds, she had proudly told me one day. The green heron, the Cara Cara and the hawk, all there in her bird field, the home for birds and the landmark that tells her she will also be home soon. I wish her mom could have seen her face when she first laid those wide, wondering eyes on each of the three beauties we spotted together.

But those birds didn't swim.

Instead, they flew, all with impressive wings and amazing lift and one even flew over the roof of the bus, making her dash to the other side, against the rules, to watch out the other window. Herons are impressive flyers and her face said it all.

"A duck?" she asked, her baby voice fuzzy with the early hour. "What do you mean?" I let the moment linger.

Then came the magic. "Look at the pond and wait just a sec," I whispered. The bus idled quietly. She followed my gaze to the strip of moonlit water. It was as perfect as glass. And then it happened.

The duck popped to the surface of the pond, right there in the middle of the moonlit stage. She squealed with surprise, all her sleepiness gone.

"A bird that SWIMS!" she exclaimed.

"Yes," I said. "A bird that swims."

I put the bus in drive and mentally thanked the moon.

75. Brave

*Anthropomorphism: the attribution of human
form, character, or attributes to non-human entities.*
(Merriam-Webster Dictionary)

It's not a sin, nor is it a law that says we can't bestow upon our
animals some human attributes that we admire. I raise my hand,
for I am guilty.

There are some people who scoff at those who treat animals
as equals, but I don't hide from scoffers. I bought a recliner
just because it fit both my dog and me. At the same time. If
Dave didn't fit, then I didn't sit because when it was time to sit,
when the day was over and dinner plates licked clean, it was our
time. He waited all day for the clock to strike "us," and for all
the hundreds of nights we watched football or Netflix together,
it was his chair as much as it was mine. He was the dog that
fit, after a few before him who had mostly gotten it right. He
taught me that being one with a dog was one of the most perfect
accomplishments a human being could aspire to, once *I* got it
right.

If you want to call me crazy, I will say just one thing. You
haven't met the right dog yet. Or cat.

Grandpa in town, who swore at dozens of cats for daring to
step foot into the yard, was surprised one day when, without a
formal introduction, the right one knocked on his door.

After years of hard work, Grandpa had retired. By then he
didn't have a dog. But a few months into his retirement, a cat

came knocking and for the rest of his life Grandpa and that cat watched The Price is Right, every day at 10 AM, sitting together in a chair big enough for two.

Someone should have told me to pay attention when that apple fell from the tree.

We should all be so lucky to have a dog in our life who thinks highly enough of us to want to share a chair every night. It got to be such a thing between Dave and me, that if I was sitting somewhere else in the house, he would do one of two things. Either he'd sit in the middle of the living room and squeak a pathetic noise that, upon translation meant simply "get in the chair," or he'd sit in the chair alone and wear the face.

He was a superb and accomplished martyr.

But beware the anthropomorphic parallels because believing in such nonsense might cause your heart to swell and someday it will burst at the loss of the best love you've ever known. Our dogs and cats just don't live long enough, but that's as it should be because they shouldn't have to live without us once they've given us *their* heart. It's like Mom said that day, as she lay on the couch in the last days of her life. That was the day I learned that she would rather die than lose her children.

And that is love.

So, here's to Dave who embodied the love of all the dogs and cats who chose me. They all lived their best lives with me, but Dave was the one who filled my whole heart and then left me holding an empty leash, sitting alone in a too-big chair.

While being the first to leave may seem an easy way out, it takes real bravery to convey such raw grief upon the person who has loved you to the core. Dave was the bravest I ever knew.

Our beloved dogs, born knowing how to sit without being told, also know instinctively that death is not better if we experience it alone. They are gifted with the courage to see our pain and help us through it, even at the moment we let them go and then, after they are gone from our life.

So, when your dog says it's time, don't be afraid. Our dogs

are uniquely qualified to drive that bus and they don't need GPS; they just need you. They've earned the right to die first, notwithstanding the thievery of age or disease. Your courage in the face of their death is the price you pay for being human.

Then, we bury our faces in their fur and breathe deep, holding tight to the warm, solid feeling of them next to us. They leave us with the memory that we were their one true love and their whole heart in human form.

As we grapple with the mortality of our beloved dogs and cats, and we dare to anthropomorphize, offer no apologies. Because throughout our lives together we are them and they are us and to take one into our heart and life, knowing that we will eventually lose them, is the bravest thing we will ever do.

76. The Tree Tunnel Road

More than ten years ago, the county road in front of our home was narrow and usually quiet, with not much regular traffic besides neighbors. The ditches were functional, carrying rainwater away with ease and, through most of the year, deceptively covered with flowering weeds. The quiet country miles were a special perk, my job at a small-town animal services program was close to home this time, and I was eagerly building strong new programs and procedures for a good city whose leadership had recognized a need for them. As I drove each morning, it wasn't lost on me that I was one of the few who didn't have to submit to the combat zones of metroplex traffic snarls and toll-road nightmares.

But the most amazing thing about our county road were the trees. Then, as it is now, the oaks, southern pecans and spindly elms grew together in solidarity, their trunks and branches growing up and reaching outward towards each other, the rows of trunks supporting an interlocking roof of leaves and branches. As if out of a fairytale, the neighborly work of the trees on both sides of the road created a tunnel of shade and light. As I drove back and forth from work to home, the tunnel through the trees often sparked my imagination.

Through the years the Tree Tunnel Road has become nearly magical, the sun dappling the asphalt between the shade of leaves and branches, the opening of the tunnel visible three-quarters of a mile ahead regardless of which direction you travel, the invitation to enter irresistible. Where engineers spend lifetimes blasting tunnels in mountains to build roads over and through, this tunnel, Mother Natures' own creation, invited peace. Looking through the windshield, it was easy to see the tunnel roof and sides as home to birds and squirrels, leaves and branches providing shelter, trunks and roots providing security and a close comfort you could feel, like a warm, weighted blanket on a cold, lonely night. Most days I was the only car driving through. Twenty years later, even with an astonishing increase in traffic volume requiring the road to be widened and the ditches cleared of weed flowers and dug deeper, the magic remains, even as the trees have been making their way, one by one, to earth in their own old age rituals.

It was on a day like this, an unremarkable summer morning in 2004, that I drove through the Tree Tunnel on my way to work. I reached the end of the road, turned right, then another left to stay on the same county road, heading west toward my office where a kennel full of homeless dogs and cats awaited care. As I left the tree tunnel behind me, one of the larger stretches of land opened up. Twenty feet or so off to my right was a blond child sitting bareback on a white-footed red pony. Her long hair was tangled in that feral-child way that makes mothers cringe. The pony was poised, his ears tipped back towards her voice, head up, waiting like an electric current behind the wall switch. Behind them, two ponds reflected the morning sun, ahead of them waited a tall, grassy berm that rose alongside the road several feet, bulldozed in place to help with erosion control. The dozer operator likely had no idea what a wonderful racetrack his berm would become for a half-wild, smiling little girl and her shiny Unicorn pony.

As I pulled even with the pony and his grinning rider, she dropped her reins and leaned forward. Her pony exploded in speed towards the berm, neck stretched out, ears pinned in effort, tiny rider embedded in his whipping mane, one hand pushing the reins onward and one hand waving to the car beside them, tangled hair flying, her smile that moment as wide as west Texas. We galloped side by side for a few hundred yards, she on her Unicorn, me in my car, and then my road continued and hers ended as the berm pathway dipped down to the creek bottom. I was breathless.

In that instant, I was transported back to 1970 as easily as if my car was a time machine, back to the memory of my own first pony, Ginger. I remembered the runaway train of my imagination at nine years old, especially when I was bareback on Ginger. We raced, we wrangled, we jumped, we stole invisible cattle herds, we flew through space and time every time I rode. I had no idea how far away those memories had gotten until I found my breath again after that race with a laughing girl-child on a shiny red pony.

Fast-forward to 2023, it was the end of the year, and we had been spending a few days a week at a local establishment having a few beers and cocktails with people from our neighborhood; people we've never met even after living here for nearly thirty years. Sometimes, conversations between the two of us would catch another ear, as our talk almost always involved conversations about dogs, cats, sheep, horses, or cows, the bits and pieces of animal minutia that have made up our lives and careers. One night we were talking about a friend with two German Shepherds and five cats when a young lady sitting a few chairs away joined our conversation.

"I have two shepherds and five cats, too!" she laughed.

We introduced ourselves. She said she had lived all her life here and still has horses not far from where we live, after we shared that information. When I realized where she lived, now with her husband, aging mom and dad, and two little horse-crazy girls, I remembered my drives through the Tree Tunnel to work those years ago, and the morning I raced with a copper-colored Unicorn pony and his waving, blond-headed fairy princess. As I began to recount the story, a smile spread across her face.

"That was me," she said.

We are never far from what makes our lives worth living, even though there are days that make it so easy to forget. I'll "remember to remember" and will always love those snapshots of time that make unremarkable mornings, or moments, remarkable. As adults, we battle time, fighting for more, working to save, hoping to forget, watching it leave us, running to catch it. But time is the unsung hero of our lives. I said goodbye to my own inner fairy princess long ago, and now I see in the mirror new wrinkles every day. But when I met this young woman, now a mom watching her own little princesses on their own Unicorn ponies, our conversation reminded me to look past the wrinkles, the tired eyes, the years I see in my grown-up mirror. I'll dig down inside myself and find the shy kid, the teenager, the new volunteer, the animal services officer, and the friend I learned to become to people and animals and then, one by one, I'll pick a memory and take it out for a wild ride, wrinkles and all.

With my eyes closed, I feel the warm, bare back of my pony again, her muscles surging under my seat bones as we fly through the fields as one. I grip her dark mane and let loose her reins, wave my free hand in pure joy and wildness and then I'm a horse crazy kid again, living her best life all over again, but this time in the sunlight of a child's imagination. If the day comes when my memory fails, I know that I'll always have the feeling of losing my breath, overwhelmed by the gifts I've received throughout my life, gifts I never expected and which time can never steal away.

77. Memory Lane

In the summer of 2024, I returned to the Rock Falls farm for the first time since the day I had left it, more than forty years ago. I took a right turn off Highway 37, then followed the school bus route down Langdell Road. Just like that I was sixteen years old again, passing by the same field where one ice-cold midnight, I stopped the car, braking hard to watch a snowy owl glide across the beam of the headlights. The owl lifted its feet at the last minute, its wings taking three big beats as it settled on top of a wooden fence post right there between the ditch and the field. As the car idled, the owl and I stared at each other. Neither of us blinked. Its white feathers were stark against the black of the winter night; she was as easy to see as if it were daylight.

On this summer day more than four decades later, I hadn't expected that memory of the owl, but there it was, the moment changing instantly from summer to winter, a backdrop of black night outlining the stars and the owl under them. She was a ghost now, but the road in front of me was real.

I kept driving, following the turns and curves of Langdell Road to the intersection with County Line Road, the corner where the bus would drop us for our walk home, no matter the weather. Keep going straight and I'd be in Rock Falls in two minutes, turn right and I'd soon see the shimmer of the Chippewa River at the bottom of the ridge. I turned left, driving the three-quarters of a mile from the bus stop to the driveway of the farm. Then it was there, the weathered, hip-roofed barn, its gray paint now faded and nearly matching the white trim around its windows. There was the riding arena where Sunny had taught me so much, the butternut tree next to the big maple tree, the same white farmhouse. Nearly everything looked as if I had just stepped out to head to the barn in my bed hair and boots, with Sunny, Star and the cows waiting behind the barnyard gate.

I drove slowly past the farm, noticed the missing boards on the riding arena, the dangling gate telling a story much like mine, that of a daughter who had moved on to a life of her own. Slowly, my truck followed the road south to the dip where the big creek flowed underneath. The creek bank was choked with low bushes, it was impossible to see the water. The beavers had always done the job of keeping the creek banks clear of brush so the clear caramel of the water was easy to see, but it looked like the beavers, too were gone. At the top of the dip, the field where the skunk was rescued was now home to several houses, their driveway entrances branching off from the place where the wire gate and its "no trespassing" sign always made me hesitate, even if I never paid attention to the warning. A half-mile up at the four corners, I turned my truck to go back the way I had come, wanting one last look at the place where my life had changed in so many ways, where my memories were still held fast and tight, where parts of my heart still lived. Then there, in the brush of the ditch a deer looked up, her mouth full of wildflowers and grass. We froze together. Then in one leap and a swirl of chestnut, she was gone behind the curtain of brush, disappearing instantly. I idled, knowing she was still there, hidden but still close, never running more than she needed, but just enough to stay safe.

Most of my life has stayed in rhythm with the seasons as they circled around. They've always kept me measured, a simple beat remembered from the winters of my younger self, the summers heavy with growth, the changes of fall and spring arriving like "ollie ollie in come free," whether I was ready or not. The patterns of my life guided me silently each day, whether I knew it or not.

My last winter, whenever that comes, is never far from my

thoughts these days, and maybe that's why the memory of all the seasons that have come before are so clear and perfect now. Maybe, like the summer deer, they are just there in the brush, out of sight but always within reach, there for me to remember.

78. Breathe

I've been a bird watcher since an icy, wind-blown winter day, a long time ago in Arkansas. Trapped inside, I sat by the window of our mobile home, amazed by the dozens of different birds coming to the porch for seed. How had I missed these beauties all my life? Most astonishing of all was the White-Throated Sparrow, truly the first sparrow to teach me that not all sparrows are created equal. Their plaintive song "Oh-Canada-Canada-Canada" will forever take me back to that day spent indoors, watching a whole new world unfold before my eyes.

As I've grown older, my eyes can't see the birds in the tops of the trees, across the pastures or between the leafy branches overhead. As a result, I've joined the ranks of those with "apps" on their phones, and one has been like a best friend these mornings and soft evenings when I sit and listen to the voices in the air. In less than ten seconds, I can open the app on my phone, hit record, and then see the name and accompanying picture of the singing bird. It's brilliant. It was just last year that I learned the repetitive song and call of the Summer Tanager had been a regular visitor here in our yard for as many years as I've lived here, and likely many more. For all their startling colors, scarlet for the males, vermilion green with soft yellow for the females, I never actually saw one until last year. How could I have missed those flashing colors? How could I not heard the Tanager's songs and calls and wondered, who is that? What bird makes her home here?

I'm grateful that I've finally heard and seen this visitor. It's a familiar thing, this recognition of things unseen but known. I find it within myself again but more easily now, having found it when I left my work to save my life. It was hard to give myself grace when the judgment came from within. It was hard to beat back that darkness, and I spent the next years searching for another purpose to keep me moving, suddenly too high in the trees for me to see. I found small bits of color through the last ten years, a glimpse here and there of the person I was. Those glimpses chipped away at the person I had become, a woman nearly lost to anger, my emotion without borders.

Animals were the ones that showed me the path forward when I was young, then walked beside me on my journey through the career that defined me. My small pack of dogs still tell me that there are joys and wonders in the world, there is still a reason to get up in the morning even if it is, almost always, far too early. Their own joy makes me smile, watching them leap to catch a ball, clamor to go for a ride in the truck, compete to be the first one to get a hello scratch when I come home from being gone for two minutes, two hours, or two weeks. Animals are still the foundation of my everyday life, but now it is not the daily onslaught of their loss but a daily litany of joy, one that I had forgotten.

Animals helped me find my way forward from the chaos and pain of loss and change, they've shown me that if I hold my hand out to lift others when they might find themselves broken, or to sit quiet and listen when it's not words they need but a shoulder, that sometimes, my healing becomes almost visible, even measurable through the days. The strength of their hearts showed me the strength of my own. And when someone looks at me funny when I tell them I can't take that vacation or I can't meet them downtown for an evening, or my budget has been blown due to an unforeseen vet bill, I smile back and ask, "Have you met my dogs?"

It's taken most of my lifetime, but I'm finally understanding the language I've been hearing all these years, the thousands of wordless conversations that have come before and still accompany what I see and feel when I am in the presence of animals. Almost 30 years of old conversations are now echoes of the fear and worry of dogs and cats waiting behind stainless-steel walls of shelter kennels, or prisoners on chains and in dirt pens with no love behind the locks and latches.

In those fading echoes I've made my way back to the sound of a fish surfacing on a shiny lake, the ripples like the silent spin of a spider web. I sit in a summer chair, ducking my head from the back-and-forth buzz of a hummingbird making decisions mid-flight. I look up into the canopy of the green above me to hear a summer tanager, her wild heart singing the song of the season, the lyrics teaching me that she's always been here, I just had to take note. Then I look down at my own dogs at my feet, who know I hear their words, and I am humbled by their dependable forgiveness for my absence, their patient wisdom knowing that I will keep my promise, giving back to them the time they have so unconditionally given to me.

The animals that have shown me such wonders have become the electric hum of life holding tension on the surface all around me. Then, in those moments when I am surrounded by the profound silence of death, no matter how it arrives, their voices are the same. I know this because I've seen it too many times and heard it whispered in songs almost lost. I've finally found comfort in knowing that each glorious voice insisted that there is joy in life and there is wonder in living it. It didn't matter if the lyrics were whispered or shouted in a dozen languages repeated a dozen times a day. The words were always the same. "Listen to me, my joy is yours, and for as long as we breathe together, yours is mine." I've listened and heard the songs. They are sung by the loves of my life.

"*Life will break you. Nobody can protect you from that, and living alone won't either, for solitude will also break you with its yearning. You have to love. You have to feel. It is the reason you are here on earth. You are here to risk your heart. You are here to be swallowed up. And when it happens that you are broken, or betrayed, or left, or hurt, or death brushes near, let yourself sit by an apple tree and listen to the apples falling all around you in heaps, wasting their sweetness. Tell yourself that you tasted as many as you could.*" Louise Erdich, "The Painted Drum" 2005

Epilogue

"Once a dogcatcher, always a dogcatcher," we used to say. My fellow dogcatchers and I, a few of whom are still solid friends, all started as rookies. We worked the same kind of streets and saw the same kind of horrors, all while trying to help animals find better lives. All of them could have written a book like this, some of them still might.

But back then we were on our own. There was no instructor to show us how to get down on our hands and knees or belly crawl to a bleeding lost dog or terrified kitten in a storm drain. No teacher to tell us how it was back in the day so we could learn from their mistakes and help animals quicker, kinder, and better. We were all battling the cartoon caricature of dogcatchers. The communities where we worked hadn't yet rewarded our passion with their support. But we all persevered. The animals needed champions.

As we learned how not to get bitten, we didn't notice the moment that we began to see every moving thing, especially if it's not where it's supposed to be. It happens that way. One day, your eye sees an animal moving about 300 yards away and you know instantly whether it has a collar and tags and whether it's a lost animal or a sassy escapee with party plans.

A closer glance tells you whether that dog will be a simple catch or a runaway train. Our dogcatcher's eye, sharpened with muscle memory.

Coming home from town early this spring, I was about a mile from our driveway when I saw a dog and a young lady standing in a field next to the road. It's been more than 13 years since I wore an animal control officer's uniform, but my first thought was "catchable." The dog wasn't running, just standing there looking at the lady.

Worry, hope, fear.

I used to know a song with those words.

I reviewed my mental dogcatcher's inventory: cable slip lead, bag of treats, decent shoes. My truck never left home without them. Its own version of muscle memory. I made a u-turn and went back to the road next to the field.

Parking my truck to the side of the road, I climbed out and slowly approached the good Samaritan. She turned to me.

"Is this your dog?" she asked.

"No," I said. "But I saw you and wanted to offer you more treats. It looks like he trusts you a bit."

From where I stood on the road, I saw that he was limping, thin, and had the eyes of a dog just a breath away from bolting. I'd seen that look so many times. Sometimes I managed to make it disappear, sometimes it disappeared with the dog into the wind. It looked like bullet wounds in his hip and hocks, the injuries likely keeping him from running, pain mediating panic.

I kept my distance, sensing his need to flee, two people nearly more than he could manage.

"I think he's been hit by a car or something," she said. Then, with little apology, "I can't stay," and she turned to go back to her car.

Just like that I became the dogcatcher again, my lazy-day sweatpants now the uniform promising a better life for this dog.

I went back to my truck and searched the driver's seat-back pocket for my cable leash, the kind that can't be chewed through, the kind a scared dog can't see coming. It has a memory, too. Just like a good lariat it holds a big loop, unlike the nylon leashes most new animal control officers carry. This leash was my magic trick; together we had saved a lot of lives. Good tools become good friends when used with skill and this leash had been with me a long while.

Rummaging around my truck I found a small bag of training treats, but looking inside the bag, saw just two tiny pieces. Heart-shaped. I could break them into smaller pieces, maybe.

The metaphor wasn't lost on me.

I made a phone call to our local shelter and sent them a quick text pic of the dog. They said it might be a while before they could send anyone. So, I began a slow approach, holding my leash close, all the while singing the song of the lost dog to this weary fellow. It wasn't a spoken song, no. This tune was one that the dog could hear even though my mouth never moved. It was a song of quiet, peace, an offer of safety, an exit from fear. I knew the words by heart, the melody carried to him on the breeze.

In a few minutes I was almost within touching distance. I turned sideways, breaking one of the heart-shaped treats into two. I offered it on my outstretched hand. He stretched forward, reaching with his nose, then licked it into his lips. Did I see his eyes soften a bit?

As the minutes ticked by, he wasn't inviting me to come any closer than too far away. It was like he knew the exact length of my leash, just like a longhorn cow knows exactly how long her horns are when she slips through the trees or tells you to leave her new calf alone. But then an animal control truck arrived. I held my breath, hopeful the officer would be someone the dog could trust.

A young man stepped out and approached us, his youthful beard and booming voice the exact thing the dog didn't need.

"Just give me your bag of treats," I said, shouting the harsh words inside my own head. Instead, I said "Do you have treats?" The young man looked confused. "For the dog," I finished. "Do you have treats for the dog? "

"Oh, right!" he said. He went back to his truck. As he returned to where I was standing, he reached into the bag and pulled out a large piece of jerky, then threw it at the dog and whistled. "Come here, boy!" he boomed with a smile.

"Well, *that's* going to work," I muttered silently.

The dog hobbled away, adding a few more yards to his distance. Then I saw another animal control truck pull up. Well, this will be a circus, I thought. The same kind where I used to end up talking loudly and not so kindly to young men with catch poles who saw me as just another old woman with no usefulness to their mission. "I kiss puppies for a living" was their favorite pick-up line, and it usually worked to get them a hot date. Patience was never their best virtue, and most puppies knew that.

Out of the second truck stepped a voice, the kind of voice that made the dog stop and turn. I followed his gaze and heard her sing-song, quiet and happy voice, one that said "Hey buddy! Nice to meet you what's your name do you need some help?" Not that she used those actual words, but in the right minute it's what stray dogs hear. They want just a little bit of hope and an open door to walk through. They want to leave the panic and fear behind. A welcome from a friend. She knew the song of the lost dog. Every note, by heart.

Between the two of us we worked the next few minutes silently, both of us singing bits of the song, praising his bravery, each of us angling closer, measuring our steps in inches. I saw him trembling, his threshold of panic nearly broken.

He looked at her, then me, then he looked away and in a millisecond my leash dropped over his head and settled perfectly around his shoulders and he reared back terrified but he heard the songs, the words coming from us both and then, at the end of the leash he spun in a circle to find his courage, then stopped to listen. I handed the leash to the officer and thanked her for her good work, then told her to keep the leash.

"Oh, I couldn't," she said.

"Keep it," I encouraged. "You have a lot more lives to save, and this leash remembers how."

I didn't thank her for also knowing the song of the lost dog. For a good dogcatcher, that's just muscle memory.

Biography

Sandra Kay has lived in the presence of animals since she can remember. She has traveled around the country, living east, west, north and south, but will always call Wisconsin home. The stories in this book describe a life lived in service to animals and the people who love them. Any good dogcatcher has done the same.

Acknowledgments

To my family and friends:

Lou, JustDave, Amelia, Parker, Penny, Archie, Gus, NFC, and Simone for your patience. Well, not Simone. You'll get there one day, we hope.

Thank you to friend, big sister, author and editor Anna M. Blake for every single day since the first phone call about a corgi no one wanted, the day you said yes. I owe a debt to every one of your smart dogs, even if I only knew them from their voices over the phone. Walter, Preacher Man, Mister, Jolene. The dogs introduced us, then sat back and barked. I couldn't be more grateful to them forever. They shared you with me. Such good dogs.

To Detective Steve Shaw, CFEI Ret. JCSO, one of the finest law enforcement officers in the country, now and forever. Tink for the miles we traveled and the lives we changed, including our own; Shelly for what you taught me about resiliency; Rowdy for being the best brother from another mother; Peggy for your perseverance when the rest of us walked away; Martha A for your early friendship and laughter in a world that was bigger than I thought possible; Dick and Suzanne for your faith in the possible, Becky and Phil for the yes you always keep handy; Janet and Paul and Linda P, who represent the few good humans I found in the kennels at Dallas, Fort Worth and Irving. All those whose names I can't remember but whose faces I'll never forget; Karen Voss, now Deeds and your best friend Bob who happened to become your husband, I and all the dogs I dragged to your training studio through the years thank you for the behavioral GPS you delivered so expertly; Stacy Smith for your fire and energy, I hope you find your own exit ramp to the world of birds soon because we're only promised one more day, the one we're in right now; Amy, the big sister I never knew I needed; Mary and Kris and Kaci, my family from another lifetime, with a lasting love I never expected.

Chris Boese, Katie, Toree, Kelly, Lori, Patti, Holly, Crystal, Denise, Gutch, Karla, Mel, Dilly, Jodi, Froj, and Diane who stood with me as we convinced a brave college professor to sponsor our university's very first gay organization and support group. There were so many strong, good women, and every one of them showed me another door worth opening.

To my beta-readers, for your patience, thoughtfulness, and sharp eyes. Thank you. Deb Reid, Leslie Fowler, Karen Deeds, Martha Armstrong, Dr. Jennifer Williams, Stacy Smith and Cheri Flett-Collins.

Brother Chris for being my best friend for as long as I can remember, Dawn for standing with him every time he needed you and always smiling; Nieces Emily, Kayla, Bailey, Gabi, Grace, Taylor, Lauren, and nephew Jordy, carrying on as parents, spouses and siblings and making your own stories shine. To my own mom and dad and the hard things you did to help us all live good lives. To the other brothers, I hope you all find that good life, where kindness and compassion and understanding are the keys to personal joy. To cousin Sarah and cousin Ann, keep telling your stories. To the Leslie family for helping me retire my bicycle and giving me the pony of my dreams.

Resa, the busy bee, for showing everyone how to keep the strength to never give up and always follow through; Rick B. for showing me that suicide should never be an option, I hope you found peace; Tammy M, Charles, Cliff, Jason, Dr. Jones, Joe, Letitia, Tham, Phu, and the entire cast of characters from six years of the most meaningful work I've ever known at the Humane Society of North Texas. Also, Samantha B, Gail B, Judy

1, Sam C, Lo S, Karlene P, May P, Corgi Nation friends Deb R, Jennifer R-P, Josie R, Lynne T, Janie, Jacque, Sandi M, Sharon B; Karen R for your constant cheer and positivity, cattle dog friend Whitney W, retired sheriff's detective Kim W.

Jo F, Jennifer A, Victoria S, Carrie M, Dee, Carrie D, Susan T, Beverly H, Kimberly J, Sarah K, David and Erin, Peggy K, Shelia K, Brenda L, Laura K, LJ, MJ MacG, Jane and Chris, Deb and Z, Hugh McE.

Every veterinarian I've ever known and had the honor of working alongside or who made the lives of my own animals better; Dr. Torres, Dr. Mandava, Dr. Egar, Dr. Monger, Dr. Bruner, Dr. Roeber, Dr. Thorn, Dr. Finn, Dr. Bove, Dr. Paul, and all the veterinarians who keep walking the hard walk and doing the hard work. The animals can't thank you, but know that they do, they really, truly, do. None of us can do what you do.

Lib Horn for raising me to become an adult; Candy C, Jerry, Gary, Judy, Kathy, Richard, Ben, Duane, David, Desiree, Philip E, for all the work, both good and bad. We did it together and I learned from each of you. To Robert, and every city manager and supervisor who didn't think animals were important until they landed on your desk.

And to the cities of Fayetteville, AR, Maumelle, AR, Dallas, Fort Worth, Burleson, and Irving, TX, I learned from all. Some good, some bad, but at the end, the truth is that you can't learn to run until you learn to fall. Help your people keep learning how to fall, then be there for them and pick them back up, because "there's nothing we can do" is never an answer for an animal in need. It takes a village to make the life of an animal better, and we are all part of a village.